D1576558

# THE PSYCHOLOGY
## OF LUST MURDER

# The Psychology of Lust Murder

## Paraphilia, Sexual Killing, and Serial Homicide

CATHERINE E. PURCELL, PH.D.

AND

BRUCE A. ARRIGO, PH.D.

AMSTERDAM • BOSTON • HEIDELBERG • LONDON
NEW YORK • OXFORD • PARIS • SAN DIEGO
SAN FRANCISCO • SINGAPORE • SYDNEY • TOKYO

Academic Press is an imprint of Elsevier

Publisher: Nikki Levy
Project Manager: Jeff Freeland
Sr. Developmental Editor: Barbara Makinster
Sr. Marketing Manager: Trevor Daul
Cover Design: Alisa Andreola
Composition: SNP Best-set Typesetter Ltd.

364 . 1523019 Pur

Academic Press is an imprint of Elsevier
30 Corporate Drive, Suite 400, Burlington, MA 01803, USA
525 B Street, Suite 1900, San Diego, California 92101-4495, USA
84 Theobald's Road, London WC1X 8RR, UK

This book is printed on acid-free paper. ∞

**Library of Congress Cataloging-in-Publication Data**
Purcell, Catherine E.
    The psychology of lust murder : paraphilia, sexual killing, and serial homicide / Catherine E. Purcell and Bruce A. Arrigo.
        p.   cm.
    Includes bibliographical references and index.
    ISBN-13: 978-0-12-370510-5
    ISBN-10: 0-12-370510-X
        1. Sex crimes—Psychological aspects.   2. Psychosexual disorders.   3. Serial murderers—Psychology.   4. Criminal psychology.   I. Arrigo, Bruce A.   II. Title.

HV6556.P87 2006
364.152'3019—dc22

                                                                    2005057238

**British Library Cataloguing-in-Publication Data**
A catalogue record for this book is available from the British Library.

ISBN 13: 978-0-12-370510-5
ISBN 10: 0-12-370510-X

For information on all Academic Press publications
visit our Web site at www.books.elsevier.com

Transferred to Digital Printing 2009

*For all victims of sexual and violent crimes*

Catherine E. Purcell, Ph.D.


*For the memory of my grandparents*

Bruce A. Arrigo, Ph.D.

# TABLE OF CONTENTS

# 1

## INTRODUCTION

# 2

## PARAPHILIA AND LUST MURDER

# 3

## SEXUAL HOMICIDE AND SERIAL MURDER:
## WHAT DO WE KNOW?

# 4

## AN INTEGRATIVE MODEL:
## WHAT DO WE NEED?

# 5

## THE CASE OF JEFFREY DAHMER

# 6

## DAHMER, PARAPHILIA, AND LUST MURDER: TESTING THE MODELS

# 7

## IN SEARCH OF MEANING: ON THEORY CONSTRUCTION AND MODEL BUILDING

# 8

## IMPLICATIONS AND CONCLUSIONS

# About the Authors

As an undergraduate student in psychology at the University of Redlands, the lead author, Catherine Purcell, worked in a transitional rehabilitation program at Patton State Hospital, a forensic in-patient psychiatric facility, where she had her first encounter with a paraphilic offender. The patient in question had an Axis I diagnosis of schizoaffective disorder 295.70 and fetishism 302.81. In addition, he harbored extremely violent and distorted sexual fantasies. His crime occurred while acting out one of his paraphilic fantasies. In his fantasy, the man cut his victim's throat while experiencing sexual intercourse with her.

This was the first time that the lead author was exposed to the notion of fetishism and the criminal manifestation of erotic and sadistically deviant behavior. Since then, both practitioner (including legal and clinical) and scientific interests have been prominently featured in her ongoing applied work. Through the course of her endeavors thus far, she has come to realize that there is a limited amount of sound research within this complex domain of criminal psychology. This has led her to conclude that both theory construction and model making are essential if the knowledge base in this area is to be meaningfully and usefully advanced. Due to this need for theory and model development, Dr. Purcell explored this idea in her graduate studies, and ultimately developed the Integrative Model for Paraphilia, the crux of her doctoral dissertation.

She received her bachelors degree from the University of Redlands, and received her Ph.D. in Forensic Psychology from the Institute of Psychology, Law and Public Policy at the California School of Professional Psychology in Fresno, California. Dr. Purcell was part of the first class of forensic psychologists at the Fresno campus. While at CSPP Fresno, she was able to work collectively with Dr. Hickey out of California State University Fresno. Since receiving her doctorate in 2000, she has continued to work with him in the capacity of a research assistant, as well as guest lecturing several criminology classes for him at CSUF.

Dr. Purcell has worked for several years as a psychologist for the California Department of Corrections. Her most recent position has been in the capacity of Mental Health Coordinator for the only maximum security juvenile detention facility in Kern County. In addition, she has taught several classes in psychology and criminology at National University in Fresno and California State University Fresno. She continues her research endeavors in the area of model and theory development of paraphilic sexual crimes, and has recently been involved in profiling such cases with law enforcement entities, as well as lecturing to audiences on forensic psychology.

Similar interests and concerns have informed Bruce Arrigo's professional endeavors. He began his career as a community mental health outreach worker in Pittsburgh, Pennsylvania, specializing in assisting the homeless and persons with psychiatric disabilities. Although his interventions were not principally targeted to individuals with paraphilic (and murderous) proclivities, several individuals spoke of such tendencies and sought out-patient treatment to address them.

As an educator, Dr. Arrigo has often explored the extreme boundaries of criminal behavior, especially given the fascination students generally express over actual clinical cases or popular movie portrayals of the same. This has led him to investigate a number of worthwhile topics, not the least of which includes paraphilia and lust murder. Whether addressing these issues in the classroom, through fieldwork practices, or by way of scholarly publication, he has found that knowledge about erotophonophilia remains mostly underdeveloped or unexamined. As such, he has surmised that a more systematic treatment of this phenomenon, anchored in sound social and behavioral science research, is one vital step toward growing the literature in this area of criminal behavior studies.

Dr. Arrigo is Professor of Crime, Law, and Society within the Department of Criminal Justice at the University of North Carolina-Charlotte. He holds additional faculty appointments in the Psychology Department and the Public Policy Program. He served as Chair of the Department of Criminal Justice at UNC-Charlotte (2001–2004) and as Director of the Institute of Psychology, Law, and Public Policy at the California School of Professional Psychology-Fresno (1996–2001). Dr. Arrigo is the author of more than 125 journal articles, book chapters, and scholarly essays. In addition, he is the (co)author or editor of 20 volumes published or in press. Recent books include *Psychological Jurisprudence: Critical Explorations in Law, Crime, and Society* (2004), *Police Corruption and Psychological Testing* (2005), *Introduction to Forensic Psychology* (2nd ed.) (2005), and *Criminal Behavior* (2006). Dr. Arrigo is Editor-in-Chief of the peer-reviewed quarterly the *Journal of Forensic Psychology Practice*, as well as the Book Series Editor for *Criminal Justice and Psychology* (Carolina Academic Press) and *Critical Perspectives in Criminology* (University of Illinois Press). He is a past recipient of the Criminologist of the Year Award (2000), sponsored by the Division on Critical Criminology of the American Society of Criminology, and is also a Fellow of the American Psychological Association (2002) and a Fellow of the Academy of Criminal Justice Sciences (2005).

Whether in the context of professional practice work, applied research, or classroom instruction, both authors believe that the fields of criminal justice and psychology can benefit from a more thorough assessment of lust murder. Admittedly, the work undertaken along these lines in the pages that follow is by no means exhaustive. No book can ever make such a claim, despite the compelling nature of its contents or the erudition of its arguments. However, in the case of this volume, our aims are decidedly modest. Having said this, we believe that the paraphilic process and the crime of lust murder warrant further exploration and careful scrutiny. Readers and reviewers alike will have to decide if our efforts represent a useful foundation for the next generation of social and behavioral scientists inclined to investigate these troubling and provocative matters.

# 1

# INTRODUCTION

## OVERVIEW

Sexually deviant or aberrant behaviors, otherwise known as paraphilias, are commonly associated with crimes that are sexual in nature (Hickey, 2005). There are literally hundreds of paraphilias. Some are more common (e.g., voyeurism) or well known (e.g., cannibalism) than others. Deviant sexual behavior exists on a continuum and varies in severity. Some of these behaviors can be classified as criminal; others represent mostly nuisance forms of conduct. An example of this continuum's breadth can be illustrated by looking at severe sexual deviance (e.g., pedophilia or rape) versus harmless variants (e.g., fetishism or peeping Toms). On the most extreme end of the paraphilic continuum is erotophonophilia, commonly referred to as lust murder (Arrigo & Purcell, 2001).

Erotophonophilia is the acting out of injurious behaviors by brutally and sadistically assailing the victim (Hickey, 2003). These actions are undertaken so that the offender can achieve sexual satisfaction. Lust murderers are likely to repeat their crimes, making them serial in nature (Egger, 2002; Hickey, 2001). Mutilation of body parts, especially the genitalia, represents a routine characteristic of this form of paraphilic deviance (Hickey, 2005; Money, 1990).

This book examines the sexual offense of lust murder. This type of killer makes a profound connection between sexual gratification and fatal violence (Holmes, 1991; Simon, 1996). The lust murderer harbors deep-seated, erotically charged fantasies in which his attacks and slayings sate, although incompletely and temporarily, the need for more sexual violence (Arrigo & Purcell, 2001; Hazelwood & Douglas, 1980; Schlesinger, 2003). For these assailants, sexual enjoyment and erotic fulfillment depend on the amount of torture and mutilation they can inflict upon their victims (Holmes & Holmes, 2002a). Thus, for the lust murderer, ultimate pleasure is derived from sadistically killing others. Clearly, then, they are motivated by a violent and powerful need for sustained sexual satisfaction (Kafka, 2003).

The extant research on the origins, onset, and escalation of paraphilias, as well as their criminogenic structure, is somewhat limited and mostly anecdotal (Hickey, 2005). Notwithstanding these deficiencies, this volume investigates the relationship between sadistic sexual deviance and lust murder, arguing that the association represents a systemic process of increasingly erotic and violent behavior. In addition, this book examines the prevailing conceptual models on sexual homicide and serial murder. The aim is to create an integrated theoretical framework that can comprehensively account for the joint effects of paraphilia and lust killing. If successfully developed, the framework or typology can help classify lust murder as a specific and distinct category of sexual homicide in which paraphilia functions as an underlying motive.

In an effort to foster meaningful conceptual synthesis, two existing models on the subject are investigated: the motivational typology developed by Burgess, Hartman, Ressler, Douglas, and McCormack (1986), and the trauma control model established by Hickey (1997, 2001). The former examines sexual killing in particular; the latter focuses on serial homicide in general (Arrigo, 2006). Both models contain interactive components that help support existing knowledge and research on paraphilic behavior. Additionally, the insights of other social and behavioral scientists that have investigated sadistic deviance and sexual violence are incorporated into the overall analysis. These observations both extend and deepen the proposed integrated model's explanatory and predictive properties.

In an attempt to comprehend the emergence and maintenance of paraphilic behavior, as well as how sexual deviance progresses within an individual, the significance of fantasy and masturbation are explored. Both fuel the offender's desires, aspirations, and actions. In this way, the integrative typology, unlike its sexual homicide and serial murder counterparts, demonstrates the unique role that paraphilias assume in the act of lust murder. In the final analysis, this book intends to provide a more accurate evaluation of this crime and a more complete assessment of this offender.

To ground the more theoretical material, the case of Jeffrey Dahmer, a convicted paraphilic lust murderer, is examined. His life story is provocative on a number of fronts and a variety of researchers have explored facets of his clinical and criminal background (e.g., Egger, 2002; Masters, 1993; Palermo, 2004; Tithecott, 1999). Despite these worthwhile accounts, efforts to explain Dahmer's behavior within the context of a serial murder and sexual homicide framework have not, until now, been systematically undertaken.

Moreover, the utility of the proposed synthetic framework has implications for professionals in the fields of criminal justice, psychology, and public policy. For example, efforts to profile, track, and apprehend offenders are vital to the effective administration of law enforcement. In addition, clinical concerns encompassing prevention, diagnosis, and treatment are crucial if the goals of rehabilitation are to have a reasonable chance of being met. Finally, sensible public policy concerning correctional and mental health hospital management necessitates a more complete understanding of the lust murderer. This is especially the case if the assailant's behaviors are more serial in nature. Thus, the practical implications stemming from the recommended conceptual framework also warrant some systematic review.

## SEXUAL HOMICIDE AND SERIAL MURDER: TOWARD THE NEED FOR INTEGRATION

Various experts have attempted to classify murder, including law enforcement personnel, applied criminologists, and criminal psychologists (Ressler, Burgess, & Douglas, 1988, p. 3; see also Douglas, Burgess, & Ressler, 1995). However, a number of these efforts do not specifically address sexual homicide; rather, they study murder without differentiating between sexual and nonsexual crimes (cf. Hickey, 2001; Perdue & Lester, 1974).

According to the Uniform Crime Reports (UCR), sexual homicide in general is classified under the "unknown motive" category. This is because investigators are unaware of the underlying sexual dynamics for such an offense. Sexual homicide, particularly lust murder, does not have a specific taxonomy or cataloguing within the UCR. As such, statistics reflecting these types of crimes are mostly intangible and often misleading (Douglas et al., 1995; Egger, 2002; Hazelwood & Douglas, 1980).

The investigations that do address sexual homicide in particular suggest the existence of two types of offenders: the rape, or displaced anger, murderer (e.g., Cohen, Garofalo, Boucher, & Seghom, 1971; Groth, Burgess, & Holmstrom, 1977; Prentky, Burgess, & Carter, 1986; Rada, 1978), and the sadistic, or lust, murderer (e.g., Becker & Abel, 1977; Bromberg & Coyle, 1974; Cohen et al., 1971; Groth et al., 1977; Guttmacher & Weihofen, 1952; Podolsky, 1966; Prentky, Burgess, & Carter, 1986; Rada, 1978; Scully & Marolla, 1985). Displaced anger murderers kill their victims after raping them, primarily as a means of escaping detection. Consequently, they do not become sexually satisfied from the rape (Douglas et al., 1995; Holmes & Holmes, 2002a). A growing, though admittedly limited, body of literature continues to explore the dynamics of the anger rapist and the serial nature of this sexual offender's murderous conduct (e.g., Graney & Arrigo, 2002).

What we know about sadistic sexual homicide is even more circumscribed than its displaced-anger-murder counterpart (Arrigo & Purcell, 2001). To date, sadistic sexual homicide has typically been viewed as a perplexing phenomenon, defying efforts at explanatory and predictive models based on some theory-driven conceptualization of the behavior (Prentky, Burgess, Rokous, et al., 1989, p. 887). What we recognize thus far, however, is that fantasy is a key component to understanding and interpreting lust murder (Holmes & Holmes, 2002a; MacCulloch et al., 1983; Money, 1990). This notwithstanding, a cogent theoretical formulation regarding its role as a driving force or motive for explaining this form of sexual crime has mostly eluded researchers.

Studies contributing to our conceptual understanding of sadistic sexual homicide include the work of MacCulloch et al. (1983), Burgess et al. (1986), and Hickey (2001). MacCulloch and his colleagues were instrumental in demonstrating how a pattern of sadistic fantasies propels sexual criminals into compulsive acts of behavior, first in the form of fantasy and then in the form of assaultive conduct. Their findings suggest that when sexual arousal is involved in the sadistic fantasy, offenders are increasingly motivated to act out their violent images understood in terms of habitual behavior. This sexual and violent habitual behavior is linked to conditioned responses and cognitive interpretations of the fantasies themselves.

Extending the cognitive model of MacCulloch et al. (1983), Burgess et al. (1986) introduced a motivational dimension to sexual homicide (see also Douglas et al., 1995). They argued that fantasy is an internal driving mechanism for repetitive acts of sexual violence. However, they also pointed out how the interaction of critical personality traits and cognitive mapping processes are integral to generating the sexual images that produce violent behavior.

Unlike MacCulloch et al. (1983), who addressed sadistic behavior and fantasy, and Burgess et al. (1986), who focused on sexual homicide per se, Hickey's (2001) work more squarely considers serial murder. Mindful of the previous literature on cognition and motivation, Hickey assesses how certain predispositional factors and facilitators lead some individuals to engage in serial murder. His model demonstrates how psychological and/or physical traumatic events occurring in the formative years of a person's life can function as triggering mechanisms where increasingly violent fantasies, fueled by facilitators (e.g., alcohol, pornography, drugs), produce homicidal behavior.

Interestingly, none of the preceding models examines lust murder with any appreciable degree of specificity. This notwithstanding, we contend that the previous work on sexual homicide and serial murder is assimilable, especially for purposes of describing an integrated theoretical model of paraphilia and its extreme variant, namely, erotophonophilia. In particular, the motivational model of Burgess et al. (1986) and the trauma control model of Hickey (1997, 2001) possess key components suggestive of a viable and useful synthesis. Clearly, both models discuss some aspects of the paraphilic process as a system of behavior. However, neither of them offers a detailed conceptualization of sadistic sexual conduct. This is surprising, especially since comprehending the paraphilic process may be of considerable significance for future clinical forensic intervention as well as police homicide practices.

The elements of and need for this synthesis are essential to this book's thesis. As such, both the operation of these respective typologies, as well as their assimilation, are thoroughly discussed within the context of this volume. However, in order to preliminarily understand how sadistic deviance and sexual violence function as a systemic process, as well as how they manifest themselves criminally, some cursory observations on the phenomenon of paraphilia are warranted.

## ON PARAPHILIA AND LUST MURDER:
## A PRELIMINARY REVIEW

Paraphilia literally means "abnormal love." *Para* is a Greek term for beyond, or outside the usual, and *philia* is a Greek term for love (Money, 1990, p. 27; Hickey, 2005). From a clinical perspective, paraphilias are a group of persistent sexual behavioral patterns in which unusual objects, fetishes, rituals, or situations are required for full sexual satisfaction (Money & Werlas, 1982, p. 58; DSM-IV TR, 2000). The average number of paraphilias is 4.8 per person (Holmes, 1991, p. 19). Multiple paraphilias are often found in an individual; however, one paraphilia typically becomes dominant until it is replaced by another (Abel et al., 1988, pp. 159–161; Hickey, 1997, p. 15).

There are a number of essential components to most paraphilic behaviors, including fantasy, compulsive masturbation, and facilitators (e.g., alcohol, drugs, and/or pornography). Research on the role of fantasy demonstrates that it principally serves to influence, induce, or motivate violent and/or deviant sexual conduct (e.g., George & Marlat, 1989; Greenlinger & Bryne, 1987; Langevin & Lang, 1985; McGuire, Carlisle, & Young, 1965; Malamuth & McLlwraith, 1988; Hickey, 2005; Prentky, Burgess, Rokous, et al., 1989). Studies on compulsive masturbation and paraphilia indicate that the former, as a reinforcer, is integral to sustaining the fantasy system. Indeed, the orgasm ultimately becomes a conditioned response to the paraphilic imagery. Thus, the fantasies are bolstered by "powerful sex drives that, in turn, facilitate some unusual behaviors" (Hickey, 1997, p. 15). Inquiries addressing the connection between facilitators and paraphilic activity suggest that alcohol, drugs, and pornography are positively correlated with sexual and serial homicide (e.g., Douglas et al., 1995; Hazelwood, Reboussin, & Warren, 1989). However, a causal connection between facilitators and the etiology of paraphilic behavior remains inconclusive (Hickey, 2005).

Paraphilias exist on a continuum, and have the potential to become more violent over time. Diagnosed levels of paraphilic seriousness include mild, moderate, or severe (Abel & Osborne, 1992, p. 675; DSM-IV TR, 2000). What distinguishes "normal" paraphilic individuals from their "abnormal" (and pathological) counterparts is that the former can function sexually without the sadistic stimuli and fantasy. The behavior is only considered abnormally paraphilic when the individual needs and depends on the aberrant fantasy for sexual arousal and gratification. In the absence of the paraphilic stimuli and fantasy, the dysfunctional individual loses his ability to behave in an appropriate sexual manner. In extreme cases, the person comes to depend on the paraphilia so much so that this reliance causes significant distress or impairment in interpersonal, social, and occupational contexts, or other important areas of everyday life (Matthews, 1996).

In order to understand how paraphilias work, it is important to conceptualize these behaviors as functioning from within a systemic process (Arrigo & Purcell, 2001). Paraphilic activities are rooted in early childhood development (Hickey, 2005). Research indicates that many individuals who engage in such behaviors experience traumatic events during pre-adolescence, usually in the form of sexual and physical abuse (Burgess et al., 1986; Hickey, 2001). For example, studies conducted on child molesters (e.g., Simon, 1996), rapists (e.g., Graney & Arrigo, 2002; Hazelwood, 2001), and lust murderers (e.g., Douglas et al., 1995; Hickey, 2005) report that offenders utilized paraphilias and fantasy in their conduct, which were precipitated by childhood trauma and triggered their sadistic/deviant behavior or serial killing. And, as others have explained, the effects of such pre-adolescent traumatization can be devastating, even producing revenge fantasies in some cases (Eth & Pynoos, 1985).

As previously mentioned, erotophonophilia or lust murder is at the most extreme end of the paraphilic continuum. Interestingly, this severest of sexual deviations is comprised of several other paraphilias. Paraphilias typically associated with lust murder include flagellationism, anthropophagy, picquerism, and necrosadism (Holmes, 1991, p. 68; Egger, 2002; Palermo, 2004). Flagellationsim is an intense desire to beat, whip, or club someone. Anthropophagy involves an intense desire to eat the flesh or body parts of another. Picquerism is the intense desire to stab, wound, or cut the flesh of another person. Often, these stab wounds are inflicted near the genitals or breasts in the act of lust killing (DeRiver, 1956). Necrosadism involves sexual contact with a dead body.

Clearly, the above-mentioned paraphilias have a common element: all are in some way sadistic in nature. According to Money (1990, p. 27), sexual sadism is an "obsessive and compelling repetition of sexual thoughts, dreams, or fantasies that may be translated into acts [where] the mental or physical suffering of a victim is intensely sexually arousing." Thus, the various combinatory and interactive effects of those paraphilias that constitute lust murder make for a very troubling, disturbing, and volatile phenomenon (Holmes & Holmes, 2002a).

In addition to the sadistic dimension of erotophonophilia is the role that lust or eroticism plays in forming and sustaining the paraphilic behavior. "The notion of lust suggests one who possesses a particular urge, not only to kill, but [also] to ravage [and devour] the victim" (Hickey, 1997, p. 69). The lust murderer is motivated and consumed by the need for ultimate sexual satisfaction. One example of this is torture. The offender tortures the victim, either pre- or post-mortem, for the sole purpose of achieving climax. The orgasm, and the sexually sadistic nature by which it is reached, symbolize complete domination by the assailant over the victim, whether the offender's prey is alive or dead (Hazelwood & Douglas, 1980; DeRiver, 1956).

Lust murderers have a proclivity to engage in serial killing (Egger, 2002; Hickey, 2003). The FBI defines and classifies erotophonophilia as murder that involves more than three victims, where the offender has a cooling-off period between murders, indicating the premeditation of each sexual offense (Simon, 1996). Both the nature and content of the assailant's fantasy system act as catalysts for each subsequent killing. Typically, the manifestation of these sexually aggressive fantasies involves inappropriate sexual behavior (e.g., touching or fondling a victim); however, as the fantasies become increasingly violent, so, too, do the offenses. This escalation in overt erotic aggression is linked to the fantasy system of the offender, who associates sex with violence (Hickey, 2005). Indeed, routine themes identified within these fantasies include power, domination, molestation, revenge, and degrading and humiliating others (Holmes & Holmes, 2002a; Simon, 1996).

## ORGANIZATION OF THE BOOK

The main research objective of this book is to illustrate the relationship that exists between paraphilia and lust murder. In addition, the aim is to demonstrate, through the use of an integrative typology, the sensible application of this association to established or future cases of lust murderers. For exemplification purposes, the clinical and criminal story of Jeffrey Dahmer, a sexually deviant lust murderer, has been selected. According to most reports, Dahmer represented the quintessential lust murderer (Palermo, 2004, pp. 121–124; Tithecott, 1999). Finally, this book intends to explore, on a provisional and speculative basis, the practical implications stemming from the integrative model, given the case in question. Concerns related to law enforcement training and administration (forensic), psychological practice, and law and public policy are all featured. Thus, the book's organization and focus unfolds with these three objectives in mind.

In Chapter 2, the relevant literature on paraphilia and lust murder is systematically reviewed. As previously stipulated, paraphilia is conceptualized as a continuum of behavior, ranging from normal to abnormal to pathological. Social and behavioral science research investigating the presence of paraphilia commonly found within clinical as well as criminal populations is discussed. This commentary is significant. It enables the reader to comprehend the full context within which sexually aberrant behaviors manifest themselves in society. This includes casual sexual behavior with a consenting partner absent harm, as well as violent and sadistic conduct with nonconsenting persons.

Chapter 2 also describes the basic components of aberrant sexual deviance, including fantasy and masturbation, and various paraphilic facilitators, such as alcohol, drugs, and pornography. Understanding paraphilia as a systemic process of behavior enables the reader to discern the relationship between sadistic deviance and sexual violence (i.e., erotophonophilia). Ultimately, this discernment is useful to the detailed assessment of the various conceptual models explored in subsequent chapters. Moreover, the chapter features relevant information on the criminogenic structure of the lust murderer's crimes as well as the psychopathological dimensions of erotophonophilia. Along these lines, useful commentary on the organized nonsocial lust murderer and the disorganized asocial lust murderer is highlighted.

In Chapter 3, the distinct theoretical models that attempt to explain sadistic homicide, serial murder, and sexual killing are all thoroughly reviewed. Delineating the specifics of each model is relevant on two fronts. First, the respective typologies build on one another, thereby yielding "added value" in the effort to understand the paraphilic continuum. Second, by specifying the dimensions of this process, a more complete (and accurate) understanding of lust murder is made possible. Jointly, these matters are suggestive for much needed future research, germane to the empirical assessment of the proposed integrative model's overall reliability and validity.

In Chapter 4, the essential features of the integrative paraphilic model are identified and examined. The synthetic typology is an amalgam of the sadistic homicide, serial murder, and sexual killing theoretical frameworks systematically reviewed in the previous chapter. Chapter 4 demonstrates where and how the new model is more comprehensive and complete than its predecessors, especially in terms of providing useful information relative to paraphilia and erotophonophilia.

In Chapter 5, the high-profile case of Jeffrey Dahmer is featured. Important background information on his life narrative is provided. Particular attention is paid to such matters as childhood experiences; early sexual identity; fantasy development; victimization tendencies; educational, criminal, and employment history; increasingly violent and homicidal actions; and paraphilic behaviors. The observations in this chapter set the stage for the detailed application work developed in the subsequent chapter.

In Chapter 6, the utility and soundness of each theoretical typology in question is carefully assessed, given the case study of Jeffrey Dahmer. In particular, this includes the motivational model, the trauma control model, and the proposed integrative paraphilic model. By interpreting the case of Dahmer through these three distinct (although related) conceptual lenses, it is possible to identify what contribution each framework makes to our understanding of the crime of lust murder and to those responsible for its serial commission.

In Chapter 7, the similarities, differences, and unique aspects of the motivational, trauma control, and integrative paraphilic typologies are systematically discussed. The aim of this exercise is to demonstrate the relative strengths and limits of the respective frameworks, especially as each one endeavors to account for the phenomenon of paraphilia and its extreme variant of erotophonophilia. Ultimately, the work undertaken in this chapter helps illustrate the rich explanatory and predictive properties of the integrative model and how its investigative capabilities exceed all other theoretical counterparts. Thus, Chapter 7 intends to show how the synthetic framework offers a more incisive and robust understanding of the paraphilic systemic process, of the manifestation of sexually aberrant (and sadistic) behavior, and of how paraphilias function as a compelling motive in sexual crimes, including the offense of lust murder.

In Chapter 8, the implications of the book's findings are very conditionally and speculatively delineated. Indeed, generalizing from the case of Jeffrey Dahmer can at best be described as a provisional exercise. However, the purpose of this final chapter is to suggest what work remains if the phenomenon of paraphilia is to be more completely understood and if the crime of lust murder is to be more effectively halted. The chapter concludes by summarizing the essential features of the overall project. Along these lines, suggestions for future research and the limits of generalizing from the integrative model are discussed.

This project was undertaken in an attempt to advance the knowledge base relative to sexual deviance, the paraphilic continuum, and the crime of lust murder. As a practical matter, these issues raise important questions about how best to clinically recognize and treat high-risk sexually sadistic behaviors and the proactive criminal justice responses necessary to protect victims.

As practitioners, researchers, and educators, our interests include how these behaviors emerge, progress, and sustain themselves, as well as how such erotophonophilic offenders can be identified, treated, and, hopefully, rehabilitated.

# 2

# PARAPHILIA AND
# LUST MURDER

## OVERVIEW

In this chapter, the etiology and development of paraphilic behaviors are examined. In addition, how these behaviors exist and function on a continuum, ranging from normal to abnormal, is delineated. By exploring the paraphilic process in this way, it is then possible to explicate how sexually aberrant behaviors manifest themselves and progress within an individual through the use of fantasy, masturbation, and facilitators. Examples of these facilitators include drugs, alcohol, and pornography.

A paucity of information (either empirical or anecdotal) regarding the etiology of paraphilia, as well as research explaining and supporting the progression of such behavior, exists in the extant literature (Hickey, 2005). However, what is known makes evident that paraphilic behaviors have their roots in early childhood development (Arrigo & Purcell, 2001; Hickey, 2001). For example, studies indicate that many individuals who engage in such conduct experience traumatic events early in their lives, usually in the form of childhood sexual assault and/or physical abuse (e.g., Hazelwood & Douglas, 1980; Hickey, 2005; Holmes & Holmes, 2002a). Accordingly, in this chapter, social and behavioral science research is presented that illustrates how such events unfold and function as motivational or catalytic dimensions (i.e., triggering mechanisms) in the etiology of sexually deviant behavior.

The ultimate paraphilia investigated in the ensuing pages is erotophonophilia, also known as lust murder or sexual homicide. As previously indicated, erotophonophilia is located on the extreme end of the paraphilic continuum. It is comprised of several other paraphilias, including necrophilia, sadism, anthropophagy, vampirism, and flagellation. Each of these sexually sadistic behaviors is briefly discussed, especially in terms of their dynamic relationship with and contribution to the emergence and maintenance of erotophonophilia.

Additionally, the development of early childhood sexual fantasies and their aggressive content are explored. Fantasy is a vital component in the facilitation of paraphilic conduct. In order to sustain the erotically charged nature of the violent image, compulsive masturbation typically is featured. Compulsive masturbation essentially reinforces the paraphilic behavior, and the person ultimately becomes conditioned to the erotic deviance and fantasy. This conditioning process is addressed within the scope of this chapter.

A major focal point in both classic and contemporary research on paraphilia is the vital role that fantasy and visual imagery play, especially in motivating and sustaining this type of sexual aberration (DeRiver, 1949; Hickey, 1997, 2005; Holmes & Holmes, 2002a; MacCulloch et al., 1983; McGuire et al., 1965; Prentky, Burgess, Rokous, et al., 1989). During the past 25 years, experts have done extensive research on the role that fantasy and aggression assume in paraphilic behaviors and violent imagery, including the act of lust murder (Hickey, 2001, 2005; Douglas et al., 1995). As such, Chapter 2 also investigates the connection between sexualized and aggressive fantasies and sadistic or otherwise violent behaviors. This commentary is useful in that it helps establish the powerful association that lust murderers make between violence and sexual arousal. However, in order to situate the following remarks on paraphilia and sexual homicide, some cursory observations on sexuality and the societal mechanisms for determining it are warranted.

## UNDERSTANDING SEXUALITY: FROM NORMATIVE TO ABNORMAL TO PATHOLOGICAL

To completely comprehend and fully appreciate the unique qualities and underlying dynamics of sexually aberrant behavior, it is crucial to understand the elements inherent in all erotic behaviors, specifically, those considered normative in orientation. So, what is considered normal sex? The answer is quite elusive and difficult, especially given the very controversial nature of the subject matter. Sex and sexuality are a function of our humanity and the manner in which people or groups distinctively express it. However, societies' regulations, as well as different cultural standards, can adversely affect the way in which sex and sexuality are perceived (e.g., Holmes & Holmes, 2002a; Kimmel & Plante, 2004; Knafla, 2002; Lancaster & Di Leonardo, 1997). Indeed, a society determines what is considered normal sexual ideation and conduct (Kimmel & Plante, 2004). Yet, depending on the culture, individuals have the right to choose their own personal preferences relative to the sexual behaviors in which they engage, as well as to determine what they consider normal and abnormal sexual conduct (Weeks, Holland, & Waites, 2003).

In a heterogeneous society with many individual differences, it is inevitable that sexuality will be personal, diverse, and manifold (Kimmel & Plante, 2004). Thus, what one person deems normal, appropriate, and healthy may be regarded as abnormal, inappropriate, and unhealthy by another individual (Lancaster & Di Leonardo, 1997). Because of varying perspectives on what is considered sexually normative, erotic behavior in general should be conceptualized as a continuum, ranging from normal to abnormal to, in the extreme, pathological (Kimmel & Plante, 2004; Weeks, Holland, & Waites, 2003). Within this framework, it is inevitable that some people will need more sexual stimulation than others, and may engage in more *perverse* behaviors in order to be sexually aroused and satisfied. However, perverse conduct may be regarded as deviant and even criminal by the society in which one lives (Holmes & Holmes, 2002b; Palermo, 2004).

## DETERMINING NORMAL SEXUAL BEHAVIOR

According to research conducted by Holmes (1991), there are at least four standards used to determine sexual *normalcy*; however, it is difficult to ascertain the applicability of each to individual circumstances, as well as which standard to regard as the most important (see also Holmes & Holmes, 2002a). Both the specified circumstance and individual differences must be considered when making a decision to cite or select a standard. The following is a list of standards associated with sexual behavior, along with corresponding summary definitions. Each standard is subsequently explored in greater detail.

*Statistical*—what most people do
*Religious*—what one's religion permits or prohibits
*Cultural*—what one's culture encourages or discourages
*Subjective*—one's judgment about one's own behavior (Holmes, 1991, p. 2)

*Statistical standards.* Statistical standards of behavior are identified if more than half of the people within a sample either commit or perform a specific act of behavior. Essentially, this percentage then validates normalcy for that given group of individuals. Statistical standards tend to function as an objective measure regarding sexual conduct. Thus, they reflect the normative and consensual approach that people appropriate regarding this form of behavior at a given historical time (Hensley & Tewsbury, 2003; Ward, Laws, & Hudson, 2002).

*Religious standards.* Historically, the role of religion has been pivotal in the development of a value system, especially as it pertains to both individuals and societies (Kimmel & Plante, 2004; Weeks, Holland, & Waites, 2003). Consequently, religious standards influence the way in which people perceive what is considered to be right and wrong. This type of decision making plays a vital role in determining what is sexually acceptable and legally permissible (Knafla, 2002).

*Cultural standards.* Culture is a normative and shared institutional structure consisting of rules, language, ideas, customs, and beliefs that govern a given society (Lancaster & Di Leonardo, 1997). There are many attempts through a society's norms, rules, codes, and criminal sanctions to control and regulate sexual behavior (Holmes & Holmes, 2002a). For example, in the state of California, it is illegal to have sexual intercourse with someone under the age of 18; yet, in the same state, having sex with a dead body (i.e., necrophilia), does not have a specific criminal code within the penal system (Hickey, 2005).

*Subjective standards.* According to some researchers, one of the most important standards for determining normal sexual behavior is the subjective guideline (e.g., Weeks, Holland, & Waites, 2003). This standard legitimates behavior in the same fashion as found among the statistical, cultural, and religious approaches; however, it does so in a very personal and subjective way (Holmes, 1991, p. 4). Moreover, as various investigators have observed, when an act of sexual or other deviance is committed, attempts are made to legitimize the behavior by way of subjective rationalization (Hensley & Tewksbury, 2003; Ward, Laws, & Hudson, 2002).

## ELEMENTS OF SEXUAL BEHAVIOR: NORMAL, ABNORMAL, AND PATHOLOGICAL

In addition to providing a baseline specifying normal sexual standards, several researchers have examined elements inherent in both normal and abnormal sexual conduct (Kimmel & Plante, 2004; Weeks, Holland, & Waites, 2003), as well as those facets located in the extremely dysfunctional and pathological variant (Holmes & Holmes, 2001a, 2001b). For example, both Hickey (2005) and Holmes (1991) have noted that fantasy, symbolism, ritualism, and compulsion are all factors identified as significant when attempting to establish some clear division or useful distinction between normal and abnormal sexual behavior.

To be sexual, one must have erotic fantasies, and without such imaging, it is impossible to be sexual (Holmes & Holmes, 2002a). Other commentators also have drawn attention to the essential role of fantasy in erotic behavior, arguing that sexual imagery is a component of normal sexual activity among most males and females (Bader, 2003; Chodorow, 1994). The creation and use of erotically charged images has been hypothesized to be an important aspect of sexual functioning in some of the earliest theories of psychology (Freud, 2000). Moreover, several contemporary accounts rely upon such formulations when assessing the parameters of normal and abnormal sexual conduct (e.g., O'Donohue, Letourneau, & Dowling, 1997; Palermo, 2004; Palermo & Farkas, 2001).

Fantasy is a fundamental aspect that accounts for extreme deviation from what is typically considered normal sexual activity (Hickey, 2005). A factor that distinguishes normal from abnormal imaging is the nature and content of the fantasy (Bader, 2003). Most abnormal fantasies contain aggressive and sadistic elements. Indeed, according to Holmes and Holmes (2002a), most violent erotic fantasies center on willing partners in consensual, though abnormal, sexual acts. This is the realm in which deviant paraphilic imagery is prominently featured (Hickey, 2005). This topic is discussed in more detail elsewhere in this chapter.

Symbolism pertains to the visual aspect of sex and sexuality (Freud, 2000; Kimmel & Plante, 2004; Lancaster & Di Leonardo, 1997). A common example of sexual symbolism is illustrated in advertisements that market alcohol, cigarettes, or other commodities. The advertisement might utilize an attractive, scantily clad, woman to sell the product to consumers. Sex is visual; sex sells (e.g., Leigh-Kile, 2001).

Holmes (1991) associated sexual symbolism with fetishes and partialisms. A partialism is a type of paraphilia in which sexual attraction is focused exclusively on a specific body part (i.e., a breast, foot, or mouth fetish). He noted that "these philias have a sexual association attached to them" (p. 6). Moreover, he intimated that every male has at least one sexual fetish (see Holmes & Holmes, 2002a). In the context of male heterosexual erotic imaging and symbols, a wide array of female articles of clothing such as bras, garter belts, and negligees are all commonly featured fetish items, as are various parts of the female body. These objects can signify sexualized activity and, when employed in a pathological context, can foster sadistically deviant and sexually violent behavior (Hickey, 2003; Palermo, 2004). For example, Jerry Brudos, a notorious serial killer, had a paraphilia (i.e., partialism) regarding women's feet. He severed them from his victims and kept them as souvenir fetishes in his refrigerator (Hickey, 1997).

Both fetishes and partialisms exist on the paraphilic continuum. They can fall into the mild, moderate, or severe range of this scale (Holmes & Holmes, 2002b). An example of a *normal* fetish might be that of a man who is attracted to feet but who can also function in an appropriate sexual manner without the presence of this stimulus. Conversely, someone with a foot fetish in the severe range absolutely requires and depends on the visual stimulus of feet in order to become erotically aroused and, ultimately, sexually satisfied (Bader, 2003).

In the context of normal or abnormal sexuality, ritualism entails a particularized recognition that one's conduct must be reproduced, mindful of a customary and predictable process (Hickey, 2005). Expressions of such sexualized routinization exist across cultures (e.g., Herdt, 2005; Young, 2003; Weeks, Holland, & Waites, 2003). With ritualism, the sexual act is performed in the same fashion and often in the same sequence (Holmes & Holmes, 2002a). This can be true for married couples as well as for sexual offenders. However, with the sexual offender, the practice of ritualism essentially becomes a form of addictive behavior (Palermo, 2004).

Sexual compulsion is an often uncontrollable urge to engage in some form of sexual conduct (Freud, 2000; Lancaster & Di Leonard, 1997). This behavior can be present in normal relationships, where there is a natural impulse and need to engage in sexual activities with a consenting partner (Kimmel & Plante, 2004). However, this tendency becomes abnormal (and pathological) when the compulsivity is so overwhelmingly potent that genuine emotions toward and authentic caring for the partner are lacking (Small, 2004). With respect to serial sexual offenders, concern for the victim is completely absent. Compulsive feelings well up inside the assailant, launching the person into action (Graney & Arrigo, 2002; Hickey, 2005; Palermo & Kocsis, 2005; Shipley & Arrigo, 2004). Such was the case with the predatory sex offender Ted Bundy. Indeed, as he indicated during his 1978 criminal interrogation in Pensacola, Florida, "there is something deep inside of me, something I can't control, it's so strong" (Holmes, 1991, p. 8).

## DEFINITION OF PARAPHILIA

Paraphilia is a biomedical term that was first used by I. F. Krauss and was adopted by Wilhelm Stekel. Stekel was a psychologist and one of Sigmund Freud's earliest followers. In 1934, a pupil of Stekel's, Benjamin Karpman, introduced the term to American psychiatry (Money & Lamacz, 1989, p. 17; see also Hickey, 2005). Karpman was a psychoanalyst who studied criminal sexual psychopaths at St. Elizabeth's Hospital in Washington, D.C. Paraphilia was officially appropriated as a replacement for the legal construct of *perversion* in the 1980 version of the *Diagnostic and Statistical Manual of Mental Disorders* (i.e., DSM-III) (Money, 1990; Palermo, 2004).

According to the *Diagnostic and Statistical Manual of Mental Disorders* (4th ed.), paraphilia is defined as sexual arousal to objects or situations that are not part of normative stimulation (American Psychiatric Association, 1994). Moreover, as the manual explains, the essential features of all philias are recurrent, intense, erotically laden, arousing images that produce sexual urges or behaviors involving either nonhuman objects (such as fetishes) or the suffering of oneself or one's partner, children, or other nonconsenting individuals (APA, 1994). The definition provided by the DSM-IV for paraphilia is utilized for purposes of this book (see also American Psychiatric Association, 2000).

The paraphilic individual seeks unusual objects, rituals, or specific situations in order to achieve full sexual satisfaction, including orgasmic pleasure (Arrigo & Purcell, 2001). Paraphilia is common almost exclusively in men, and multiple partialisms are frequently employed (Hickey, 2005; Palermo, 2004). However, as investigators note, one paraphilia usually becomes dominant until replaced by another (Holmes & Holmes, 2002b; Hickey, 2001, 2003). Interestingly, in one study examining multiple paraphilic diagnoses among sex offenders, the findings reported that several such partialisms occurred simultaneously, but at different frequencies (Abel et al., 1988). This suggests that in some paraphilic males, the presence of sadistic deviance and sexual violence manifests itself in various forms concomitantly.

## ETIOLOGY OF PARAPHILIA

In order to understand the etiology (or origins) of paraphilias, it is important to briefly comment on a number of factors germane to their pathogenic cause.

These factors include an explanation of the paraphilic continuum, the distinction between their normative and criminal manifestation in individuals, their presence and operation in criminal and clinical populations, and their association to fantasy. Each of these matters is briefly reviewed in the following.

## THE CONTINUUM OF PARAPHILIA

Paraphilias are conceptualized as a continuum of behavior, ranging from mild, moderate, to severe (Abel & Osborne, 1992; Arrigo & Purcell, 2001). Conceiving of paraphilias as operating on a continuum is quite significant, in that this spectrum depicts the clear manifestation and potential progression of such forms of conduct. Moreover, by specifying the mild-to-severe range, it is possible to distinguish innocuous types of paraphilia, such as the use of restraints (i.e., bondage) in consensual sex, from pathological and criminal manifestations, where bondage and sexual force is exercised against nonconsenting persons.

One factor that differentiates the functioning of persons in the paraphilic normal range from their abnormal and pathological counterparts is that *normal paraphiliacs* can behave sexually without fantasy and stimuli (Hickey, 2005; Palermo & Farkas, 2001). Indeed, the behavior is considered dysfunctionally paraphilic only when the individual comes to compulsively rely upon the paraphilic stimuli and fantasy for sexual arousal and gratification (Arrigo & Purcell, 2001; Holmes & Holmes, 2002a). The individual loses his ability to express himself in a sexually healthy fashion without sustained dependence on the paraphilic inducements and imagery. He eventually becomes so reliant on the partialism(s) for orgasmic relief that the paraphilia causes significant distress or impairment in the routine social, interpersonal, and occupational facets of daily life (Hickey, 2005).

## NORMAL PARAPHILIA

According to the American Psychiatric Association, people frequently employ paraphilic fantasies for sexual excitement (Abel & Osborne, 1992; APA, 2000). Normal paraphilic behavior typically goes unreported unless the behavior has brought the individual into conflict with sexual partners or with society (Ward, Laws, & Hudson, 2002). A common paraphilia typically found within the mild and moderate range of the spectrum is fetishism or partialism (Lancaster & Di Leonardo, 1997; Krips, 1999).

A fetish is when a person is sexually aroused by an inanimate object (Hickey, 2001). Specifically, the fetish is required or, at least, strongly preferred in order to foster erotic arousal, sustained excitement and, ultimately, orgasmic pleasure (Bader, 2003). As previously noted, the most common fetishes include female articles of clothing, such as undergarments, shoes, or gloves. Partialisms are an attraction to a specific part of the human body. Similar to fetishes, they are also very common. Partialisms can include a preoccupation with legs, feet, hair, or other aspects of the physical self.

Much like all other paraphilias, fetishes can be situated on the mild-to-severe continuum. An example of this range is depicted in the following scenario of four men, all having a fetish for women with long hair. The first man might have a mild fetish for women with long hair simply because he has always perceived the longer length to be more sexually appealing. The second man, functioning in the mild-to-moderate range, might whistle at and call out to an otherwise unattractive female with long hair yet remain silent when an extremely attractive woman with short hair walks past him. The third man, operating in the moderate-to-severe end of the continuum, might be unable to achieve an erection during intercourse unless he wears a long-haired wig or his partner has long hair. The fourth man might be able to attain an orgasm simply by looking at or touching the desired object. This behavior demonstrates that the individual functions at the severe pathological end of the paraphilic spectrum. The absence of deploying such fetishes in the extremely paraphilic-prone individual can cause erectile dysfunction (APA, 2000). In those instances where the use of fetishes is featured, masturbation is common, especially while the person holds, rubs, or smells the sexualized object (Hickey, 2005).

The example above illustrates the salience and progression of paraphilias. However, based on the degree to which paraphilic behavior is utilized, it is difficult to determine with precision the frequency of deviant behavior within the general population (Hensley & Tewksbury, 2003), unless voluntary treatment is sought or contact with the criminal justice system has been established (Palermo, 2004; Palermo & Farkas, 2001). Moreover, reporting one's deviant proclivities is often deemed a socially undesirable response that could potentially result in self-incrimination for the commission of an unlawful act (Abel & Osborne, 1992; Hickey, 2005; Holmes & Holmes, 2002b).

## CRIMINAL PARAPHILIA

Paraphilic behavior is typically illegal, especially in its abnormal and pathological variants (Palermo & Kocsis, 2005). Moreover, the majority of the research in this area is taken from the criminal population (Kafka, 2003; Palermo & Farkas, 2001). Having said this, it is difficult to accurately ascertain the frequency of arrests for various paraphilic behaviors. While arrests for illegal sexual activities are tabulated regularly by the criminal justice system, these crimes are reported and classified only under one of two categories: forcible rape or other sexual offenses (Abel & Osborne, 1992). This clearly indicates that there is no specific category by which to group paraphilic sexual offenses (Hickey, 2003).

It is even more difficult to attain accurate and specific information regarding the frequency of erotophonophilia or lust murder (Arrigo & Purcell, 2001; Kafka, 2003). The Uniform Crime Reports (UCR) compiled annually by the FBI provides data regarding the number of homicides committed. Based on the UCR, there are five distinct categories in which homicide has been indexed. As Ressler et al. (1988, p. 2; see also Hickey, 2005) indicate, these categories include the following:

1. Felony murder (occurring during the commission of a felony)
2. Suspected felony murder (elements of felony are present)
3. Argument-motivated murder (non-criminally motivated)
4. Other motives or circumstances (any known motivation that is not included in a previous category)
5. Unknown motives (motive fits into none of the above mentioned categories).

With the above indexing in mind, we note that sexual homicide, particularly lust murder, can only be classified in the UCR's "unknown motive" category. This is despite the fact that erotophonophilia is a unique phenomenon with underlying sexual dynamics characteristic of the offense. Given the UCR classification for lust murder, statistics reflecting these types of offenses are often intangible, misleading, or inaccurate (Arrigo & Purcell, 2001). The twin problems of indexing and reporting have led some researchers to assert that under appropriate conditions of confidentiality, self-report data might be a more accurate way to assess the frequency of paraphilic behavior, as well as the phenomenon's pathogenic manifestation and criminogenic progression (Palermo, 2004). However, the best source of accurate information regarding participation in deviant sexual behavior is the paraphilic offender himself (Abel et al., 1988; Hickey, 2003; Palermo & Farkas, 2001).

## PARAPHILIA IN CRIMINAL AND CLINICAL POPULATIONS

Paraphilias commonly found in the clinical as well as criminal arenas include exhibitionism, fetishism, frotteurism, pedophilia, voyeurism, and sexual sadism (Hickey, 2005; Holmes & Holmes, 2002b; Palermo, 2004). Each of these phenomena is relevant to an understanding of paraphilia in general and erotophonophilia in particular (Kafka, 2003). The use of fetishes and partialisms has been explained in discussion of normal, abnormal, and pathological sexuality. As such, they will not be prominently featured here. However, some summary observations on the other paraphilic constructs are warranted.

Exhibitionism is the exposure of one's genitals to a stranger. It is common for the individual to masturbate or experience a sexual fantasy while engaged in this act. More often than not, however, the offender is unable to obtain an erection during these instances. This notwithstanding, for the exhibitionist exposure of the genitalia followed by later masturbation serves to reinforce the behavior, resulting in repetitive compulsive conduct (Hickey, 2001). As with all paraphilias, fantasy is an essential element in facilitating the behavior; thus, masturbation is a reinforcer in this activity (Hickey, 2005). Indeed, the individual conditions his orgasm to the paraphilic stimuli and fantasy, eventually losing all sense of sexual normalcy (Arrigo & Purcell, 2001).

In some cases, the exhibitionist is aware of a desire to surprise and shock his observer. It is this shock value that excites the offender (Maxmen & Ward, 1995; Palermo & Farkas, 2001). However, in other instances, the individual experiences a sexually arousing fantasy in which the observer becomes erotically stimulated or excited (Holmes & Holmes, 2002b). The offender ultimately benefits from a momentary sense of power and control from the imagined encounter (Hickey, 2001).

Frotteurism involves touching and rubbing against a nonconsenting person, usually in a crowded place. The selection of a well-populated locale enables the offender to easily escape detection or to blend into the background if necessary (Holmes & Holmes, 2002a; Palermo & Farkas, 2001). Typically, when the assailant is engaged in his paraphilic conduct, he imagines sharing an exclusive caring relationship with his victim (APA, 2000; Holmes & Holmes, 2002b). Indeed, it is the touching rather than the coercive nature of the act that sexually satisfies him (Hensley & Teksbury, 2003; Maxmen & Ward, 1995).

Pedophilia is an adult's sexual attraction to and relationship with a prepubescent child, generally age 13 years or younger (Arrigo, 2006). According to the *Diagnostic and Statistic Manual*, pedophilia entails "recurrent, intense [and] sexually arousing fantasies, sexual urges or behaviors . . ." (APA, 1994, p. 528). These erotically charged impulses and images can be directed toward either or both sexes and can be found among males or females (Hickey, 2001). The aggression displayed ranges from the very passive to the extremely violent, depending on the fantasy of the individual perpetrator (Palermo, 2004).

A voyeur or peeping Tom receives sexual pleasure by looking at private or intimate scenes (Ward, Laws, & Hudson, 2002). This is usually done by looking through the windows of unsuspecting victims who are naked, in the process of disrobing, or engaged in sexual activity (Kimmel & Plante, 2004; Maxmen & Ward, 1995). In these instances, the offender's intention is not to have direct contact with the victim; it is to masturbate while watching the victim (Davis, 2002). In addition, the voyeur fantasizes that the victim, usually a female, feels "helpless, mortified or terrorized by the fact that a 'peeping Tom' is observing her" (Maxmen & Ward, 1995, p. 326).

Sadism is when the individual derives sexual excitement or gratification from the psychological or physical suffering, including humiliation, of the victim (APA, 1994; Holmes & Holmes, 2002a). The fantasies of this offender typically involve complete control and dominion over the victim, who is terrified in anticipation of the sadistic act (Palermo, 2004). The use of torture is clearly evident with the sadistic paraphilic assailant and usually increases in severity over time (Hickey, 2005). There is a wide variety of sadistic acts; however, the most common include burning breasts, electrocution, and body dismemberment (Hickey, 2003).

Erotophonophilia is the acting out of sexually sadistic behavior by murdering one's victims (Arrigo & Purcell, 2001). Lust killers are likely to repeat their offenses, making their crimes serial in nature. Erotophonophilia is comprised of several other paraphilias (Holmes & Holmes, 2002a). The most frequent of these include flagellation, picquerism, anthropophagy, vampirism, and necrosadism. Because of their relevance to this volume's expressed purpose, each of these phenomena is summarily reviewed.

Flagellation is a form of sadomasochism in which sexual satisfaction is achieved by whipping others or by being whipped (DeRiver, 1949; Hickey, 2001). Beatings and clubbings are also common manifestations of this behavior. For the lust murderer, arousal and orgasm are linked to the intensity, frequency, and duration of the pain inflicted or received (Hickey, 2005).

Picquerism is a profound desire to stab, wound, or otherwise cut the flesh of another (DeRiver, 1956; Holmes & Holmes, 2002a). In lust killings, these stab wounds are usually inflicted on or near the genitalia or breasts (Arrigo & Purcell, 2001). The erotophonophiliac experiences sexual excitement and satisfaction through these acts, especially since they fuel the desire to reach climax.

Anthropophagy is a form of cannibalism in which the offender either eats the victim's flesh directly from the body or slices it off for consumption. Some lust murderers are "known to have eaten the breasts [of victims], while others have cooked portions of the [person's] thighs in a casserole" (Hickey, 1997, p. 16). Once again, the ritualized and sexualized violence of this act makes it possible for the assailant to experience ultimate erotic pleasure.

Vampirism entails the smelling or drinking of blood for purposes of sexual stimulation and gratification (DeRiver, 1949; Hickey, 2001; Holmes, 1991). Typically, the blood that is consumed belongs to the immediate or previous victim. Lust murderers who engage in this type of paraphilic behavior may partake of the victim's blood before, during, and after the individual is assaulted (Holmes & Holmes, 2002a).

Necrosadism and necrophilia involve the desire to have sexual intercourse with a dead body. However, necrosadists murder their victims for the express purpose of having postmortem sex (Holmes & Holmes, 2002a). When linked to erotophonophilia, the behavior becomes serial in nature. Indeed, over time, the only way this type of lust murderer can experience sexual fulfillment is through intercourse with a corpse (Hickey, 2005).

## THE ROLE OF FANTASY

As previously described, sexual fantasy is necessary in acts of eroticism and, without such imaging, it is impossible to be sexual (Holmes & Holmes, 2002a). Fantasies fall along a continuum, with content ranging from rather insipid and benign to bizarre and violent (Bader, 2003; Palermo, 2004). This imaging is an integral element in the emergence and maintenance of most paraphilic behaviors; several influential theorists have implicated paraphilic fantasy in the etiology and maintenance of deviant and violent erotic behavior (e.g., George & Marlat, 1989; Greenlinger & Bryne, 1987; Langevin & Lang, 1985; Malamuth & McLlwraith, 1988; McGuire et al., 1965; Prentky, Burgess, Rokous, et al., 1989). Collectively, the insights derived from these researchers have helped to establish the emerging literature on paraphilia and lust murder (Hickey, 2005).

Understanding the inherent role of fantasy in relation to the nature of paraphilic sexual offenses (i.e., lust murder) is significant for another reason: Formulating treatment and prevention strategies depends on the clinician's capacity to correctly interpret such erotically laden images (Arrigo & Purcell, 2001). Several behavioral and social science researchers have endeavored to address fantasy and paraphilias. Protter and Travin (1987), for example, not only implicated the role of fantasy as a motivating force operating behind and through paraphilic crimes, but they also proposed a bimodal approach in the treatment of paraphilic disorders. Although their observations are incorporated into this book's overall analysis, some summary (and targeted) comments are serviceable here.

Within their work, Protter and Travin (1987) examined both the behavioral and psychodynamic paradigms as they pertain to the theoretical underpinnings of fantasy, particularly fantasy as a driving force underlying paraphilic thoughts, impulses, and conduct. As they noted, the behavioral and psychodynamic treatment approaches have developed their own unique conceptualizations regarding the operation of fantasy (Protter & Travin, 1987; see also Bader, 2003). The authors also specified how paraphilic fantasies could include a series of conscious mental images similar to those that manifest themselves within a daydream.

The psychodynamic perspective regarding fantasy was originally developed within the work of Sigmund Freud (2000). Freud systematically explored both conscious and preconscious aspects of fantasy as being deterministically linked to a person's sexual desires. Notwithstanding more contemporary accounts of its psychodynamic underpinnings (e.g., Bader, 2003), Laplanche and Pontailis (1973) and Protter and Travin (1987) have criticized a number of Freud's more mechanistic contentions.

Specifically, Protter and Travin (1987) relied on more recent psychoanalytic theories for their research, focusing principally on relationship structure. This unique aspect of psychoanalysis emphasizes the enduring need for human relatedness and the importance of a well-formed, secure, and cohesive sense of self and personal identity (e.g., Hendrix, Hunt, Hannah, Luguet, & Mason, 2005; Simpson & Rholes, 1997). According to this perspective, issues central to a more complete psychodynamic assessment emphasize interpersonal relatedness, attachment styles, and general intimacy (Guntrip, 1971; for applications in the criminological and psychological literature see Shipley & Arrigo, 2004). When such factors are underdeveloped or inappropriately established in a person, especially during childhood, behavioral problems surface (e.g., underage drinking, truancy, and other forms of delinquency). Moreover, when coupled with environmental stressors, such as a lack of parental role modeling or care taking, the individual retreats into fantasy as a coping strategy (Bader, 2003). In those situations in which the sense of self and identity remains mostly arrested or negatively constructed, the person's image-making can become increasingly aggressive, sadistic, and violent (Shipley & Arrigo, 2004). This is especially the case for the paraphilic individual (Hickey, 2005). Psychodynamically speaking, the conscious and perverse fantasies that emerge have some kind of representational value that psychically relate to preconscious and unconscious meanings for self and others (Arrigo & Purcell, 2001; Hendrix et al., 2005).

The behavioral perspective on sexual deviance suggests that these actions are a result of classical learning and reinforcement theory (see, e.g., Sapp, 2004; Ward, Laws, & Hudson, 2002). More specifically, this perspective examines the role of fantasy and masturbation in maintaining erotic stimulation (e.g., paraphilia). In the classic works of McGuire et al. (1965), these investigators hypothesized that sexual deviations are conditioned behaviors. They explained this process by drawing attention to the role that masturbation typically assumes in sustaining sexually aberrant conduct. They further suggested that when sexual fantasy precedes orgasm, this becomes a process of conditioned behavior. Any stimulus, circumstantial or deliberate, that regularly precedes ejaculation becomes increasingly sexually exciting and erotically satisfying. McGuire et al. (1965) argued that deliberate stimuli, such as a specific sexual situation or a particular erotic fantasy, represents the process by which most sexual deviations are acquired, developed, and sustained (see also Protter & Travin, 1987).

In addition to studies addressing the psychodynamic and behavioral approaches to fantasy and its role in treating sadistic deviance and sexual violence are efforts to comprehend both specifically in relation to the crime of murder. When examining the motivating factors behind this offense, external precipitating factors have been noted in the literature (e.g., Holmes & Holmes, 2002a). Examples include the heat of passion, accidental killing, or premeditated intentional acts of violence. However, researchers have also identified internal mechanisms for homicide, particularly sexual homicide (Hickey, 2001). Along these lines, Prentky, Burgess, Rokous, et al. (1989) investigated the role of fantasy as an internal drive or psychic force for repetitive acts of sexual violence. They hypothesized that paraphiliac individuals manifest a higher prevalence rate for intrusive fantasies as compared with their non-paraphiliac counterparts. In addition, results from their study indicated that brutal and sadistic images were present in 86% of the serial murderers versus 23% for the single-murder offenders. The researchers concluded that a functional relationship existed between fantasy and repetitive assault behavior (Prentky, Burgess, Rokous, et al., 1989).

The authors relied on the work of MacCulloch, Snowden, Wood, and Mills (1983) to support their contentions. MacCulloch et al. examined 16 sadistic offenders and found that 13 of the 16 individuals were motivated by *internal circumstances* (MacCulloch et al., 1983). Their results indicated that offenders experienced recurring masturbatory fantasies based on aggression and cruelty. Moreover, respondents compulsively pursued outlets to act out their internal daydreams. These efforts initially manifested themselves in the form of imagined events and actors. Eventually, however, these tendencies intensified and featured violent dimensions, including the use of force and the act of sexual assault. As the researchers noted, increased cognitive rehearsal of the fantasy ultimately resulted in the establishment of a more powerful and aggressive content for these offenders.

Fantasy is a safe, private, and powerful reality (Bader, 2003). The paraphiliac individual is socially unable to approach potential partners in a sexually appropriate manner. Given the lack of appropriate sexual socialization and emotionally blunted self-esteem, paraphilic activities become a substitute for healthy human relationships. The individual becomes so immersed in his erotically perverse fantasies that he eventually loses all contact with reality, only to find himself suddenly compelled to actualize, to experience, the full sexual image (Arrigo & Purcell, 2001; Bader, 2003). This process happens repeatedly and compulsively by drawing human objects into the fantasy (Hickey, 2005; Reinhardt, 1957).

Other investigators have reached similar conclusions about the role of fantasy in the commission of sexualized deviance or violence. For example, McGuire, Carlisle, and Young (1965) examined a group of 45 sexual deviates. Their results indicated that over half of the participants, prior to the development of their respective paraphilias, experienced feelings of physical and social inadequacies. In other words, these feelings were not a consequence of their partialisms; rather, they preceded the individual's aberrant sexual thoughts and impulses. The researchers concluded that this felt sense of inadequacy drove individuals away from the expression of normal or healthy sexuality and toward a fantasy world. As McGuire et al. (1965) noted, this was a world in which the subjects of the study imagined increasingly sadistic and violent erotic encounters. When dwelling in a rich, nonjudgmental fantasy world—one free from the personal rejection or criticism routinely found within the external environment—the paraphiliac individual ultimately experiences complete dominion over his sexual partners and assignations. Masturbation following identification of the desired paraphilic stimuli reinforces the fantasy as a potent elixir; that is, as a powerful intact system controlled only by the individual. This enables the paraphiliac individual to experience sexual pleasure and ongoing satisfaction. Consistent with the behaviorally oriented observations of Protter and Travin (1987), this process, as a recurrent system of erotically charged behavior, is best understood in terms of classical conditioning.

Given the various research findings outlined above, it is evident that fantasy is integral to sustaining paraphilic-based sexual offenses. However, the manner in which the paraphilic fantasy initially develops needs further elucidation. Returning to the work of McGuire et al. (1965) offers some intriguing suggestions. The investigators examined sexual deviations as conditioned behavior and posited that the onset of aberrant sexual proclivities was linked to a developmental change. This change included the transition from a normal sexualized fantasy life to that of a paraphilic masturbatory fantasy life.

According to their research, fantasy is based on memory. Memory is subjected to a psychological process consisting of the recall of an event. When recalling an event from memory, distortion and selection of certain cues take place. When emphasis is placed on a cue, the cue becomes more and more dominant because of the positive feedback involved in the conditioning. The more sexually stimulating the fantasy becomes, the greater the likelihood that the progression to a masturbatory fantasy will occur. Consequently, through conditioning, it is the fantasy itself that becomes more and more erotically arousing.

McGuire et al. (1965) offered a paraphilic case example to illuminate this fantasy progression. A 17-year-old male had witnessed a young girl changing clothes through an open window. He was initially stimulated by this encounter and subsequently took to masturbating while remembering the incident. With the passage of time, the memory of the actual event became vague. However, advertisements and shop window displays of women's lingerie continually reminded him of the initial image. These visual cues were used as part of his fantasy and, through the course of 3 years, his sexual interests in women gradually and consistently changed to include an erotic fascination with female undergarments. To sustain his paraphilic fantasy, the man either bought or stole these items.

When examining the fantasy system of lust murderers, it is apparent that these types of offenders associate sex with aggression (Arrigo & Purcell, 2001; Kafka, 2003). A common theme found within these fantasies is the presence of power, domination, molestation, and revenge, as well as the desire to degrade and humiliate others (Simon, 1996). Ultimately, the lust murderer transforms his fantasies into predatory criminal behavior. Additional commentary regarding the role of fantasy in the commission of erotophonophilia is discussed in the subsequent section of this chapter. However, before addressing this particular concern, it is important to more fully explicate both the criminal and clinical facets of erotophonophilia and the sadistic behavior of the lust murderer.

## LUST MURDER OR EROTOPHONOPHILIA

Erotophonophilia can be distinguished from other forms of homicide, including those that are classified as sexual in nature (Hickey, 2005). Lust murder is the commission of a sexual killing and is a distinct subcategory of homicide (Holmes & Holmes, 2002b; Simon, 1996). It is not the same as sadistic homicide. Lust murder involves a mutilating attack, such as the displacement of the breasts, rectum, or genitals from the victim's body (Hazelwood & Douglas, 1980; Holmes & Holmes, 2002a). It is also common for the genitalia to have been subjected to stabbing or slashing with a sharp instrument (Arrigo & Purcell, 2001).

As previously noted elsewhere in this chapter, the body's mutilation typically takes place postmortem (Hickey, 2001). Moreover, the victim's death often occurs shortly following the assailant's abduction or attack. Killing is an integral part of the sexual excitement (Simon, 1996). Dr. J. Paul DeRiver, an early researcher on the phenomenon of lust murder, commented on the essential criminogenic dimensions of this behavior in his book, *Crime and the Sexual Psychopath* (1956):

> [T]he lust murderer, usually after the killing, tortures, cuts, maims or slashes the victim in the regions on or about the genitalia, rectum, and breasts in females. It is also common for this offender to cut on or about the neck, throat and buttocks, as usually these parts serve as a sexual stimulus. (as cited in Hazelwood & Douglas, 1980 p. 40)

The notion of *lust* murder suggests one who possesses a particular urge not simply to kill but also to ravage his victim(s) (Arrigo & Pucell, 2001). The lust murderer is motivated by the need for ultimate sexual satisfaction, exemplified by the acts in which the offender engages, either pre- or postmortem. The sexualized persecution at the core of the assailant's behavior is principally inflicted as a means of sustaining arousal and attaining orgasm.

Lust murderers exhibit a progression of brutality (Hickey, 2005), and each subsequent murder becomes more vicious and sadistic. Erotophonophiliacs establish a violently sexualized relationship in their minds that they have rehearsed repeatedly while masturbating. They may initially experience innocuous paraphilia; however, as their fantasies and daydreams become more aggressive in nature, the paraphilic stimuli also progresses in intensity, frequency, and duration (Arrigo & Purcell, 2001). Indeed, each time the paraphilic fantasy is acted upon, increasing levels of sadistic deviance and sexualized violence are required in order to reach orgasm. These offenders experience an exhilarating rush of erotic excitement and satisfaction from their actions. They are quite impulsive (and compulsive) in their behavior and are unable to escape their fantasy world. This is a sexualized imagined realm that is robust with themes of power, control, sex, violence, and mutilation (Hickey, 2001).

The lust murderer's victims represent objects or props in which the assailant acts out his fantasies (Kafka, 2003; Simon, 1996). Investigators note that the victims can be male or female (Holmes & Holmes, 2002a), are primarily heterosexual in orientation, and come from different racial/ethnic groups (Hickey, 2005).

The impetus for lust murder is the sexually aggressive images and cognitions harbored within the thought processes of the individual (Holmes & Holmes, 2002a). Traumatic pre-adolescent events and a lack of structure and support from the home environment fuel these fantasies (Hickey, 2001). Consistent with this notion of a *lost childhood*, research specifically indicates that sexual murderers are created within early childhood development, particularly before the age of 5 or 6 (Hickey, 2005; Douglas, Burgess, & Ressler, 1995).

In terms of ascertaining the relationship between thinking patterns containing aggressive fantasies and sexualized death, some research suggests that the assailant's thought configurations are established early and exist in a context of social isolation (Hickey, 2001; Douglas et al., 1995). According to the psychological research, serial sexual killers usually reach their peak for killing in the late 20s, with a range in age from the early 20s to the mid-30s (Dietz, Hazelwood, & Warren, 1996; Simon, 1996). Moreover, their fantasies generally begin in mid-adolescence, 10 to 15 years before the first slaying (Hickey, 2005).

One study examined behavioral indicators in childhood and adolescence among 36 sexual murderers. The results indicated that the factors motivating offenders to kill included daydreaming and fantasy (Ressler, Burgess, Harman, Douglas, & McCormack, 1986; see also Douglas et al., 1995). Another internal component that was identified was compulsive masturbation. Within the same study, over 50% of the subjects reported specific behavioral indicators that were consistent in childhood, adolescence, and adulthood. The following internalized behaviors were also noted within the research: (a) childhood—82% daydreaming, 82% masturbation, 77% isolation; (b) adolescence—81% daydreaming, 82% masturbation, 77% isolation; (c) adulthood—81% daydreaming, 81% masturbation, 73% isolation (Ressler et al., 1986; see also Dietz et al., 1996).

The information obtained from this self-report data helps to support the contention that a systemic process of paraphilic behaviors contributes to the emergence and maintenance of the lust murderer's actions. Subsequent research (e.g., Douglas et al., 1995; Dietz et al., 1996; Kafka, 2003; Hickey, 1990a, 2001) confirms this hypothesis. However, what remains to be thoroughly explored is the full operation of the paraphilic process, mindful of the existing typologies on serial murder and sexual homicide. This issue represents the substance of what Chapters 3 and 4 investigate. As we contend, by investigating the existing models on the subject (i.e., the motivational and the trauma control typologies) and by proposing how the two can be usefully assimilable (i.e., the integrative model), our understanding of the paraphilic systemic process will be deepened and our understanding of the lust murderer's behavior will be more complete. Both are relevant for purposes of police administration and management, clinical treatment and prevention, and law and public policy. However, before turning to these matters, this section concludes with some summary descriptions of the established typologies on lust murder.

## FBI TYPOLOGIES FOR LUST MURDER

To date, some law enforcement efforts have been undertaken in order to determine the sort of person capable of committing erotophonophilia. Indeed, along these lines, special agents working within the Behavior Science Unit of the Federal Bureau of Investigation have developed profiles of potential lust murderers. According to their classification schema, two types of individuals engage in erotophonophilia: the *organized nonsocial* and the *disorganized asocial* personality (Hazelwood & Douglas, 1980; see also, Douglas et al., 1995; Douglas, Burgess, Burgess, & Ressler, 1992; Hickey, 2005). The relationship between the two typologies is discussed in the next subsection. A cataloguing of the unique properties for each, as well as a synopsis detailing the nature of the lust crimes they respectively commit, follows thereafter.

## Similarities Between Organized Nonsocial and Disorganized Asocial Lust Murderers

The common denominator for both types of lust murderers is the essential role of fantasy (e.g., Canter, Alison, Alison, & Wentink, 2004). As others have reported, fantasy is the principal motivating factor in erotophonophilia (e.g., Hickey, 2001; Holmes & Holmes, 2002a). Because of this, acts of organized and disorganized lust murder are considered crimes of premeditation. Indeed, situated within the assailant's fantasies is the *blueprint* or unrealized image for the offense's likely commission.

Interestingly, erotophonophiliacs can act on their fantasies somewhat impulsively or on the *spur of the moment*, especially when the "right" opportunity presents itself (Hazelwood & Douglas, 1980; Douglas et al., 1995). Moreover, lust murderers typically utilize a variety of fetishes in the commission of their sadistic crimes (Hickey, 2001). As we have noted, this sexual offender collects souvenir fetishes such as an object of clothing from the victim or a specific body part (e.g., a finger, a lock of hair, a limb infused with sexual signification) (Simon, 1996). In the case of one lust murderer, the offender decapitated his victim, shampooed the slain person's hair, applied make-up to the individual, and then had sexual intercourse with the severed head while showering (Hickey, 1997, p. 17). The primary function of a souvenir fetish is so that the offender can relive the actual event within the context of the fantasy, usually while masturbating to maintain sexual arousal and achieve orgasm (Canter et al., 2004).

The distinguishing characteristic of the lust murderer involves extreme mutilation and body dismemberment of those assailed. For example, it is common for this sex offender to gnaw on or bite off the victim's breasts, buttocks, neck, abdomen, thighs, or genitals, since these body parts possess a potent sexual connotation for the lust murderer (Palermo, 2004). In addition, the erotophonophiliac frequently amputates limbs or breasts, and is even inclined to completely dissect and eviscerate his victim (Holmes & Holmes, 2002a).

The most frequent methods of killing for both the organized nonsocial and the disorganized asocial lust murderer include strangulation; blunt force; or stabbing with a sharp instrument (Canter et al., 2004; Douglas et al., 1995). It is uncommon for the lust murderer to rely on a firearm; there is scant psychosexual gratification when utilizing such an impersonal weapon (Hazelwood & Douglas, 1980; Holmes & Holmes, 2002a).

## Organized Nonsocial Type: A Profile

The organized nonsocial lust murderer is self-centered and egocentric (Hickey, 2005). He has problems respecting the rights of others as well as society. He harbors resentment toward people; however, he makes no attempt to avoid being put in social situations. Instead, he manipulates others for his personal gain, including the desire for ultimate sexual satisfaction. This type of lust murderer revels in the pleasure he receives, given the impact of his crime and its interpretation by the social order. The organized nonsocial lust murderer is fully cognizant that killing innocent people is the most extreme way in which he can inflict havoc on and seek revenge from society. Consequently, he is capable of distinguishing between right and wrong.

### Crimes of the Organized Nonsocial Type

The organized nonsocial lust murderer is cunning and methodical, which is usually demonstrated in the commission of his criminal acts (Hazelwood & Douglas, 1980; Douglas et al., 1995). Typically, victim selection is arbitrary. This sexual offender frequently lives some distance from the actual crime scene and employs *cruising* time to seek out a victim. The organized nonsocial erotophonophiliac generally carries his weapon of choice both to and from the crime scene. Additionally, this assailant is more likely to commit his crime in an isolated locale and then transport the body to a venue where there is a high probability that it will be discovered. Generally speaking, the offender is excited by the discovery of the slain body, as well as by society's reaction (Hickey, 2005).

The organized nonsocial lust murderer may dissect the victim's body in an attempt to hinder identification (Hazelwood & Douglas, 1980). Penile penetration of the victim is a common characteristic of this sex crime (Palermo & Farkas, 2001; Palermo, 2004). As previously described, this penetration can occur as an expression of postmortem sexual intercourse otherwise known as necrophilia.

Investigators note that it is unlikely that the nonsocial organized erotophonophiliac will leave any physical evidence behind at the crime scene (e.g., Douglas et al., 1995). This is principally because this sexual offender is organized, cunning, and methodical, which decreases the likelihood of detection and apprehension (Holmes & Holmes, 2002a). Both the nonsocial and asocial lust murderers are inclined to visit the scene of their crimes. However, the nonsocial organized type does this as a way to assess the progress of the investigation, as well as to verify if the body has been discovered. Researchers report that it is common for this sexual offender to obsess over the police investigation, even to the point of frequenting after-hour law enforcement establishments (Hazelwood & Douglas, 1980; Hickey, 2005). The planned intent is to eavesdrop on discussions of unsolved crimes or to otherwise participate in the actual criminal inquiry.

### Disorganized Asocial Type: A Profile

This type of lust murderer is regarded as a loner, a social introvert, or as an "outsider" (Douglas et al., 1995). He prefers his own company and has difficulty establishing or maintaining interpersonal relationships. The disorganized asocial erotophonophiliac often feels rejected by others, which fosters and confirms a profound sense of loneliness, despair, and helplessness. This sexual offender engages in serial sexual homicide in a very chaotic fashion. Indeed, the crimes committed by this offender often appear random and unplanned. Questions persist about the mental state of this sex offender, especially whether he possesses the capacity to distinguish between right from wrong and whether his offenses are a chronic product of the lack of impulse control (Palermo, 2004).

### Crimes of the Disorganized Asocial Type

The disorganized asocial killer commits his crimes in a more frenzied, less methodical manner than his organized nonsocial counterpart. The disorganized asocial erotophonophiliac is more likely to use a weapon of opportunity, such as a sharp object, which is then left behind at the crime scene (Hazelwood & Douglas, 1980). It is this very behavior that contributes to this sex offender's designation as a disorganized lust murderer. The crimes committed by the disorganized asocial lust murderer are frequently committed close to either his residence or place of employment. These locations provide him with a deep sense of security. This sense of safety or sanctuary creates a calming effect, engendering control over the situation, the victim, and the violence that unfolds (Hickey, 2005). Additionally, the disorganized asocial erotophonophiliac typically leaves the victim's body at the crime scene, making no effort to conceal the corpse or his violence.

Some investigators note that the asocial disorganized lust murderer is likely to smear the victim's blood on the victim, on himself, or the surface on which the body is resting (Douglas et al., 1995). This typifies the frenzied-like nature of the attack (Hazelwood & Douglas, 1980; Kafka, 2003). Interestingly, this erotophonophiliac is motivated by a curious need to acclimate himself to the sexually significant parts of the dead victim's body (Holmes & Holmes, 2002a), which he does by exploring various parts of the sexual anatomy to determine how they function and appear beneath the skin. This fascination often compels the assailant to insert foreign objects into various body orifices, resulting in masturbation and ejaculation on or near the victim (Hickey, 2005). It is also common for this offender to revisit the scene of his crimes, allowing him to either engage in more mutilation of the corpse or to relive the exhilarating sexualized experience in his mind.

## SUMMARY AND CONCLUSION

This chapter addressed a number of important research themes germane to our overall project on lust murder, sadistic deviance, and sexualized violence. In particular, the construct of sexuality was examined, mindful of the relevant literature on its normal, abnormal, and pathological variants. Both the definition for and the etiology of paraphilias were delineated, the paraphilic continuum was described, and the role of fantasy (and masturbation) in the emergence and maintenance of various partialisms was reviewed. Indeed, as the chapter explained, erotic fantasies function as a major motivating factor in the acting out of sundry paraphilic behaviors.

Aberrant sexual behaviors are diverse and manifold. However, when they manifest themselves in extreme form, they are both dysfunctional and criminal. On the paraphilic continuum, this is the realm in which lust murder is situated. The chapter concluded by exploring a full range of issues pertinent to a proper clinical and criminological assessment of erotophonophilia. Specific topics examined included FBI typologies for lust murder (i.e., organized nonsocial and disorganized asocial types), as well as the context in which both types of offenders behave similarly. Several distinctive features related to these lust murderers were enumerated, including attention to their respective clinical profiles and criminal actions.

At this juncture, it remains to be seen how the existing models on sexual homicide and serial murder account for the crimes perpetrated by the lust murderer. To address this matter, both the motivational and the trauma control models are prominently featured in the following chapter. As we contend, understanding their respective theoretical components is both logical and prudent. These frameworks give us useful clues about the paraphilic process, especially as an entrenched system of behavior. Moreover, if it can be shown how these models operate when carefully integrated, then greater prospects for scientific explanation and prediction are realizable. These matters are profoundly relevant and sorely needed, especially as society endeavors to comprehend the crime of lust murder and those who commit such acts.

# 3

# SEXUAL HOMICIDE AND
# SERIAL MURDER:

## WHAT DO WE KNOW?

## OVERVIEW

The previous chapter endeavored to situate this book within the relevant literature on sexuality and, more specifically, paraphilia. On the extreme end of the paraphilic continuum is erotophonophilia, the realm of sadistic deviance and sexualized violence. Central to this book's thesis on lust murder are the existing models or typologies that account for the behavior of serial murder and sexual homicide. As we previously argued, these explanatory frameworks contribute to an understanding of the paraphilic process as a system of behavior. Within this process, if aberrant expressions of erotic deviance are left untreated or if they are incorrectly diagnosed, they can escalate and intensify, resulting in sadistic, predatory acts. Regrettably, little is know about the operation of this system, particularly as it relates to the emergence and maintenance of erotophonophilia and the sex crimes this offender commits. In order to remedy this deficiency in the literature, Chapter 3 systematically examines the relevant typologies on sexual homicide and serial murder.

The motivational model developed by Burgess and colleagues (1986) conceptually accounts for sexual murder. The trauma control model constructed and refined by Hickey (1991, 1997, 2001) theoretically explains repetitive homicidal acts. Both typologies are prominently featured in this chapter. In order to extend, deepen, or otherwise complement the presentation of this material, the contributions of MacCulloch et al. (1983), as well as Brittain (1970), are strategically incorporated into the analysis. As we contend, each model examined within the scope of this chapter contains fundamental social, psychological, cognitive, and/or biological aspects that help further explain the phenomenon of paraphilia and its etiology, as well as how paraphilic behaviors work in concert as a systemic process.

In order to address these matters, the chapter begins with some brief commentary on the relevance of the motivational and trauma control models, especially as identified in the extant literature. These observations provide a necessary context for understanding why these respective typologies were selected for investigative purposes in the first place. Moreover, they help clarify why and how these models represent a useful conceptual basis by which to explore the phenomenon of lust murder.

Next, the essential features of the MacCulloch et al. (1983) typology are delineated. Emphasis is placed on elucidating the role of fantasy in the commission of violent and sadistic crimes including, most especially, sexual homicide. The framework developed by MacCulloch et al. is characterized as a classical conditioning model. Linked to this discussion is the work of Brittain (1970) and his efforts to account for the sadistic murderer and to identify the sadistic murderer syndrome.

This commentary is then followed by a careful assessment of the Burgess et al. (1986) motivational model. Particular attention is given to the psychosocial and cognitive components of their typology. These elements form the basis of their theory on sexual homicide and those offenders who engage in these behaviors.

Next, the trauma control model of Hickey (1997, 2001) is presented. Useful to this enterprise is his focus on early (and unresolved) childhood events and how they represent a developmental framework that explains the crime of serial murder and those who commit it. Although previous investigators had identified certain events as contributing to the emergence of the sexual murderer, Hickey also identifies a series of predispositional factors and routine facilitators that fuel a person's proclivities toward serial killing. These additional matters are thoroughly reviewed in this portion of the chapter, particularly as they relate to the offender's low self-esteem, increasingly violent fantasy life, and traumatized condition.

The chapter concludes with some commentary on the explanatory and predictive limits of the classical conditioning model, the motivational typology, and the trauma control framework. These observations demonstrate the need for an alternative or more synthetic framework by which to account for the crime of lust murder. These concluding remarks set the stage for the more integrative work undertaken in Chapter 4.

## BACKGROUND ON THE MOTIVATIONAL AND TRAUMA CONTROL MODELS

There are several dimensions of the motivational model on sexual homicide and the trauma control typology on serial murder that are clearly, unmistakably, and usefully associated with the etiology and operation of paraphilic behaviors.

These dimensions or factors are all systematically examined in the subsequent sections of this chapter. In brief, they include the following: adverse psychosocial and developmental effects stemming from early childhood traumatic events; environmental, sociological, and biological predispositions toward criminal behavior; low self-esteem and social isolation; the role of fantasy in sustaining violent and sexualized thoughts; and the use of facilitators in motivating and/or contributing to homicidal behavior. To some extent, each of these notions was previously identified as underscoring (and informing) the criminal activities of the organized nonsocial and disorganized asocial lust murderer. However, we note that the social and behavioral science research community's ability to specify these factors as relevant to a proper assessment of sexual homicide and serial murder has not occurred in an intellectual vacuum. The insights of Burgess et al. (1986) and Hickey (1997, 2001) emerged within a context. And it is this context that warrants some consideration.

The Federal Bureau of Investigation conducted research on the motivational model of sexual homicide through its Behavioral Science Unit located in Quantico, Virginia. Academic and mental health consultants contributed to these scientific endeavors. This work represented the first law enforcement–oriented behavioral science research project regarding the construction of a criminal personality. It was based on a sample of 36 sexually deviant serial murderers (Douglas et al., 1995). The overall purpose of the study was to elicit information regarding each offender's developmental history; physical and personality characteristics; modus operandi; pre- and post-offense behavior; victim selection, manipulation, and control; as well as techniques used to successfully evade detection, apprehension, prosecution, and confinement (Depue, 1986; Hickey, 2005). The comprehensive nature of the research, as well as its significant contribution to the extant literature, are the principal reasons why this model was chosen for our own project on paraphilia and lust murder. Each element examined in the Burgess et al. (1986) study has direct implications relative to the etiology, maintenance, treatment, and prevention of erotophonophilia, as well as the criminal prosecution of paraphilic offenders, particularly lust murderers.

This invaluable work is complemented by studies conducted by Eric Hickey on the phenomenon of serial murder. In addition to providing vital information on the general structure of serial murder and the personality profiles of those who commit this crime, Hickey detailed the devastating effects of this behavior, particularly in relation to victims and their family members. Hickey was the first to provide a comprehensive, empirical examination of serial murder within the United States (see Hickey, 1997). Along these lines, his original volume, *Serial Murderers and Their Victims* (1991), helped define the fundamental psychological constituents that underpin this behavior and the predatory and repetitive nature of the offender's criminality. Related research conducted by Hickey focuses on several linked themes, including female offenders, missing and murdered children, predatory victimization, and lust murder (e.g., Hickey, 1985, 1986, 1990a, 1990b, 1996, 2005).

The second edition of Hickey's volume *Serial Murderers and Their Victims* (1997) offers a broader conceptualization of this form of criminal conduct. Individual case studies as well as a *typology* for serial homicide are prominently featured. Specifically, Hickey identified and examined the psychological processes in which perpetrators of serial murder find themselves immersed and caught, a self-perpetuating cycle of violent fantasy and sadistic offending. This cycle includes the use of facilitating agents such as drugs, alcohol, and pornography. As Hickey explained, this self-generating and self-perpetuating form of criminal conduct is profoundly linked to traumatic events that adversely affected the offender's development. For Hickey, arrested development, traced to early (and unresolved) childhood trauma, represents the origins of serial homicide and the likely commission of such criminal actions. The third edition of his work, published in 2001, elaborates on many of the pressing issues delineated in the first two editions. The soundness of Hickey's research on serial murder and the compelling linkages between his efforts on this subject matter and the search for a cogent explanation regarding erotophonophilia (e.g., the role of fantasy, predispositional factors, the effect of facilitators) contribute to our selection of his model for purposes of explaining the paraphilic process and lust murder.

Other investigators also have appropriated the insights of Burgess et al. (1986) and Hickey (1997, 2001), especially when accounting for various facets of sadistic deviance, sexual violence, and murder. These ancillary studies further legitimize and justify our decision to rely on both models when attempting to construct an integrative explanatory typology concerning erotophonophilia. To illustrate, several investigators have turned to the work of Burgess et al. (1986) when examining the phenomenon of serial sexual murder, including the theoretical underpinnings of this homicidal act (e.g., DeHart & Mahoney, 1994; Holmes & Holmes, 2003; Grubin, 1994; Prentky, Burgess, Rokous, et al., 1989). Moreover, despite the subsequent editions of Hickey's volume on serial murder, his original work has been the basis for a number of studies addressing the nature of violent crime and criminals, including the wayward actions of the mass murderer (Egger, 1990; Holmes & Holmes, 2000; White, 2001) and the serial homicide offender (Douglas et al., 1995; Holmes & DeBurger, 1988; Holmes & Holmes, 1998). Clearly, then, what these efforts collectively suggest is that the motivational model developed by Burgess et al. (1986) and the trauma control model established by Hickey (1997, 2001) represent a protean basis by which to explore the conceptual contours of the paraphilic process as a system of behavior that underscores the crime of lust murder and explains the conduct of the erotophonophiliac.

## THE CLASSICAL CONDITIONING MODEL

Several influential theorists and notable social scientists have attempted to ascertain the underlying dynamics of sexual and sadistic homicide (e.g., Brittain,

1970; Burgess et al., 1986; Hickey, 2001; MacCulloch et al., 1983; McGuire et al., 1965; Ressler, Burgess, & Douglas, 1988). However, it is the hypothesis-driven work of MacCulloch and colleagues (1983) that in many ways is quite distinctive, especially given its overall contribution to the literature. In particular, these investigators proposed a model in which the role of fantasy was identified as a crucial internal mechanism accounting for the onset of sexual homicide. And, as we have repeatedly suggested based on the existing research, the content of these images is pivotal to comprehending the emergence, development, and maintenance of paraphilic behaviors.

Several investigators have extensively utilized MacCulloch et al.'s (1983) conceptualizations on sadistic fantasy and sexual offending (e.g., Burgess et al., 1986; Douglas et al., 1995; Grubin, 1994; Prentky, Burgess, Rokous, et al., 1989; Ressler, 1988; Ressler et al., 1986). Indeed, MacCulloch et al.'s (1983) work fundamentally informs the motivational model of sexual murder as developed by Burgess et al. (1986). However, before turning to this particular explanatory framework, it is useful to specify the essential features of the MacCulloch et al. (1983) model.

This work examined a sample of sadistic sexual criminals and found that a pattern of violent fantasies influenced the men to engage in compulsive behaviors. As MacCulloch et al. noted, the sexual offenders first imagined these acts and then they committed assault. The authors' findings suggested that when sexual arousal was involved in the sadistic fantasy, the nature and content of the fantasy could be understood on the basis of classical conditioning. This perspective is consistent with the more behaviorally oriented approach as developed by McGuire et al. (1965). Chapter 2 delineated the significance of the classical conditioning model proposed by McGuire et al., especially in relation to the role that fantasy and masturbation assume in sustaining erotic excitement (e.g., paraphilias).

However, in the MacCulloch et al. (1983) model, the more routinely (i.e., compulsively) the individual relied on the sexualized image for arousal and orgasm, the more likely it was that a progression of violent fantasies and habituation occurred. The greatest amount of sexual pleasure, either normal or abnormal, is derived during that period of sexual excitement preceding an orgasm. The investigators found that the subjects of their study experienced perceivable levels of sexual arousal without subsequent orgasm over significant periods of time (MacCulloch et al., 1983, p. 20). It is this absence of sexual fulfillment that fuels the desire for more images with more intense erotic and sadistic content, especially since the goal for the offender is to maximize sexual pleasure.

MacCulloch et al. (1983) relied on the classic work of Brittain (1970), who had previously conducted research on the sadistic murderer. Brittain's efforts resulted in the creation of a checklist of characteristics or a personality inventory that represented the sadistic murderer syndrome. Specifically, Brittain's work gave a clinical description of the sadistic murderer that included the following features: (a) introverted and timid; (b) low self-esteem, yet extremely egocentric; (c) over-controlling mother; (d) social isolation; (e) sexually prudish, reserved, and inexperienced; (f) sexually deviant (i.e., prone to voyeurism, fetishisms, or transvestitism); and (g) rich fantasy life with violent pursuits.

Brittain (1970) maintained that the above-mentioned traits interacted with one another and contributed to the social isolation of the offender. In addition, he surmised that the sadistic killer was more prone to murder, especially when his self-esteem was challenged or otherwise in jeopardy. Brittain's work examined external precipitating factors as causal motivating agents for violent offending.

MacCulloch et al. (1983) went beyond the descriptive work of Brittain and provided evidence that fantasy, functioning as an internal precipitating agent, was more likely to be the primary impetus behind sadistic criminal activity. These investigators further believed that the characteristics proposed by Brittain were insufficient to account for sadistic behavior and the clinical implications that stemmed from such diagnostic assessments. However, they did agree with Brittain (1970) that "the more precise the offender's description, the more probable . . . their early detection" (MacCulloch et al., 1983, p. 21).

For purposes of their research, MacCulloch et al. (1983) offered a working definition for the sadistic behavior of the offender. As they explained, this conduct is best understood as follows:

> the repeated practice of behavior and fantasy which is characterized by a wish to control another person by domination, denigration or inflicting pain, for the purpose of producing mental pleasure and sexual arousal (whether or not accompanied by orgasm) in the sadist. (MacCulloch, 1983 p. 20)

In addition to providing this definitional account, the authors conceptualized sadistic behavior as having varying degrees of control and domination. They further asserted that sadistic behavior represented a common component in *normal* sexual functioning that could manifest itself in numerous ways. The research sample included a total of 16 sadistic murderers, each with a diagnosis of psychiatric disorder.

Of the 16 subjects, 13 self reported that prior to the time of the indexed offense, they had conjured a fantasy linked to sexual arousal and pleasure wherein the manufactured image was identical to all or part of the crime. Their fantasies consisted of rape, sodomy, kidnap, bondage, flagellation, anesthesia, torture, and killing (MacCulloch et al., 1983). Thus, their indexed offenses represented behavioral expressions of their fantasies. Respondents also reported that masturbation was integral to the sadistic images they constructed. In addition, these same 13 subjects described an association between recurrent sadistic fantasies and sexual arousal, as well as experiencing erotic excitement and mental pleasure while committing their offenses.

## THE MOTIVATIONAL MODEL

Burgess et al. (1986) conducted a study examining the motivational factors of 36 sexual murderers. The researchers developed a five-phase motivational model to help explain various factors influencing this behavior. In addition, they identified specific behavioral patterns linked to the criminal activities of their subjects. Figure 3.1 visually depicts the elements of the motivational model and the relationships that exist among its various constitutive parts. In this section of the

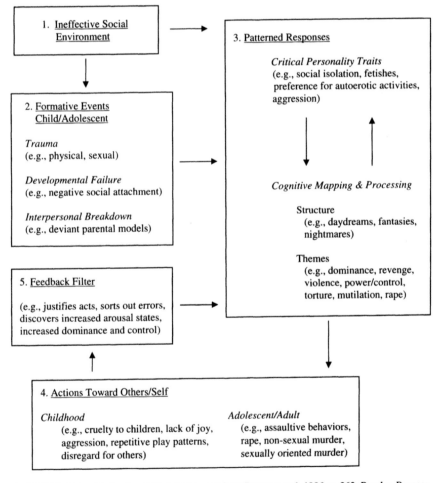

**FIGURE 3.1**   Motivational Model (Adapted from Burgess et al. 1986, p. 262; Ressler, Burgess, & Douglas, 1988, p. 70)

chapter, we systematically review the function of the motivational model. In addition, we explain how Burgess et al. (1986) utilized their framework as a conceptual basis by which to account for sexual homicide.

Burgess et al. (1986) operationalized sexual homicide to be murder with evidence or observations that indicate the crime had a sexual component. Factors they considered sexual in nature included: (1) victim attire or lack thereof; (2) exposure of the victim's sexual parts; (3) sexual positioning of the victim's body; (4) insertion of foreign objects into the victim's body cavities; (5) evidence of sexual intercourse (oral, anal, or vaginal); and (6) evidence of substitute sexual activity and interest in sadistic fantasy (Ressler et al., 1988, p. xiii).

The motivational model focused principally on psychosocial and cognitive factors. The authors theorized that the men in their sample were motivated to kill by their way of thinking. The study's respondents indicated that they had developed early in their lives an actively aggressive fantasy life (daydreaming), had subsequently experienced sexual reinforcement (compulsive masturbation), and had detached themselves from the conventional rules of everyday interaction and conduct (i.e., they engaged in social isolation) (Burgess et al., 1986). As well as these behavioral characteristics, the motivational model specifically included the following five elements: (1) ineffective social environment; (2) formative events; (3) critical personality traits and cognitive mapping processing; (4) actions toward self and others; and (5) feedback filter (Burgess et al., 1986). Each component is summarily examined in the following.

## INEFFECTIVE SOCIAL ENVIRONMENT

This component of the model specifies several factors that Burgess et al. (1986) believed contributed to the quality of an individual's social environment. In particular, they reviewed the developmental aspects of a child's formative years and the salience of that life within the family structure. They noted that healthy family interaction and the child's positive perception of the environment were important aspects for his prosocial development. Moreover, as the child matured, the investigators explained that the quality of the attachments to his parents and other members of the immediate (and extended) family were critical in determining how he related to and valued other members of society (Burgess et al., 1986, p. 261; for additional applications in the psychological and criminological literature, see Shipley & Arrigo, 2004). These early childhood attachments are also referred to as *bonding* styles (e.g., Ainsworth, Blehar, Waters, & Wall, 1978; Bowlby, 1969, 1973; Levy & Platt, 1999; Rothbard & Shaver, 1994).

All of the subjects within the study either failed to positively bond with their caregivers as children or developed selective and limited ways of attaching themselves to others. This is because their parents or primary care providers ignored, rationalized, or normalized various dysfunctional behaviors through their own criminal behavior or illicit substance abuse (Burgess et al., 1986). These ineffective social bonds helped contribute to the child's negative perceptions of reality as well as to the manifestation of cognitive distortions about self, others, and social situations.

## FORMATIVE EVENTS IN CHILDHOOD
## AND ADOLESCENCE

Three distinctive elements can influence or affect the formative events that unfold during childhood and adolescence: trauma, developmental failure, and interpersonal breakdown. Each of these is reviewed in the context of the Burgess et al. (1986) motivation model.

The investigators proposed that there are two types of traumatic experiences that can adversely impact a child's development. These experiences can be normative and non-normative in nature. Normative events include such things as illness, divorce, or death. Non-normative events include such things as physical, psychological, or sexual trauma, where the child is directly or indirectly impacted. When experiencing trauma in concert with an ineffective social environment, the pre-adolescent often feels unprotected and confused about the event and its significance in his life.

One assumption operating within the motivational model regarding early traumatic events is that the child's memories of frightening and upsetting life experiences shape his developing thought patterns (Burgess et al., 1986, p. 263). This supports the assertion that thinking patterns can emerge in the form of daydreams and fantasies, and that the child can both profoundly and thoroughly retreat into the fantasy world. In this instance, the socially isolated individual may come to relive (in imaginative form) the trauma he literally experienced or witnessed. If the child is unsuccessful in resolving these early traumatic event(s), the failure to reconcile them can reinforce feelings of hopelessness, helplessness, and despair. Thus, fantasy and daydreaming represent socially desirable ways in which the individual escapes the troubled and frightening reality where the child lacks control. Indeed, fantasy enables the child to have ultimate control and dominion over any situation manufactured or any individual imagined.

Developmental failure is the second factor that contributes to the formative event component of the motivational model. This failure occurs when the quality of the relationship between the child and the primary caregiver is unhealthy, negative, or dysfunctional in overall orientation. In these instances, the child is unable to attach to the parent or parental surrogate (Ainsworth et al., 1978; Bowlby, 1969, 1973), resulting in a negative social attachment. As such, the child may feel generally neglected and emotionally deprived.

The third factor, interpersonal breakdown, pertains to the failure of the adult caregiver to serve as an appropriate, positive role model for the child during the course of the pre-adolescent's development. It also refers to the primary caregiver's lack of prosocial involvement in the child's life. Thus, if the child's home environment is one in which violence is routinely experienced, these aggressive acts may become unconsciously associated with the adult caregiver's inappro-priate sexual behavior (Burgess et al., 1986, p. 264).

## CRITICAL PERSONALITY TRAITS AND COGNITIVE MAPPING PROCESSING

Within this component of the model are two subcategories: critical personal-ity traits and cognitive mapping processing. When these two elements interact with one another, they generate fantasies (Burgess et al., 1986).

Personality traits can either be positive or negative in nature. Positive per-sonality traits are a result of a growth and maturing process wherein the child engenders feelings of security, autonomy, and trust in others. Facilitating this is the nurturing and caring relationship the parent as caregiver provides and/or cul-tivates with the developing child. Ongoing exposure to these experiences enables the pre-adolescent to establish positive, genuine, and meaningful relationships with and attachments to others. Indeed, when operating in tandem with the pres-ence of an effective social environment, the child individuates and establishes competency and autonomy (Burgess et al., 1986, p. 264).

When negative personality traits are encouraged in the child's early develop-ment, he has difficulties forming prosocial emotional bonds (Ainsworth et al., 1978; Bowlby, 1973; Levy & Platt, 1999). As a result, the child is unable to approach others in a confident manner, and the likelihood of social isolation increases. Social isolation allows the child to become reliant on fantasy as a sub-stitute for the human encounters he is now incapable of experiencing. Moreover, the child's personality structure is such that the youth becomes heavily (indeed, excessively) dependent on the fantasy life and its dominant themes, rather than on any routine or healthy social interaction (Burgess et al., 1986, p. 246).

In addition to social isolation, the child increasingly harbors a cynical and neg-ative view toward others, as well as toward the society that rejects him. Thus, what emerges is a genuine lack of regard for people, institutions, and the social order. In adulthood, if these feelings of utter disregard for others and the trou-bling personality traits linked to them are not appropriately addressed in a ther-apeutic context, they manifest themselves in deviant and criminal ways. In short, the profound sense of social isolation, along with the anger and hostility that fer-ments, combine in the form of fantasy and aggression. This individual is only able to relate to others through the use of an imaginary system. Indeed, fantasy rather than real lived experience becomes the primary source of emotional arousal. Over time, this emotion transforms itself into a confused mixture of sadistic deviance and sexualized violence (Burgess et al., 1986, p. 265).

The personality traits critical to the development of the murderers examined in the Burgess et al. (1986) study are worth noting. They include a sense of social isolation, preferences for autoerotic activities, fetishes, rebelliousness, aggres-sion, chronic lying, and a sense of privilege or entitlement (Burgess et al., 1986, p. 264). As the researchers noted, these characterological features signify the embodiment of a severely disturbed individual.

The second component of the motivational model is cognitive mapping. This process essentially functions as a filtering system for the individual. The filtering system enables him to interpret new information as well as to give identifiable meaning to events that arise within his life. Cognitive mapping and processing can take the form of daydreams, fantasies, nightmares, and thoughts with strong visual components. Common themes specified for the 36 subjects of the Burgess et al. (1986) study were fantasies that centered on power, control, dominance, revenge, violence, mutilation, rape, torture, and death. Respondents also displayed a lack of regard for established social norms, complete disdain for other human beings and their feelings, and a general attitude of self-entitlement. These themes and cognitions led the researchers to conclude that the sexual offenders possessed antisocial views of reality. Moreover, Burgess et al. noted that the cognitive mapping processing activities for their subjects were clearly depicted in the crimes they committed.

For this individual, fantasy and thinking patterns become a substitute for prosocial relationships. The imagined world influences and supports the individual's troubled self-image because the fantasy realm represents a place of complete and unfettered control. The fantasy functions as a substitute for a lack of control over his internal and external experiences with reality. Escaping into this *pseudo-reality* ultimately enables the person to experience sexual stimulation. In turn, this arousal reduces the individual's tension, stress, and anxiety. This process of retreating into a fantasy world eventually contributes to further isolation from reality. Moreover, it becomes the principal source of psychic energy for his emotional life (Burgess et al., 1986).

In addition to the cognitive mapping processes and critical personality traits, Burgess et al. indicated that the subjects of their study experienced a neurohormonal influence relative to their sensory arousal levels. As they observed, compulsive, aggressive fantasy activity could account for a psychobiological mechanism in which certain stressors impacted the operation of the central nervous system, causing a more primal response (Burgess et al., 1986). This suggests that the murderers encountered a sense of pleasure, that is, an aped response to internal or external stressors or events. Through the use of fantasy, these individuals re-exposed themselves to their traumatic triggering experiences. This exposure elicited a primitive response, and the individuals embodied a sense of sexual relief. As a result, their preoccupation with aggressive themes, their detailed cognitive activity and mapping processes, and their elevated kinesthetic arousal states eventually compelled them to embark on sexualized criminal action (Burgess et al., 1986).

## ACTIONS TOWARD SELF AND OTHERS

Behavior patterns of children, adolescents, and adults reflect their private, internal worlds. Consistent with the various themes identified in the cognition component of the model, the behavior patterns of the 36 sexual murderers revealed that their internal worlds were preoccupied with troublesome, joyless thoughts and primarily focused on domination over others (Burgess et al., 1986, p. 266).

Preoccupation with thoughts of power, control, and domination manifest themselves at various stages along the developmental continuum (Arrigo, 2006). In childhood, they are expressed through negative play, cruelty toward animals, setting fires, destroying property, and a genuine disregard for others. In adolescence as well as adulthood, these dysfunctional behavioral patterns can become progressively more serious and more intensely violent (Shipley & Arrigo, 2004). Examples include such things as burglary, arson, and assaultive actions toward others; rape and nonsexual murder; and, in the extreme, homicidal actions involving sadistic deviance and sexualized violence (Burgess et al., 1986, p. 266).

Burgess et al. believed that failing to therapeutically intervene and address the nature of these thoughts, the content of the fantasies, the developmental failure, the ineffective social environment, and the early isolative and/or traumatic experiences to which the child was initially exposed would significantly impair that person's capacity to function appropriately in society. The researchers noted that the individual's cognitions, steeped in images of sexualized violence, would operate as a catalyst, resulting in ongoing and increasingly intense abusive behavior. Moreover, if the child was not counseled on his (or her) responsibility in the commission of these early expressions and deviant activities (e.g., cruelty to animals, setting fires), the behavior would be reinforced. If no adverse consequences attach to negative behavior, children continue to engage in such activities and come to regard them as normative. Juveniles who engage in negative or dysfunctional behaviors have a more difficult time establishing appropriate and healthy friendships with others (Bowlby, 1969, 1973). This failure to make genuine prosocial contact leads to isolationism and retreatism. Moreover, as the investigators concluded, it interferes with the abilities to effectively resolve conflicts, to develop positive empathy, and to control impulses (Burgess et al., 1986, p. 267).

## FEEDBACK FILTER

*Feedback filter* refers to the way in which an individual reacts to and evaluates his actions toward himself and others. The way in which the individual responds to and assesses his environment both affects and influences his future conduct. Burgess et al. (1986) observed that the subjects of their investigation justified their wayward actions and analyzed their behavioral errors. However, in response to these failures, the respondents made mental corrections in order to preserve and protect their internal fantasy worlds. This was undertaken to avoid possible restrictions on or limits from the external environment (Burgess et al., 1986, p. 267).

Given these activities, the fantasy life of the individual was then escalated, especially in terms of the arousal state and the feelings of power, domination, and control. The sexual murderers reported acquiring increased knowledge regarding avoiding detection and punishment. They assimilated and accommodated this knowledge into their self-other-society schema. Collectively, then, this overall evaluative process confirmed (and justified) their assessment of their actions. As such, it functioned as a feedback filter contributing to and sustaining the other elements of the motivational model.

## THE TRAUMA CONTROL MODEL

Hickey (1997) proposed a trauma control model to help explain the onset and maintenance of serial murder. His research addressed many of the aspects delineated in the motivational model for sexual homicide as described by Burgess et al. (1986). In addition, however, Hickey (1997, 2001) examined a number of predispositional factors and frequently employed facilitators that could induce an individual to commit serial acts of murder. Figure 3.2 graphically depicts the operation of the trauma control model. In the subsequent subsections of this chapter, the details of this typology are systematically reviewed.

### PREDISPOSITIONAL FACTORS

According to Hickey's (1997) model, some serial killers are known to have certain predispositional factors that can influence their behavior. These factors are biological, sociological, and psychological in nature, or some combination of these elements. An example of a biological factor is the "extra Y" chromosome theory, which is believed to explain violent behavior (e.g., see Raine, 1993). Psychological factors include mental illness, personality disorders, or psychoanalytic

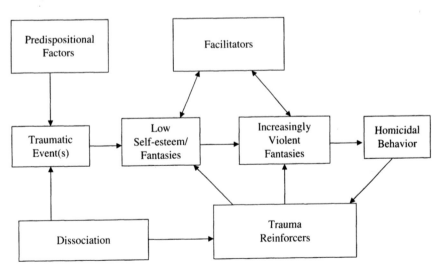

FIGURE 3.2   Trauma Control Model (Adapted from Hickey, 1997, p. 87)

phenomena (Arrigo, 2006). Sociological factors focus on how the environment influences developing behavior, particularly during the formative years (e.g., see Reckless [1950] 1973).

## TRAUMATIC EVENTS

As previously stated, traumatic events can have a profoundly adverse affect on the pre-adolescent's overall maturation and general personality structure. This is especially the case if such traumatizations occur during the formative years of the child's life. As Burgess et al. (1986) noted, examples of deeply distressing encounters either experienced or witnessed include an unstable home environment and sexual, physical, and mental abuse, among others.

Hickey (1997, 2001) asserted that ongoing social and environmental issues might exacerbate these early childhood traumas. And, when made manifest over time, these issues could seriously compromise a person's capacity to interact appropriately. Hickey's trauma control model, much like the motivational typology, addressed the debilitating effects of childhood abuse by an adult caregiver. Indeed, as he observed, the youth often feels a deep sense of anxiety, mistrust, and confusion when psychologically or physically assaulted by a parent or parental surrogate (Hickey, 1997). The adverse personal effects stemming from the experience of violent and traumatic events are also addressed in Hickey's model.

So, what do we know about childhood trauma? We know that it can manifest itself in many ways (Kennerley, 2000; Sanford, 1992). However, the research indicates that the most common form of childhood trauma is rejection (Terr, 1992). In the context of serial offenders, the rejection these individuals experience usually comes from a relative or a parent (Douglas et al., 1995). In addition, an unstable, abusive home life represents one of the primary forms of childhood rejection (Hickey, 1997, p. 87).

## LOW SELF-ESTEEM/FANTASIES

Other manifestations of rejection can include feelings of personal failure, a sense of hopelessness and helplessness, ostracism in school, and exclusion from social groups and activities (e.g., Asher & Coie, 1990; Kennerley, 2000). When children experience traumatic events in their early development, the events foster feelings of inadequacy, self-doubt, low self-esteem, and worthlessness. Moreover, fantasy and daydreaming typically function as a substitute for their flawed social relationships or their absence of healthy bonding (Moorman, 2003; Schore, 2003). Often, these interpersonal deficiencies are traceable to low self-esteem and lack of confidence (Glenn & Nelsen, 2001; Terr, 1992). This aspect of Hickey's (2001) trauma control model is compatible with the patterned response factor in the motivational model as developed by Burgess et al. (1986).

## DISSOCIATION

When children experience psychological or physical trauma in their early development, they are unable to effectively confront and cope with it (Kennerley, 2000). As such, these children may perceive themselves and their surroundings in a distorted way. In fact, a process of dissociation can occur (Putnam, 1997). During this process, the individual attempts to regain the psychological equilibrium lacking in and taken from his life by those in positions of authority (e.g., parents, teachers) by constructing a mask, facade, alter ego, or even a veneer of self-confidence and self-control (Hickey, 1997, p. 88). These youths typically want others to believe that they maintain absolute command of themselves and their behavior. In actuality, however, they are mostly socially bankrupt and morally inept (Schore, 2003).

During the dissociative experience, it is common for the individual to suppress the traumatic event so much so that he is unable to retrieve the event's particulars or to remember the overall circumstances surrounding it. This lack of recall is often referred to as *splitting off* or *blocking out*. Hickey (1997, 2001) examined the work of Tanay (1976), Danto (1982), and Vetter (1990) to help substantiate the notion of dissociation as it pertains to serial murderers. For example, Tanay (1976) reviewed the phenomenon of an ego-dystonic homicide, in which the murderer carried out his crime in an altered state of consciousness. Danto (1982, p. 6) observed that a dissociative reaction was attributable to a state of stress and disquietedness wherein the individual's mind was "overwhelmed and flooded with anxiety."

## TRAUMA REINFORCERS

For an adult serial murderer, childhood traumas ostensibly serve as triggering mechanisms, resulting in his inability to cope with the stress of certain problematic and disappointing (but otherwise routine) life events (Hickey, 1997, p. 87). These routine events may be physical or psychological in nature, or they may manifest themselves as a combination of several traumatizations. An example of a triggering factor is rejection from a girlfriend or criticism from a supervisor. When the individual encounters this feeling of rejection or criticism as an adult, he is either ill-equipped or thoroughly unable to cope with the event in a constructive manner. Consequently, the adult serial offender conjures up emotions and sentiments linked to previous (early childhood) experiences whose nature and content were negative. The individual also retreats into his internal fantasy world; this is a haven in which the relived feelings of rejection are abated and the relived feelings of criticism are eliminated. Thus, he receives temporary relief from an otherwise psychically unbearable situation (Hickey, 2001; see also Douglas et al., 1995; Holmes & Holmes, 2002a).

## FACILITATORS

Through the course of the trauma control process, it is customary for the offender to immerse himself in the use of various facilitators. The most frequently used include alcohol, drugs, and pornography. Indeed, as Hickey (1997, p. 89) explained, "Alcohol [and other illicit substances] appear to decrease inhibitions and inhibit moral conscience and propriety, whereas pornography fuels growing fantasies of violence." Generally speaking, the assailant employs a combination of facilitators in order to amplify and sustain the fantasy's sadistic imagery (Hickey, 2005; Holmes & Holmes, 2002a).

The serial murderer may become addicted to the facilitating behavior. This form of addiction is similar to the habituation encountered by those who are dependent on drugs and alcohol (Hickey, 1997; Cleveland, 2002; Jung, 2000). The offender's use of sexually explicit material helps explain the general facilitative process.

Initially, the individual experiences the physiological and psychological effects of the pornographic material. This generates stress in his daily and routine activities (Hickey, 2005). As a result, the individual transitions into the next phase in the facilitative process, identified as the escalation stage. During this period, the offender's appetite for more intensely bizarre, deviant, and sexually explicit material is heightened (Hickey, 1997, p. 89). Eventually, the individual becomes so desensitized to the graphic content, no matter how violent, that he acts out the sadistic imagery in which he has repeatedly immersed himself. For the serial murderer, failure to engage in this behavior would mean that his sense of self would remain diminished (Hickey, 2001).

## INCREASINGLY VIOLENT FANTASIES

Traumatic events occurring in the formative years of a child's development can adversely influence the youth's perception of the world and others, as well as his evolving sense of self. Fantasy and daydreaming become a refuge from the world in which the pre-adolescent lives. This internal escape provides a safety net, a haven from a lifetime of perceived external rejection. The consequence of this internal retreat—especially when coupled with the experience of dissociation, adult trauma reinforcers, and the use of facilitators—produces a synergistic effect that makes the emergence and maintenance of increasingly violent fantasies possible.

## HOMICIDAL BEHAVIOR

According to Hickey (1997, 2001), the experience of killing may generate new images of brutality. Each subsequent act of violence represents an attempt to completely satisfy and fully realize the perpetrator's fantasies. Indeed, one serial murderer remarked that "he felt good about himself and more in control of his life directly following a murder" (Hickey, 1997, p. 93). In the same interview, he also revealed that when he experienced a personal failure in his life, such as a criticism at work or rejection from a girlfriend, the event would act as a catalyst that triggered profound feelings of depression and low self-esteem. As Hickey's (2001) trauma control model specifies, these deep-seated sentiments foster self-pity, a loss of confidence, and a general sense of rejection. The frequency, intensity, and duration of these feelings significantly influence, indeed compel, the individual to engage in a behavioral pattern consisting of increasingly sadistic fantasies. Ultimately, the fantasies can (and do) result in the serial torture and killing of men and/or women (Hickey, 2001, 2005; Holmes & Holmes, 2002a).

## LIMITATIONS OF THE CLASSICAL CONDITIONING, MOTIVATIONAL, AND TRAUMA CONTROL MODELS

The classical conditioning, motivational, and trauma control typologies clearly provide conceptually useful (and scientifically testable) information concerning sexual homicide and/or serial murder. However, these frameworks are limited on a number of fronts. In this final section of the chapter, these limits are summarily described. Although these models collectively advance our understanding of those assailants whose actions involve sadistic deviance and sexualized violence, they remain theoretically underdeveloped. This is especially problematic when accounting for how the paraphilic process both underscores and sustains such behaviors.

First, each model delineated reports on a distinct category of murder (serial or sexual); however, the typologies themselves do not explain the unique phenomenon of lust murder. The classical conditioning model articulated by MacCulloch et al. (1983) explores violent sexual offending. However, their framework was based in part on Brittain's (1970) sadistic murderer syndrome. The motivational model proposed by Burgess et al. (1986) investigates sexual homicide in general. According to their own definition, all homicides that had a sexual component were included in their study. The trauma control model developed by Hickey (1997) examines serial murder. This emphasis on repetitive homicide does not necessarily include offenses with an underlying sexual component. Thus, each of the typologies, while certainly suggestive in its regard for erotophonophilia, fails to specify the psychological and criminological elements constituting the distinct category of lust murder.

Second, the three models address different, rather than similar, factors when accounting for the emergence and maintenance of sexual homicide or serial murder. To some extent, this is understandable, especially given the distinctness of these particular crimes and offenders. MacCulloch et al.'s (1983) classical conditioning model focuses on the role of sadistic fantasy and masturbation as a reinforcer for the commission of sexual homicide. Burgess et al.'s (1986) motivational model principally investigates psychosocial and cognitive factors as motivating determinants in sexual homicide crimes. Hickey's (1997, 2001) trauma control typology examines various predispositional factors and various facilitators that fuel and sustain the behavior of the serial murderer. None of these frameworks, however, reviews the influence of neurobiology or genetics as contributory factors in the etiology of serial sexual homicide. This criticism is significant, given the current research on biology, neuropsychology, and paraphilia (e.g., Kafka, 2003; Schlesinger, 2003).

On this latter observation, the insights of Money (1990) are especially noteworthy. He argued that certain biological factors influence paraphilic behavior. Indeed, he asserted that the onset of all paraphilias, particularly sexual sadism, was "due to a disease in the brain affecting the centers and pathways responsible for sexual arousal, mating behavior, and reproduction of the species" (Money, 1990, p. 27; see also Hickey, 2005). This perspective investigates a neurological deficit within the area of the brain known as the limbic system (Arrigo & Purcell, 2001), which is responsible for predation and violence in defense of both the self and the species (Raine, 1993). When confronted with the neuropsychological phenomenon of sexual sadism, the brain is pathologically activated to send messages of attack simultaneously with messages of sexual arousal and mating behavior (Money, 1990, p. 28; Kafka, 2003).

Third, each model fails to provide any conceptual depiction of paraphilia's etiology, as well as its operation as a systemic process of increasingly violent and sexualized behavior. This is especially troubling given that some subjects within each respective research sample manifested clear behavioral signs indicative of reliance on paraphilias. Consequently, the role of aberrant sexual deviance, while certainly present within each study, is not fully explained. As we demonstrate in the subsequent chapter, explicating the paraphilic process as a system of behavior is integral to explaining the operation of erotophonophilia and essential for comprehending the actions of the lust murderer.

## SUMMARY AND CONCLUSION

This chapter explored the most prominent theoretical models that account for sexual homicide and serial murder. This exercise was undertaken in order to provide a conceptual backdrop for advancing our own explanatory theory regarding erotophonophilia. The classical conditioning typology of MacCulloch et al. (1983), the motivational framework of Burgess et al. (1986), and the trauma control model of Hickey (1997, 2001) were all systematically reviewed. As we noted, each organizing schema is useful in its own right. However, the three typologies are limited, especially when accounting for the paraphilic process that underscores the emergence and maintenance of serial sexual homicide.

In Chapter 4, a more comprehensive model is proposed. As we contend, this typology builds on the conceptual insights of those researchers whose typologies were examined in this chapter. However, unlike its predecessors, the synthetic framework identifies testable and discrete elements that further explain the etiology of paraphilia. Moreover, the integrative model accounts for how these partialisms, operating as a coordinated system of complex behaviors, function as a psychic catalyst for the crime of lust murder.

# 4

# AN INTEGRATIVE MODEL:

## WHAT DO WE NEED?

## OVERVIEW

This chapter delineates the elements of an integrative typology that accounts for the paraphilic process as a system of behavior, especially in relation to its role in the etiology of erotophonophilia. This organizing schema represents a logical synthesis of the motivational model developed by Burgess et al. (1986) and the trauma control framework constructed by Hickey (1997, 2001). Several aspects of the MacCulloch et al. (1983) model are also incorporated. We contend that this more comprehensive and synthetic organizing schema, as systematically described in this chapter, helps to establish paraphilia as a pivotal component (i.e., motive) in serial sexual offenses, particularly, the crime of lust murder.

In order to specify the elements of the integrative model, this chapter is divided into four substantive sections. First, the extant and relevant literature recommending the creation of a synthetic framework is summarized, especially in relation to a cogent (and testable) explanation for serial murder and sexual homicide. Second, some background commentary on the synthetic paraphilic model itself is provided, generally accounting for the particular elements of the typology and their discrete relationship to one another. Third, the operation of the integrative framework is delineated. Throughout this exposition, the organizing schema is systematically linked to erotophonophilia. Fourth, the limits of the integrative theoretical framework are specified. These observations suggest what additional model-building work is needed, particularly if the proposed typology is to increase its explanatory and predictive properties.

## SUPPORT FOR AN INTEGRATIVE MODEL ON
## SERIAL MURDER AND SEXUAL HOMICIDE

As explained in the previous chapter, both the motivational typology and trauma control model contain elements that suggest paraphilic behavior. Consider, for example, the adverse effects stemming from negative and unresolved childhood and/or adolescent development. If the specific circumstances surrounding these experiences are traumatizing, the child will likely mature without self-esteem, which increases social isolation and reliance on daydreaming and fantasy (Kennerley, 2000; Sanford, 1992). Over time, the subject's inward retreat will lead to imaginary constructions of self, others, and situations in which sadistic deviance and sexualized violence could be prominently featured. Social isolation and erotically aggressive fantasies are characteristic of paraphilic offenders. From our perspective, paraphilic criminality needs to be distinguished as a separate Uniform Crime Report (UCR) indexed category. Paraphilic homicides (i.e., lust murder) are often classified as serial, sadistic, or sexual killings. This categorization obfuscates, rather than clarifies, the role of paraphilia in the commission of different types of murder. Given these concerns, both theory building and model development that establish lust murder as a separate subcategory of homicide is clearly warranted.

The practical problems identified above have not gone unnoticed by other investigators. Research on serial murder has examined various causal agents for this type of criminality, including biological, behavioral, psychodynamic, and cognitive dimensions (Egger, 2002; Giannangelo, 1996; Holmes & Holmes, 1998). DeHart and Mahoney (1994) reviewed the various theoretical motivations that explain the phenomenon of serial homicide. In particular, they argued that future investigators would do well to construct a more integrated model when accounting for this violent crime and those offenders responsible for its commission (see also Canter, Alison, Alison, & Wentink, 2004; Canter & Wentink, 2004).

Consistent with this position, Giannangelo (1996) constructed a two-pronged typology regarding the serial murderer's development. His schema included biological factors and psychological anomalies that would predispose an offender to engage in acts of serial murder. Additionally, however, the author explained how traumatic environmental circumstances could function as stressors that, when triggered, would activate a cyclical and patterned response of violence in persons already predisposed to this conduct. Building upon the insights of DeHart and Mahoney (1994) and Giannangelo (1996), other social scientists have considered possible approaches to consolidating theories about serial murder (e.g., Egger, 2002; Holmes & Holmes, 1999, 2003). Collectively, researchers note the need for both theoretical and empirical efforts that address the etiological and motivational dimensions of this type of criminality.

Social and behavioral scientists have recommended future analyses that integrate the existing conceptual research on sexual homicide (Schlesinger, 2003), including studies that describe the phenomenon from a feminist perspective (Cameron & Frazer, 1988). An examination of sexual murder conducted by Grubin (1994) emphasized the importance of establishing an integrative typology for paraphilia, especially in relation to the crime of lust murder. Grubin explained that the lack of scientific inquiry specifically on the phenomenon of sexual homicide was a function of the considerable attention given to sadistic and serial offenders. Consequently, knowledge about sexual homicide is underdeveloped and remains mostly in its infancy. More recent efforts exploring the limits of this phenomenon echo these sentiments (Hickey, 2005; Holmes & Holmes, 2002a).

As previously specified, serial, sexual, and sadistic homicide are often collapsed into the same category of murder although they are composed of quite distinct (but in some ways similar) underlying dynamics. The differences among these crimes are decidedly beyond the scope of this volume. However, what is relevant for purposes of our thesis on the paraphilic process and erotophonophilia is that the establishment of an integrated typology, if systematically developed, could significantly help address the concerns voiced by experts on sexual homicide and serial murder.

## DEFINING THE ELEMENTS OF THE INTEGRATIVE TYPOLOGY

The purpose of creating an integrative model is to help establish lust murder as a separate category for sexual (and serial) homicide, as well as to specify how paraphilias operate as an underlying motive in the commission of erotophonophilia. The proposed synthetic schematization attempts to explain the etiology of paraphilia, as well as how paraphilic behaviors emerge, progress and intensify, resulting in acts of sadistic deviance and sexualized violence.

Figure 4.1 visually depicts the elements of the integrative theoretical model. The first four components of the integrative framework explain the systemic composition of paraphilic behavior. These elements include: (1) formative development; (2) low self-esteem; (3) early fantasy development; and (4) paraphilic development. Formative development (which consists of predispositional factors and traumatic events), low self-esteem, and early fantasy development are all factors investigated as etiological agents. Paraphilic development, paraphilic fantasy/stimuli, facilitators, and the orgasmic conditioning process are interactive elements. Collectively, they comprise the paraphilic process. This is a process in which increasingly violent fantasies materialize and, when insufficient to establish sexual arousal and/or gratification, give way to behavioral manifestations. Given the fundamental role of the paraphilic process in the commission of sex crimes, these behavioral manifestations include, in the extreme, lust murder.

At the outset, we note that the integrative model is presented in a way that not only explains the development of paraphilic behaviors but also illustrates how

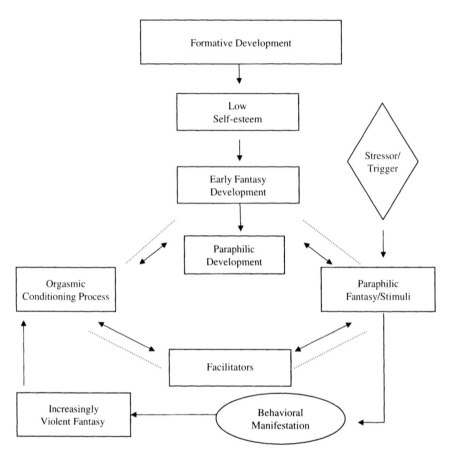

FIGURE 4.1   Integrated Model on Paraphilia and Lust Murder. ◄───►, Paraphilic Process;
············, Internal/External Stimulus Effect; ◄─────, Feedback Loop (Reinforcer). (Adapted from
Arrigo & Purcell, 2001, p. 20)

they function developmentally, sustained by several elements of the paraphilic system itself. Thus, the ensuing organizing schema conceptually describes both the etiology of this phenomenon as well as its essential disposition.

Initially, a stressor, either internal or external, functions as a trigger to past, unresolved (childhood) trauma. The stressor causes a momentary lack of control for the paraphilic individual. A response to that stressor is a behavioral manifestation. If the individual is unable to cope with the triggering stimulus, he retreats back into the paraphilic process, where comfort and relief are found. A feedback loop is shown to help illustrate how the behavioral manifestation of paraphilia can escalate and intensify, especially if the individual chooses to act on his fantasy.

Typically, in-vivo tryouts of the paraphilic fantasy and stimuli are enacted in an attempt to preserve, satisfy, and reify the person's internal thought processes. As a result, the individual experiences an exhilarating rush of sexual satisfaction, as well as an increased need for more erotic stimulation. However, for the lust murderer, this felt sense of pleasure is ephemeral.

Masturbation (as linked to orgasmic conditioning) is a component of the paraphilic process. When violent erotic imagery no longer sates the person's sexual appetite, behavioral manifestations follow. Behavioral manifestations include sadistic deviance and sexualized criminality (e.g., homicide). When coupled with masturbation, these actions become reinforcers that are sequenced back into the overall fantasy system. The cyclical paraphilic process, as an increasingly violent system of sexualized imagery and conduct, sustains itself, especially following the individual's repeated failure to maintain arousal or achieve orgasm. The intensity, duration, and frequency of the process are dependent on the effects of the etiological elements themselves, as well as the interactive agents, particularly in relation to the individual in question.

## AN INTEGRATIVE THEORETICAL TYPOLOGY OF LUST MURDER

### FORMATIVE DEVELOPMENT

This initial dimension of the integrative model functions as the foundation where paraphilic behaviors originate. Formative development refers specifically to childhood and early adolescent experiences. It is comprised of several elements contained within the motivational and trauma control models. In particular, it is a direct integration of the "ineffective social environment" and the "formative events" components of the motivational model, as well as the "predispositional factors" and "trauma events" features of the trauma control model. Thus, consistent with the explanations provided by Burgess et al. (1986) and Hickey (1997, 2001), a person's formative development significantly impacts the manner in which he appropriately and successfully experiences psychosocial adjustment throughout the lifecourse. For simplicity, we collapse the essential features of the paraphilic individual's formative development into two interdependent concepts: (a) predispositional factors and (b) traumatic events.

### Predispositional Factors

The motivational and trauma control models implicitly recognize that there are certain predispositional factors that can either work alone or in combination to influence offender behavior. Indeed, Burgess et al. (1986) address how dysfunctional family surroundings during childhood can adversely affect the early attachments youths cultivate with their primary care provider(s). Hickey (1997, 2001), too, identifies this environmental breakdown as a sociological predispositional factor, understood as a developmental failure. Burgess et al. (1986) contend that this disintegration has a direct bearing on the interpersonal failure of both the primary care provider as well as the maturing child. According to Hickey, the interpersonal problems that emerge represent psychological predispositional factors.

As previously mentioned, Hickey (1997) also explains how certain biological factors can influence offender conduct (e.g., the extra Y chromosome syndrome) (see also Giannangelo, 1996; Raine, 1993). Other research also indicates that certain biological factors influence paraphilic behavior. This perspective on the psychopathology of crime in general and sexual homicide in particular investigates the limbic system of the brain. The limbic system is responsible for predatory conduct, as well as violence designed both to preserve and defend the self and maintain the survival of the species (for applications in the psychological and criminological literature, see Arrigo & Griffin, 2004).

Money (1990) observed that with the disease of sexual sadism, "the brain [was] pathologically activated to transmit messages of attack simultaneously with messages of sexual arousal and mating behavior" (p. 28). This suggests that paraphilias are constituted by certain predispositional factors (e.g., sociological, psychological, biological) that can, in some instances, result in erotically sadistic, aggressive, and even homicidal behavior.

**Traumatic Events**

In addition to indicating specific factors that predispose an individual to engage in certain deviant behaviors, the motivational and trauma control models address how particular disturbances (e.g., sexual, psychological, physical) and/or their combinatory effects can adversely affect childhood and early adolescent development. An individual's inability to confront and work meaningfully through the pain of a harrowing event will likely foster feelings of self-doubt, hopelessness, and helplessness. Ultimately, this inability will interfere with the positive development of his ego-identity.

Research on the paraphilia of lust murder indicates that the early years of psychological adjustment "are crucial to the personality structure and development of these offenders" (Hazelwood & Douglas, 1980, p. 21; see also Douglas et al., 1995; Holmes & Holmes, 2002a). It is rare for the lust murderer to come from a nurturing family environment free from abuse, alcoholism, drug use, or other factors that could cause great childhood pain and suffering (Hickey, 2005; Money & Werlas, 1982; Simon, 1996). Thus, it follows, consistent with Burgess et al.'s (1986) and Hickey's (1997, 2001) assessment of trauma, that paraphilias originate in part from largely unresolved or inappropriately addressed debilitating life circumstances that occurred during childhood and early adolescence.

## LOW SELF-ESTEEM

The events occurring in the formative stage of the lifecourse are critical to creating a solid basis on which a child can develop a positive self-image and learn prosocial behavior. The largely dysfunctional background of the paraphilic individual mitigates this possibility (e.g., Abel et al., 1988; Douglas et al., 1995; Holmes, 1991; Holmes & Holmes, 2002b). The motivational and trauma control frameworks acknowledge the consequence of traumatic events in an adolescent's life. The child is likely to experience a deep-seated sense of personal failure and a genuine lack of regard for others and the society from which he feels rejected. Ultimately, this interferes with the child's ability to form positive attachments with others. Daydreaming and fantasy become a stand-in for the social relationships he is incapable of forming.

Burgess et al. (1986) explain how negative personality traits, in conjunction with a contrary and cynical attitude toward others/society, act as catalysts to generate fantasies. These fantasies become patterned responses, fueled by incessant feelings of inadequacy and self-doubt. The anger the individual feels as a result of previous trauma and rejection is expressed in the content of his image-making. According to Hickey (1997), the person's anger and hostility combines with the social isolation the individual routinely confronts to form violent fantasies.

## EARLY FANTASY AND PARAPHILIC DEVELOPMENT

A cyclical conceptualization of paraphilias is unique to the integrated conceptual model, in that the focus is on several factors occurring simultaneously, essentially producing a synergistic effect. Social isolation arising concurrently with the early development of sexualized fantasy mobilizes the paraphilic system into operation. Eventually, this mobilization becomes a process in and of itself. Fantasy, compulsive masturbation, and facilitators, along with paraphilic stimuli (e.g., fetishes, unusual objects, sadistic and erotic rituals) function to sustain the paraphilic process.

Burgess et al. (1986) specifically identified personality characteristics within the patterned response component of the motivational model that are indicative of the paraphilic process described above. These characteristics include social isolation, a preference for autoerotic activities, and fetishes. As others have noted, "the internal behaviors most consistently reported over the murderers' three developmental periods were daydreaming, compulsive masturbation, and isolation" (Ressler, Burgess, & Douglas, 1988, p. 30).

The Burgess et al. (1986) study examined killers who were sexually abused as children, as well as those who were not. Eighty-three percent of the sexually abused offenders engaged in fetishistic behaviors, whereas 57% of the non-abused offenders did not. This finding strongly suggests that paraphilic stimuli (i.e., fetishes) are introduced at some point in the context of social isolation and fantasy.

It is difficult to ascertain the exact process by which an individual develops paraphilic stimuli and engages in sadistic behavior; however, fetishes have been described as symbolic links to persons of importance in the life of a sexual killer (e.g., Simon, 1996; Holmes, 1991; Hickey, 2001). One early theorist suggested that a fetish possesses some quality associated with a person the offender was closely involved with during childhood. This significant other is both loved and needed, but is also responsible for the adolescent's traumatization (Bancroft, 1985). The analysis implies that in the formative years of the offender's life, he makes a connection between the paraphilic stimulus and a traumatic event.

## PARAPHILIC PROCESS

The integrated conceptual model illustrates how the paraphilic process becomes a system of behaviors. As previously stipulated, the paraphilic process is cyclical and consists of the following mutually interactive elements: (1) paraphilic stimuli and fantasy; (2) orgasmic conditioning process; and (3) facilitators (e.g., alcohol, drugs, pornography). Each of these elements is briefly explained.

### Paraphilic Fantasy and Stimuli

In their research, MacCulloch et al. (1983) examined the sadistic fantasies of sexual offenders. They found that their subjects experienced difficulty in both social and sexual relationships at a young age. As previously described, a lack of social sexual bonding produces feelings of inadequacy, which drive a person into a world of fantasy and isolation (e.g., Burgess et al., 1986; Hickey, 1997). Over time, the images become more violent and erotic, incorporating assorted fetishes, rituals, and/or unusual and sexually charged objects as stimuli. The repetitive nature of the fantasy furnishes a sense of personal relief from the individual's internal failures. The felt sexual arousal in conjunction with the sadistic fantasy reinforce one another by means of classical conditioning. The conditioning increases the likelihood of escalation and habituation. The conditioning model of MacCulloch et al. (1983) explains not only the strength and permanence of sadistic fantasies in abnormal personalities, but accounts for their progression from non-sexual to sexual as well. We contend that this research further supports the notion of a paraphilic process of ongoing sadistic and erotic behaviors.

Fantasy is very influential in facilitating the paraphilic process. It is a safe, private, and powerful elixir. Individuals become so immersed in the images they create that they dwell in their image-making, losing all contact with reality. With a rich fantasy world free from any rejection, the sexual deviant has complete control over his imagined encounters. When the fantasy systems of lust murderers are examined, it is apparent that sex is associated with aggression (e.g., Douglas et al., 1995; Hazelwood & Douglas, 1980; Holmes & Holmes, 2002a; Liebert, 1985; Schlesinger, 2003). Common themes associated with their fantasies include power, domination, exploitation, revenge, molestation, and degrading and humiliating others (Simon, 1996).

### Orgasmic Conditioning Process

Compulsive genital stimulation enables the individual to experience sexual satisfaction. The person fantasizes and rehearses the paraphilia, and then masturbates to the point of orgasm. This is a conditioning process in which the individual eventually loses all sense of normalcy and depends on the paraphilic fantasy for both erotic arousal and satisfaction. Initially, a person might experience "normal" paraphilias; however, as the nature and content of the fantasy becomes increasingly violent and sexual, the paraphilias progress in intensity and frequency.

### Facilitators

The use of drugs, alcohol, and pornography are important components to the paraphilic process. Hickey's (1997) trauma control model examined the use of these facilitating agents in relation to serial murderers (p. 89). Additionally, Ressler et al. (1988) studied a sample of sexual killers. They found that over half of their subjects reported interests in pornography, and 81% expressed "interests in fetishism, voyeurism, and masturbation" (p. 25). Other investigators have similarly commented on the role of facilitators in sustaining and contributing to the manifestations of sadistic sexual homicide (e.g., Holmes, 1991; Simon, 1996; Hazelwood & Warren, 1989; Prentky et al., 1989; Schlesinger, 2003).

Consistent with Hickey's (1997) analysis of serial killers, these facilitators manifest themselves as addictions. The paraphiliac individual becomes firmly entrenched in a cycle of addiction, experiencing dependency and craving more of the stimulus for sexual gratification. The reliance on the alcohol, drug, and/or pornography escalates, until he becomes desensitized to the facilitator. The paraphiliac individual may eventually act out his fantasies, including lust murder.

### STRESSORS

Burgess et al. (1986) described the manner in which the offender is motivated to respond to circumstances based on how he thinks. This is steeped in formative and unresolved traumatic experiences. As the adolescent matures, the precipitating events from his childhood and the feelings associated with them may function as "trigger mechanisms" (Hickey, 1997, p. 87).

The integrative model proposes that triggering factors (e.g., rejection, isolation, ridicule) are stressors that constrain or thwart the individual's capacity to cope adequately with everyday life. These stressors are akin to Hickey's (1997, 2001) trauma reinforcers, which make it impossible for the person to deal effectively with routine conflict or strife. Depending on the nature and severity of the triggering mechanism, the person may experience a momentary loss of control. The stressor activates childhood trauma and rekindles the feelings associated with them (Ressler et al., 1988, pp. 45–46; see also Douglas et al., 1995). This triggering effect cycles back into the paraphilic process by way of a feedback loop. The behavior is sustained through masturbation, facilitators, and fantasy. In extreme cases, the response to the stress may manifest itself in erotic and sadistic conduct, including erotophonophilia.

## BEHAVIORAL MANIFESTATIONS

The feedback loop has the potential to escalate into behavioral manifestations if the person feels compelled to execute his fantasy. By enacting the paraphilic fantasy and stimuli, the individual attempts to satisfy, complete, and reify his illusions. He experiences an exhilarating "rush" of carnal satisfaction, as well as an increased need for stimulation each time the behavior is inaugurated. The behavior, whether criminal or not, functions as a reinforcer, and sequences back into the fantasy system.

Both the motivational and trauma control models depict this process. The former focuses on the offender's need to evaluate his actions toward others and himself by way of a feedback filter (Burgess et al., 1986). In addition to examining the homicidal behavioral component of the motivational model, the trauma control model specifies how the fantasy life of the individual escalates, generating new images and sustaining existing ones (Hickey, 1997).

## INCREASINGLY VIOLENT FANTASIES

As the fantasies become increasingly violent, the paraphilic stimuli also progress in intensity, duration, and frequency. Each time an individual carries out the fantasy and stimuli, the need for increased stimulation becomes apparent. This need for continued violent arousal is a part of the paraphilic feedback loop, and cycles in the process accordingly.

The trauma control model specifically designates an increasingly violent fantasy component when explaining the behavior of serial killers (Hickey, 1997). We contend that this component essentially serves the same function as outlined in the integrated paraphilic model. The motivational model also supports our theoretical analysis. In this typology, two components account for increasingly violent imagery: actions toward others and the feedback filter.

Burgess et al. (1986) indicate that when the actions-toward-others factor occurs "in adolescence and adulthood, the murderer's [conduct] becomes more violent: assaultive behaviors, burglary, arson, abduction, rape, nonsexual murder, and finally sexual murder involving rape, torture, mutilation and necrophilia" (p. 266)." Thus, the offender's behaviors grow more intense and predatory as a direct result of an increasingly violent and complex fantasy system.

The feedback filter component explains how the sexual deviant reacts to and evaluates his actions toward others and himself. Feelings of dominance, power, control, and increased arousal all cycle back into the offender's "patterned responses and enhance the details of the fantasy life" (Burgess et al., 1986, p. 267). Here, too, we see how violent imagery is sustained and intensified by the sexual killer. This is consistent with our integrative conceptual analysis regarding the paraphilic process.

## THE LIMITS OF THE INTEGRATIVE
## THEORETICAL TYPOLOGY ON LUST MURDER

Although the proposed organizing schema on lust murder synthesizes several elements of the classical conditioning, motivational, and trauma control models, it is not without its own shortcomings. Generally speaking, these deficiencies are the basis for future theory testing. Scholars of sexual homicide and serial murder are encouraged to investigate these limitations in greater detail and to assess the explanatory and predictive properties of the overall integrative framework. Having said this, the following observations summarily outline the more noteworthy limitations of the integrative paraphilic model.

First, the literature on serial, sexual, and sadistic murder is not clearly delineated. Often, these offenses are classified as types of murder without a systematic assessment of their unique as well as similar properties. Although a focus on paraphilic murder specifies the inherent problem with this practice (especially on a theoretical level), the proposed typology on lust murder does not provide any further categorization for these separate forms of homicide. In other words, the organizing schema does not specify how the paraphilic process is distinctively implicated in sadistic homicide, serial murder, or sexual killing. This is problematic, particularly when considering the fact that sadistic deviance, serial and predatory behavior, and violent sexuality are all a part of the pathologically driven paraphiliac individual.

Having said this, the thesis examined in this volume is whether a synthesis of the motivational and trauma controls models (and, where appropriate, the classical conditioning typology) provide a more comprehensive theory for and better predictor of erotophonophilia. Future investigators would do well to conceptually examine the discrete personality traits and behavioral factors of the paraphilic process, especially in terms of accounting for sadistic, serial, and sexual murder. These formulations should then become the basis for ongoing theory testing.

Second, many of the constructs specified in the integrative paraphilic typology are not fully or discretely operationalized. Additionally, they are not normed, mindful of race, gender, or class differences. A more global account of the paraphilic process as a system of increasingly aggressive and erotic behavior is enumerated. This more nomothetic explanation, as principally developed from the Burgess et al. (1986) and Hickey (1997, 2001) frameworks, is only broadly linked to the crime of lust murder through the integrative exercise. Subsequent examinations on the topic of erotophonophilia would do well to provide greater and more precise definitional clarity on the etiological and interactive elements constituting the proposed synthetic framework. Efforts such as these are essential, particularly if the model is to represent a reliable and valid measure of the emergence, progression, and maintenance of lust homicide, as well as function as a useful and dependable forecaster for those individuals likely to engage in this behavior.

Third, the integrative paraphilic typology is based on limited studies exploring the phenomenon of sexual homicide and serial murder. Indeed, much of what we know about these offenses is anecdotal or otherwise stems from very small data sets. The absence of more robust and statistically animated investigations potentially leads to theory construction that materializes in something of a vacuum. This is problematic, especially if the goal is to develop a logical and sensible typology, one that possesses significant explanatory and predictive capabilities for the social and behavioral science communities.

This concern notwithstanding, the integrative conceptual framework clearly builds on the prevailing research. Moreover, although certainly limited, both the motivational model and the trauma control typology are routinely identified in the extant literature as the approaches that account for sexual homicide and serial murder, respectively (e.g., Douglas et al., 1995; Egger, 2002; Giannangelo, 1996; Holmes & Holmes, 1999, 2002a; Schlesinger, 2003). As such, incorporating the insights of these two very promising perspectives as a basis to fashion an integrative conceptual paraphilic framework represents a strategic and useful model building enterprise.

## SUMMARY AND CONCLUSION

This chapter delineated the specifics of an integrative theoretical typology regarding erotophonophilia. The typology specifies the role that paraphilia assumes as a motive underlying the commission of sexual homicide in general and the crime of lust murder in particular. As such, the organizing schema suggests how erotophonophilia represents a completely separate subcategory of homicide, especially those killings that are classified as sexual in nature. Finally, the chapter demonstrated how the synthetic framework provides a more comprehensive understanding for the etiology of paraphilia, as well as how the phenomenon functions as a systemic process involving increasingly aggressive and sexualized cognitions, fantasies, impulses, and ultimately behaviors.

The integrated paraphilic model builds on many of the observations described in the MacCulloch et al. (1983) classical conditioning framework, the Burgess et al. (1986) motivational model, and the Hickey (1997, 2001) trauma control approach. The impetus for paraphilic behavior is the violent and erotic fantasies harbored deep within the individual's thought processes. Moreover, traumatic and unresolved childhood events, as well as a lack of prosocial and healthy structure from the home environment, fuel these increasingly sadistic and aggressive images.

The unique aspect of the integrative paraphilic model is that it specifically addresses the process of aberrant sexual deviance and how a person can become *fixed* within this cycle of behavior. This process is comprised of the paraphilic stimulus and fantasy, compulsive masturbation, and facilitators such as drugs, alcohol, and pornography. When an internal or external stressor occurs in the life of the paraphilic individual, those pressures are exacerbated by past feelings of rejection or anxiety from a harrowing event experienced in the person's early childhood development. As suggested, the individual lacks the necessary skills to effectively resolve the tension that surfaces and feels profoundly debilitating distress. Given that he perceives that no other outlets exist, the individual retreats into the paraphilic cycle of behavior. Withdrawing into this pathological sequence creates a sense of relief, satisfaction, and control. The cognitive processes of the individual, in conjunction with the orgasmic conditioning of the fantasy and the paraphilic stimulus, sustain and perpetuate not only the aberrant sexual and sadistic behavior but also the nature and content of the violent fantasy.

It remains to be seen whether the proposed integrative theoretical typology usefully accounts for the crime of lust murder. In order to respond to this matter, the case of Jeffrey Dahmer is examined in the following chapter. According to several investigators, Dahmer was a paraphilic lust murderer (e.g., Masters, 1993; Palermo & Farkas, 2001; Tithecott, 1999). However, the psychological (and criminological) context in which this determination has been made warrants additional commentary. Indeed, as we propose, the application of the integrative paraphilic framework both extends and deepens our understanding of Dahmer's homicidal acts of sadistic deviance and sexual violence. In order to situate our more typologically oriented assessment of Dahmer within its appropriate analytical framework, the following chapter systematically outlines his life narrative.

# 5

## THE CASE OF
## JEFFREY DAHMER

### OVERVIEW

This chapter specifically addresses the highly publicized case of Jeffrey Dahmer, a serial lust murderer responsible for the death and mutilation of 17 young men. In an attempt to create a working profile, several factors linked to Dahmer's social and family history, sexuality, education, employment status, fantasy system, and criminality are discussed. In Chapter 6, this developmental portrait is linked to the three principal theoretical models discussed within Chapters 3 and 4. Specifically, Chapter 6 explores what insights the motivational, trauma control, and integrative paraphilic typologies offer in their accounts of Jeffrey Dahmer's criminal behavior. This exercise is particularly useful since the goal is to ascertain the extent to which each conceptual schema advances our understanding of serial sexual homicide (i.e., lust murder) and those persons who commit this act.

This chapter is divided into two sections. First, several methodological issues germane to our overall assessment of Jeffrey Dahmer are delineated. Given that our approach emphasizes the case study investigatory strategy, a number of remarks relevant to this line of analysis are warranted. Some observations regarding the elements of the case study method are specified, several justifications for the selection of a qualitative approach are outlined, and a description of the data is supplied.

Second, both historical and biographical information concerning Dahmer's life is provided. These data are sequenced chronologically, commencing with his early childhood development and moving all the way to his violent fantasies, criminal conduct, and paraphilic behaviors. Profiling his case in this way allows the reader to assess the merits of the general organization and facilitates a more comprehensive and seamless evaluation within the application work undertaken in Chapter 6.

## METHODOLOGICAL CONCERNS

Jeffrey Dahmer is perhaps one of the most notorious contemporary examples of a serial lust murderer (Egger, 2002; Tithecott, 1999). Various biographical and historical accounts illustrate a life replete with paraphilic interests and sexually violent fantasies (Palermo & Farkas, 2001). But the sensationalism surrounding his offenses must not overshadow the varied experiences that constitute the fullness of his life narrative. Describing these circumstances is essential to a proper understanding of this individual. Indeed, this is how useful personality profiles are constructed (Palermo & Kocsis, 2005).

### BACKGROUND ON AND ELEMENTS OF THE CASE STUDY METHOD

In order to establish a workable as well as a testable portrait of Jeffrey Dahmer, the method by which the profile is constructed must be explained. We employ the case study method. Case study research occupies a long, prominent, and illustrious history across many fields of academic inquiry (Stake, 1995). Case study analysis has been used by decision makers in the governmental and private sectors for informal policy guidance, as well as by historians, political scientists, psychologists, and other academic researchers for specific analysis and exposition (Creswell, 1998; Stake, 1998). Case studies are geared toward identifying and incorporating contextual influences that would otherwise be disregarded as confounds in quantitatively oriented research (McGrath & Johnson, 2003).

Generally speaking, a case study is defined as an exploration of a bounded system or a case over time through detailed, in-depth data collection involving multiple sources of information that are rich in content. This bounded system is conditioned by time and place, and is the case itself being investigated (Creswell, 1998). For purposes of our inquiry, the bounded system in question is an individual, namely, Jeffrey Dahmer. Multiple sources for this study include the use of various public domain documents and reports. The context of the case involves situating it within its physical, social, historical, or economic setting (or any combination of these and related contexts), provided they are relevant to the particular life narrative under review (Stake, 1995; Creswell, 1998).

The goals of case study research entail the summation of information that is unique and, therefore, not yet captured in the scientific literature (Lowman, 2001). Moreover, this method of inquiry describes the application of knowledge in a way that makes it easier to apply the principles of the case to similar situations (Stake,

1995). By summarizing how one particular situation is addressed, the researcher can react to it by suggesting alternative conceptualizations and interventions that might also be effective or that might lead to different outcomes in or interpretations of the life narrative being scrutinized (Lowman, 2001). The goal is not to learn about a single situation; rather, the aim is to use the case in order to develop a theory, to engage in practice consistent with the findings, and to fine-tune and revise the theory to guide future empirical investigations (for applications of this approach in the overlapping psychological and criminological literatures, see Graney & Arrigo, 2002; Claussen-Rodgers & Arrigo, 2005). It is in this context, then, that the case study method makes possible certain generalizations regarding the issues to which the case itself is bound (Lowman, 2001).

Several representative examples of single case study designs are discernible in the extant research. Generally speaking, these are efforts that integrate the relevant psychological and criminological literatures in order to fashion a systematic assessment of controversial and infamous criminals. Three such instances are worth noting.

In their examination of the power serial rapist, Graney and Arrigo (2002) reviewed the case of Gilbert Escobedo, the "Ski Mask" rapist, to explain how this type of sexual offender selects potential victims. The authors were able to provide greater clarity for the behavior, motivation, and personality structure of the power serial rapist. This included the development of a more sophisticated and integrated typology than previously articulated in the literature pertaining to the victim selection process.

In their investigation of the female homicide offender, Shipley and Arrigo (2004) evaluated the case of Aileen Wuornos, a woman who engaged in predatory serial murder, assailing seven men. Based on their inquiry, the authors were able to explain why psychopathic women who experience severe attachment disorder are likely to kill repeatedly. Their research significantly contributed to the literature on the female homicide offender, demonstrating that some women commit the crime of murder instrumentally; that is, for material gain or profit. Contrary to much of the existing research on the subject, the authors showed that the motivational forces and personality structure of the female serial killer extend beyond the popular explanations of ongoing victimization, fear for her life, and partner abuse.

Finally, in their treatment of police corruption and psychological testing occurring at the pre-employment screening phase, Claussen-Rodgers and Arrigo (2005) considered the case of Robert Philip Hanssen. Hanssen was a former FBI agent convicted of selling nuclear war plans and other highly classified United States documents to the former Soviet Union and Russia in exchange for money and diamonds. The authors demonstrated how the personality constructs of conscientiousness and non-sociability (e.g., deviance, corruption) could be psychometrically tested among would-be police officers by relying on the NEO-Personality Inventory-Revised and the Inwald Personality Inventory assessment tools. The assimilation of these psychological testing instruments, if appropriately administered during the pre-employment screening phase, could yield rich data on which to base a hiring decision. By proposing a novel, theoretically driven evaluation strategy, the researchers significantly contributed to the literature on policing, corruption, and psychological testing.

There are various models of case study research (Stake, 1995). An *intrinsic* case study focuses on a singular instance, phenomenon, or story that requires investigation because of its uniqueness. A *collective* case study is utilized when more than one instance, phenomenon, or narrative is studied. An *instrumental* case study focuses on an issue (or issues), with the case used instrumentally for illustrative purposes (Shipley & Arrigo, 2004). *Issues* are "matter for study regarding the specific case. Starting with a topical concern, researchers pose foreshadowed problems, concentrate on issue-related observations, [and] interpret patterns of data that reform issues as assertions" (Stake, 1998, p. 92).

An instrumental case study approach is the qualitative methodology employed in the current study. More specifically, in this book, the high-profile case of Jeffrey Dahmer, a convicted lust murderer, is used to address the issue of how paraphilia functions as an underlying motive in instances involving sexual homicide and serial murder. By relying on the data collection process of the instrumental case study method, a detailed description of the case emerges, wherein an analysis of issues (or themes) can be conducted and an interpretation of the life narrative can be supplied (Creswell, 1998).

Regardless of the specific case study format utilized, several essential features must be incorporated into this type of methodology. These features include a detailed, accurate, and objective description of specific case events and variables; diagnostic interpretations about the data, derived from the case events; an identification of the specific interventions made; an assessment of the measured effects of these interventions; and a plausible alternative explanation of the results in their specific context (Lowman, 2001). In addition, there are several overriding principles that are imperative to the data collection of any case study. These include the following: utilizing multiple sources of evidence that confirm the same set of facts or findings; a formal assembly of evidence; and identifying links between the propositions, the data, and the conclusions (Yin, 1989). Collectively, these features and principles inform the five components of a case study design. Accordingly, these elements are incorporated into the overall presentation of Jeffrey Dahmer's life narrative.

## JUSTIFICATIONS FOR SELECTING A QUALITATIVE METHODOLOGY

Qualitative research questions whether an objective conception of reality can truly exist and suggests that other forms of investigation are necessary to increase the understanding of certain social and psychological issues (Cafasso, Camic, & Rhodes, 2001). The strengths of qualitative research derive primarily from its

inductive approach, its specific focus on situations and individuals, and its emphasis on words rather than numbers (Maxwell, 1996). Findings from qualitative
studies have a quality of "undeniability" (Miles & Huberman, 1994, p. 263).
Stated differently, words, especially when organized into incidents or stories,
have a concrete, vivid, and meaningful flavor that often proves far more convincing to professionals than pages of summarized numbers (Stake, 1998).

A significant feature of qualitative research is that it focuses on naturally
occurring, everyday events in organic settings. In other words, qualitative
inquiries endeavor to capture a snapshot of what ordinary life is like in relation
to the particular instance investigated (Miles & Huberman, 1994). The
researcher's capacity to confidently and accurately depict ordinary occurrences
in the case is reinforced by the phenomenon of local groundedness, a process by
which data are collected in close proximity to a specific individual or situation
(Stake, 1995). As such, the focus is uniquely on a specific case, a bounded phenomenon, rooted in its manifold contexts (Miles & Huberman, 1994). The influences of these contexts are not ignored. Indeed, they are strategically evaluated.
In this way, the researcher seeks to determine whether there is a strong likelihood
that these influences or forces underpin or otherwise inform the issues of the case,
thereby creating greater understanding of the phenomenon in question (Creswell,
1998; Miles & Huberman, 1994).

There are various research purposes for which qualitative studies are especially well suited. First, this method generates deeper comprehension of the
meaning of the events, situations, and actions involved. Unlike more quantitatively oriented research, qualitative studies are not merely interested in physically
measurable events and behaviors. While these are certainly noteworthy objects
of inquiry, social scientists that appropriate a qualitative methodology also
concern themselves with how participants make sense of their conduct and how
this knowledge influences their ongoing behavior and interactions (Maxwell,
1996).

In addition, qualitative investigations endeavor to grasp and explore the
particular cultural, historic, economic, political, psychological contexts, among
others, within which the participants act, and the influence that this overall context
has on the actions of individuals. In a single case study research design, the
subject pool is limited to a data set of one. By maintaining the integrity of the
methodology and the process by which it unfolds, the individuality of the subject
in question can be preserved (Maxwell, 1996). In short, by adhering to the principles and features of the qualitative research design, an understanding regarding
the interplay of actions, events, and meanings emerges (Stake, 1998). This is
insight and discernment shaped by and derived from the unique circumstances of
the case itself (Maxwell, 1996).

Finally, adopting a qualitative methodology promotes awareness with
respect to the natural process by which events and actions take place. A major
strength of qualitative analysis is that it enables the researcher to access and

ascertain the unique processes that led to specific outcomes (Miles & Huberman, 1994). These are processes of interaction and comportment that experimental and survey research are often ill-equipped to identify or otherwise interpret (Maxwell, 1996).

## DESCRIPTION OF THE DATA

In the context of the present study, the case of Jeffrey Dahmer is presented through a series of techniques, including the chronology of major or important life events, followed by an in-depth, detailed discussion about several key incidents (Creswell, 1998). This description of the case represents a body of relatively uncontested data. And, as previously specified, this information, both historical and biographical in content as well as chronologically and systematically sequenced, forms the basis of our overall assessment.

The data sources utilized for purposes of this study, although varied, were somewhat limited. This problem is not atypical when relying on a single case (i.e., Dahmer) to instrumentally explore the relationship between a number of social and psychological phenomena (i.e., sexual homicide, serial murder, and paraphilia) (Creswell, 1998). Notwithstanding this restriction, pertinent information was collected from various newspaper and journal articles. This data collection was a function of a careful search in psychological and criminal justice abstracts featuring the constructs "serial murder," "sexual homicide," "lust killer," and "paraphilia." This search spanned the 1992–2005 publishing period. Those articles featuring accounts of Dahmer (especially historical and biographical commentary) were utilized; those articles that did not were discarded. In addition, the Time Life (Flaherty, 1993) text addressing the compulsion to kill was incorporated into our construction of Dahmer's life narrative. This volume was selected because of its considerable detail on matters related to pertinent developmental information. Moreover, it provides a more exacting cataloging of Dahmer's acts, including personal statements from Dahmer relative to some of his early fantasies and subsequent criminal history. Finally, a number of monograph-length works exploring the clinical and offender dynamics associated with Dahmer's personality structure and sexual assault inclinations were utilized. The insights from these volumes were delineated, particularly when they confirmed accounts found in other sources of available information.

Collectively, then, various newspaper reports, journal articles, the Time Life volume, and several monograph-length works represented the data set. Mindful of the specific elements pertaining to a case study research design, these sources were organized and sequenced so that a portrait of the offender could be sensibly and logically established. Where possible, items specified in one source were cross-checked with items identified in other outlets. When this occurred, a theme was established relative to the life narrative of Jeffrey Dahmer. These overarching themes formed the basis of the historical and biographical content constituting his personality structure and general profile.

## HISTORICAL AND BIOGRAPHICAL ACCOUNT
## OF JEFFREY DAHMER

In order to achieve a more complete understanding of Jeffrey Dahmer and grasp the assorted components of his criminal behavior, a recounting of important dimensions of or phases regarding his life must be chronicled. Along these lines, factors specifically considered include the following: early childhood and adolescent development, early sexual identity and fantasy development, first victim and post-high school acts, early criminal conduct, and employment history, as well as paraphilic system of behaviors. Each of these historical and biographical elements is methodically presented in the ensuing subsections.

### EARLY CHILDHOOD DEVELOPMENT

Jeffrey Dahmer was born on May 21, 1960, at Deconess Hospital in Milwaukee, Wisconsin, to Lionel and Joyce Dahmer (Flaherty, 1993; Schwartz, 1992). At the time of his birth, his mother was a homemaker and his father was a graduate student in chemical engineering. Dahmer's father eventually earned his PhD in chemistry from Iowa State University in Ames, Iowa. In 1966, Jeffrey's mother gave birth to a second son, David Dahmer. Jeffrey was 5 years of age when his brother was born. Over time, the family settled into Bath, Ohio, an affluent area north of Akron (Davis, 1998; Flaherty, 1993).

As a young boy, Dahmer was fascinated by and became preoccupied with dead insects, animals, and other organisms, as well as with their deteriorating remains. It was not uncommon for him to collect the entrails of the animals he would find in the woods behind his home or on the side of the road. On one occasion, he discovered a dead dog along side a nearby street. He disemboweled and decapitated it, and then impaled the animal on a stick near his residence (Egger, 2002; Tithecott, 1999).

Dahmer kept his souvenir collection of dead animals and insects in a shed behind the family home, often referring to them as his "fiddlesticks" (Flaherty, 1993, p. 8). A friend later described Dahmer's collection as "tons and tons of jars of animals and pieces of animals in which he seemed fascinated by the decomposition" (Flaherty, 1993, p. 7; see also Palermo & Farkas, 2001, p. 103). Dahmer used a chemistry set his father had given him to preserve the remains of these decaying organisms. The kit also enabled him to dissolve and remove the skin of these decomposing creatures. He was intrigued with the insides of the animals and how things worked underneath the surface of their skins (Davis, 1998). In addition to his fetishistic shrine of dead organisms was an animal cemetery of Dahmer's own making in his back yard (Masters, 1993). This pet cemetery was the same place where Jeffrey Dahmer scattered the bones of his first victim, Stephen Hicks (Flaherty, 1993; Martens & Palermo, 2005).

Within the Dahmer household, there was constant family discord and marital strife (Palermo & Farkas, 2001). Eventually, his parents divorced during

Dahmer's senior year in high school (Davis, 1998; Hickey, 1997). These incidents served to alienate him through his formative developmental period, a stage during which he found great comfort and companionship within a rich fantasy world (Tithecott, 1999). Dahmer's emotional focus in life was his fear of being abandoned and alone (Egger, 2002; Martens & Palermo, 2005). After his final arrest in 1991, in a subsequent psychological examination, Dahmer disclosed that both of his parents were under-involved in his life. His mother was hospitalized for psychiatric reasons during his early childhood, and his father was often absent from home addressing work-related matters (Davis, 1998).

Commenting on the tumultuous and troubled period of Dahmer's early childhood, Martens and Palermo (2005) offer a number of insightful summary observations. As they indicate:

> When Jeffrey was 5 years of age, his brother David was born and for the first time, Jeffrey felt neglected. His mother, who suffered from occasional depression and suicidal ideation, was very self-involved, his father was involved in doctorate activities, and Jeffrey had to share the sparse attention of his parents with his brother. As a child, Jeffrey was shy but displayed impulsive and angry behavior (tantrums). . . . Between the ages of 6 and 8, Jeffrey's family moved three times. He was occasionally isolated and was regarded by other children as odd and bizarre, and at age 10 he reportedly felt guilty about his mother's emotional disorder. . . . It appears that Jeffrey remained unattached during his childhood and never really bonded with anyone except a few high school friends with whom he had only superficial relations. . . . [H]e was frequently apathetic and demonstrated no normal emotions, and he felt that he was an outcast, belonging neither to family nor any other social network. (Martens & Palermo, 2005, p. 300)

## ADOLESCENCE

Friends, neighbors, and teachers regarded Dahmer as a social outcast who had considerable difficulties in his relationships with others (Tithecott, 1999). Throughout the course of his adolescent development, Dahmer preferred the relief and comfort of fantasy to the pain and disappointment of reality (Davis, 1998; Flaherty, 1993; Hickey, 1997). However, despite his identification as socially isolative with a morbid fascination toward and penchant for dead animals, Dahmer seemed to be active in an array of school-related activities (Schwartz, 1992; Tithecott, 1999).

For example, during his freshman year, he participated in the high school band, where he played the clarinet. He also was involved with intramural tennis in his sophomore through senior years (Masters, 1993), and worked on the school's newspaper during his junior year (Davis, 1998). However, it was common for him to attend class inebriated or otherwise under the influence of illicit substances (i.e., marijuana) (Davis, 1998). Dahmer relied heavily on intoxicants or stimulants (Tithecott, 1999). Indeed, on many occasions, he would drink Scotch whiskey from a styrofoam cup during class (Flaherty, 1993).

Dahmer was also regarded as something of a prankster or class clown (Dahmer, 1994). Fellow classmates recall Dahmer stumbling drunk through the local mall, harassing patrons and pretending to have epileptic seizures. One classmate recollected that "the performance was fun to watch, but more than a little frightening, for we were always a little bit wary of him. He was a big guy, and we had the feeling that if he went off, you didn't want to be in the way" (Flaherty, 1993, p. 9).

In addition to the mall outing as an indicator of Dahmer's practical jokester tendencies was his uninvited attendance at the school's National Honor Society photo session, when he unceremoniously inserted himself into the photo shoot (Masters, 1993). Editors blacked out his face before the photograph was printed in the school yearbook. It was also common for Dahmer to draw chalk outlines of bodies throughout the school corridors (Tithecott, 1999). As some commentators have remarked, it was as if he were an actor on a stage, a peripheral figure who never really let down his act (Flaherty, 1993, p. 9; see also Palermo, 2004).

### EARLY SEXUAL IDENTITY

Dahmer seemed somewhat indifferent when it came to having relationships with females (Egger, 2002). More precisely, "[H]e was very shy toward girls but aggressive toward authority figures." He longed for attention and seemed to be seeking it everywhere (Martens & Palermo, 2005, p. 300). Dahmer's one adolescent sexual experience occurred at around the age of 14 and involved kissing and fondling another boy (Flaherty, 1993). At the age of 15, he stole a manikin on display at a local store. He took the dummy home and rested with it in his bed while his parents were out of the house (Tithecott, 1999). This was the point at which Dahmer developed necrophilic fantasies that fueled his homosexual desires (Masters, 1993; Martens & Palermo, 2005).

Throughout adolescence, Dahmer struggled with his sexual identity, often feeling that his homosexual cognitions and impulses were wrong (Schwartz, 1992). As a result of this intra-psychic struggle and confusion, he frequently contemplated suicide, while at the same time developing increasingly violent and sexualized (necrophilic) fantasies, including the lustful domination of others (Hickey, 2001, 2003). These thoughts and desires were the product of intense loneliness, emotional turmoil, and social isolation (Egger, 2002; Palermo, 2004).

In addition to the inner conflict surrounding his sexual identity, Dahmer faced debilitating environmental stress and hardship due to his parents' failing marriage. During his senior year in high school, there was increased tension within the household (Dahmer, 1994). Unable to maintain a functional and healthy relationship, Dahmer's parents divided the family home, with each parent occupying his or her own space. To further demarcate this division, Lionel Dahmer constructed a string with hanging keys in his dwelling area. This alerted him when his estranged wife trespassed into his space (Flaherty, 1993).

Complicating the tension-filled interactions between Damher's parents was the bitter custody battle that ensued with their divorce. By this time, Jeffrey was 18 years of age, and his brother David, who was 12 years old, was the center of controversy during the divorce proceedings (Davis, 1998). It was during this period that Dahmer's reliance on alcohol increased and his emotional resources declined, resulting in profound withdrawal and depression (Martens & Palermo, 2005).

Throughout the divorce and custody proceedings, each parent claimed the other was cruel toward and extremely neglectful of both boys (Masters, 1993). Additionally, Lionel alleged that Joyce had a chronic mental illness and vigorously argued against David's placement with her (Schwartz, 1992). Despite these assertions, Joyce was awarded custody of David. The adverse affects for Jeffrey Dahmer stemming from this very toxic and public experience were considerable. Indeed, as he said, "[I]t was at this time when I began having fantasies of killing people; these fantasies overcame my feelings of frustration and emptiness" (Golman, 1991, p. A8).

### EARLY FANTASY DEVELOPMENT

Interestingly, Dahmer admitted to having contemplated what it would be like to take the life of other human beings; these fantasies existed long before his first slaying. As others have suggested, social isolation and sadistic images were integral to Dahmer's adolescent development (Martens, 1993; Palermo, 2004; Tithecott, 1999).

As a teenager, Dahmer often fantasized about having sexual intercourse with other men (Schwartz, 1992). Continuing to struggle with his own sexual identity, Dahmer envisioned possessing a totally compliant, unconscious lover, someone who would never leave his side (Egger, 2002; Holmes & Holmes, 2002a). A common theme of these fantasies was the desire that his lover be dead, dismembered, and disemboweled (Flaherty, 1993). Dahmer's capacity for killing was enhanced by his increasingly aggressive erotic fantasies, which included the urge to control and to harm others as a way to regain command over his deteriorating life (Palermo, 2004).

Dahmer reported that one of his first elaborate and contrived fantasies occurred when he was 15 years old (Masters, 1993). He had an obsessive fascination with an unknown jogger who would frequently run past his family's residence. He imagined how he would meet this attractive young man (Flaherty, 1993, p. 9), but feared the jogger would reject any of his advances. As part of his fantasy, he formulated a plan in which he hid in the bushes close to the jogger's path. As the runner passed by, he would leap out, slug him with a baseball bat, and drag the unconscious body off into the woods, eventually having sexual intercourse with him (Flaherty, 1993, p. 9). That particular fantasy remained unfulfilled. The fictitious jogger never ran past his dwelling (Tithecott, 1999).

### FIRST VICTIM

A few weeks after Dahmer's high school graduation, on June 18, 1978, he murdered and dismembered his first victim, 17-year-old Steven Hicks (Davis,

1998; Martens & Palermo, 2005). Dahmer encountered Hicks, stripped to the waist and hitchhiking, so he offered to give him a ride. Dahmer was 18 years old. Hicks accepted, and Dahmer recommended that they go back to his parents' house for a few beers, since the house was vacant. Dahmer's mother and brother had gone to Wisconsin, and his father was staying in a nearby motel (Schwartz, 1992). Without food, money, or contact from kin, Dahmer had been alone and isolated in the family residence for weeks.

According to Dahmer's account, he and Hicks got along well, lifted weights, shared a 12-pack of beer, and smoked some marijuana. However, there was no homosexual encounter because Dahmer did not believe Hicks was gay (Flaherty, 1993). Dahmer reported that "the guy wanted to leave and I didn't want him to leave" (Schwartz, cited in Davis, 1998, p. 127). Upset at Hicks's departure, Dahmer knocked him unconscious with a barbell and then strangled him by pressing the barbell into his throat. As he was killing his victim, Dahmer experienced an increased sense of personal pleasure (Martens & Palermo, 2005). Indeed, his most exciting fantasy had come true: an attractive, helpless man lay beneath him (Flaherty, 1993). Dahmer sexually assaulted his slain victim, dismembered the body, and disposed of the pieces (Egger, 2002).

## POST HIGH SCHOOL

After high school, Dahmer attempted a college career at Ohio State University in Columbus; however, he flunked out in December of his freshman year. His heavy drinking and low academic marks contributed to his failure (Masters, 1993). Dahmer then joined the Army (Schwartz, 1992). However, given his propensity for routine intoxication, Dahmer was eventually discharged from the military for alcohol abuse (Hickey, 1997).

One of Dahmer's fellow servicemen recalled his typical conduct while on the base or in the barracks. As the associate noted, "[I]t was common for Dahmer to lie on his bunk all weekend, with earphones on his head, listening to heavy metal music and drinking martinis until he passed out" (Baumann, cited in Davis, 1998, p. 29). Despite a history of excessive alcohol consumption, Dahmer managed to steer clear of any difficulties during his 2-year stint with the military. Commenting on this period, Flaherty (1993, p. 14) observed that "alcohol abuse, homosexual pornography, masturbation, heavy metal music and a busy work schedule kept him out of serious trouble" (see also Holmes & Holmes, 2002a).

## EMPLOYMENT HISTORY

Futile attempts at college and the Army left Jeffrey Dahmer vacillating between unemployment, technical work, and various unskilled laborer and factory jobs (Tithecott, 1999). For example, in 1982, he worked briefly at a blood bank as a phlebotomist, but his employment was eventually terminated. However, Dahmer found steady employment in 1985 as a mixer at the Ambrosia

Chocolate Company in Milwaukee, where he worked the night shift (Flaherty, 1993; Hickey, 1997). He retained his employment there for 7 years but was fired for continued tardiness and increased absenteeism just weeks prior to his final arrest, in which he was charged with killing and mutilating 17 young males (Egger, 2002).

## EARLY CRIMINAL HISTORY

After Dahmer's military discharge in 1981, he returned to Bath, Ohio. He was unemployed, depressed, and relying heavily on drugs and alcohol to escape the loneliness of each day and experience relief from his inner torment (Tithecott, 1999). A few weeks following his return, Dahmer had a brush with the law. Refusing to leave a local Ramada Inn, he was taken into custody and charged with disorderly conduct, having an open container of liquor, and resisting arrest (Davis, 1998). Subsequently, on August 8, 1982, while attending the Wisconsin State Fair, Dahmer was fined $50 for drunk and disorderly conduct. More than 20 people alleged that Dahmer had indecently exposed himself (Flaherty, 1993).

On September 8, 1986, there was another incident of exhibitionism. Dahmer was arrested for masturbating in front of two 12-year-old boys. This resulted in an initial charge of lewd and lascivious conduct; however, the offense was later reduced to disorderly conduct (Holmes & Holmes, 2002a). In court, Dahmer confessed to this incident as well as to five other similar episodes. Moreover, he agreed that he had a problem and promised to solicit help (Flaherty, 1993, p. 17). Dahmer was sentenced to 1 year of probation as well as to mandatory counseling (Hickey, 1997).

Dahmer's police record continued to worsen. On January 30, 1989, he was found guilty of sexually assaulting a 13-year-old Laotian boy named Somsack Sinthasomphone (Davis, 1998). Dahmer met Somsack on the street by his apartment and asked him to pose for money. The boy accepted Dahmer's offer. Once they were inside Dahmer's apartment, he gave the boy coffee mixed with Irish Cream and sleeping pills. He then fondled the boy and took a few photographs (Masters, 1993). Upon his return home, the boy's parents were suspicious of their son's incoherent condition. They contacted local authorities, which led to Dahmer's apprehension and conviction. However, the events that followed were gruesome and tragic and, more profoundly, helped to establish the serial nature of Dahmer's compulsions (Egger, 2002).

On May 27, 1991, in a fit of retaliation, Dahmer, now on parole for his previous offense, attacked and killed Somsack's 14-year-old brother, Konerak (Hickey, 2001). Ironically, this was the point at which law enforcement officials could have apprehended and ultimately prevented Dahmer from killing as many as 14 more victims (Kline, 1995). Before meeting his final fate, Konerak managed to escape Dahmer's Milwaukee apartment. Naked and bleeding, he attracted the attention of local authorities, but the police made the incalculable mistake of bringing him back to Dahmer's residence. Dahmer had followed after Konerak, once realizing that he had escaped. Finding him on a street corner nearby, Dahmer explained to the paramedics and local authorities that Konerak was 19 years of age. Dahmer provided the police with his ID and intimated that the injured man was his roommate and boyfriend. Despite the outcry from witnesses at the scene, the police did not conduct a database check on Dahmer. Instead, they determined that Konerak's injuries were somehow related to a homosexual lover's fight. And so, they left. Had the police taken a report and run Dahmer's name through their computer tracking system, they would have discovered that just 2 years earlier he had been convicted of sexually assaulting Somsack Sinthasomphone, Konerak's younger brother (Davis, 1998).

## INCREASINGLY VIOLENT FANTASIES AND HOMICIDAL BEHAVIOR

Between 1982 and 1988, before moving into an apartment of his own, Dahmer occupied the basement of his grandmother Catherine's house in West Allis, Wisconsin. He used the basement as a place to which he would lure victims, drug them, and then sexually assault them while they were unconscious (Flaherty, 1993). This ritualized behavior enabled Dahmer to act out his fantasies (Hickey, 2001).

Dahmer was known to frequent adult bookstores, peep shows, gay bars, and bathhouses, places where he would engage in consensual homosexual activities (Tithecott, 1999). During this period (1982–1987), his fantasies intensified and consumed the remaining vestiges of his reality. Typically, Dahmer would rent a $10-a-night private room at the bathhouse and slip his lover a concoction of alcohol laced with Halcion (a sleeping pill), rendering him unconscious (Davis, 1998). Throughout the course of a weekend, it was not uncommon for him to take three to four companions to his room. This was a place where Dahmer's tastes grew increasingly peculiar (Palermo, 2004). For example, he experienced immense sexual gratification and became increasingly aroused by the sound of his sleeping lovers' hearts (Egger, 2002; Flaherty, 1993).

Dahmer was eventually suspected and questioned by the bathhouse's management after one of his companions, unable to recover from the drug, needed serious medical assistance. His victim was hospitalized for 2 weeks as a result; however, he was unwilling to press charges against his assailant (Flaherty, 1993). As a result of the incident, the management of the bathhouse banned Dahmer from the premises.

Jeffrey Dahmer's capacity for killing was enhanced by the increasingly violent and deviant images he conjured (Holmes & Holmes, 2002a; Martens & Palermo, 2005). Eventually, he succumbed to his growing internal cognitions and impulses by killing a second time. On September 15, 1987, Dahmer met Steven Tuomi at the Ambassador Hotel in Milwaukee, Wisconsin, a seedy establishment frequented by prostitutes (Flaherty, 1993; Tithecott, 1999). After inconspicuously slipping tranquilizers into his companion's beverage, rendering him unconscious,

Dahmer himself passed out from consuming too much liquor. According to Dahmer's own testimony, he remembered nothing more until he awoke, lying naked on top of Tuomi's dead body (Flaherty, 1993, p. 19). After storing Tuomi's body in a fruit cellar for over a week, Jeffrey cut the corpse up into several pieces (Egger, 2002). He later told a psychiatrist that he became aroused when he slit open Tuomi's abdomen and examined the colors and textures of his victim's entrails (Flaherty, 1993, p. 19). Dahmer discarded the body parts, crushed the bones with a hammer and, after calling a taxidermist for information on how to preserve the bones, bleached Tuomi's skull, fetishistically using it to fuel and sustain his fantasies (Flaherty, 1993; Martens & Palermo, 2005).

Dahmer continued to lure potential victims back to his own apartment by offering them money to pose in the nude (Golman, 1991; Hickey, 2001). After he rendered his victims unconscious by drugging them, he would engage in sexual intercourse with them. As in his fantasies, they were completely dominated by him. Because he could not bear the thought of them leaving and being alone, he would kill them by strangulation (Egger, 2002). In an interview after his arrest, Dahmer explained that "it was better to have them with me dead, then to have them leave" (Golman, 1991, p. A8). Killing by ligature strangulation is a favored method, especially for those who yearn for the death of another to be intimate (Davis, 1998), precisely what Jeffrey Dahmer craved.

Dahmer's fantasies and actions progressed to necrosadism by 1988 (Martens & Palermo, 2005). He would kill his victims and then engage in necrophilic sex with them (Egger, 2002). Necrosadistic killers murder for the express purpose of having intercourse with their dead victims (Douglas et al., 1995; Hickey, 2005). Dahmer would perform oral and anal sex on his slain victims (Davis, 1998; Hickey, 2001). He would then mutilate the corpses (Tithecott, 1999). Dahmer would become sexually aroused by looking at the colors and textures of the bodies' entrails (Flaherty, 1993; Holmes & Holmes, 2002a).

Dahmer also engaged in souvenir fetishes, saving the remains of his victim's body parts (Hickey, 1997). It was common for Dahmer to save genitals, scalps, and skulls as cherished mementos (Flaherty, 1993; Palermo, 2004). Collecting such items enabled him to masturbate to orgasm and relive the paraphilic experience within his internalized fantasy system (Egger, 2002; Hickey, 2005). Indeed, as Dahmer explained, he experienced "sexual pleasure in the body parts he collected from his victims, and . . . he wanted to feel close to them" (Davis, 1998, p. 29).

The killings progressed in frequency and remained ritualistic in nature (Martens & Palermo, 2005). He drugged, killed, and dismembered several other victims while his fantasies launched him toward new levels of murder (Tithecott, 1999). One particular instance amply demonstrates this increase in aggressive imagery. Dahmer completely removed the skin of one victim, and then hung the skeleton from the head of his shower (Hickey, 1997). He then photographed the skeleton so that the picture could be used as another souvenir memento (Flaherty, 1993). Relying on a camera enhanced the quality of his fantasies (Davis, 1998).

Dahmer also engaged in cannibalism as a way of remembering both the killing and the victim. By consuming his victims, they would become part of him and

make him more powerful (Hickey, 1997, p. 98). Commenting on his cannibalism, Dahmer observed, "I suppose in an odd way it made me feel as if they were
more a part of me" (Cyriax, cited in Davis, 1998, p. 29; see also Palermo, 2004;
Palermo & Farkas, 2001). This was sexually arousing to Dahmer, and he regarded
the heart and biceps as sources of considerable strength and life (Flaherty, 1993,
p. 28; Egger, 2002). Dahmer would drink heavily and watch pornographic videos
as he ate the flesh of his victims (Hickey, 2005; Tithecott, 1999).

His fantasies continued to progress and escalate in severity. He wanted to
possess a *sex slave* and tried to transform his victims into zombies or servants by
performing lobotomies on them (Egger, 2002; Hickey, 2005). He drilled holes
into the heads of his unconscious, living victims, utilizing a syringe and a turkey
baster to inject acid into their brain cavities (Flaherty, 1993).

Dahmer's ultimate fantasy was to build a shrine of body parts from his victims
by using souvenir mementos such as skulls and skeletons (Martens & Palermo,
2005). He imagined having his two favorite victims, fully skeletonized, standing
on either side of him while he sat in a large black chair, similar to the one used
by Darth Vader in the movie *Star Wars* (Hickey, 1997, p. 96). Additionally,
Dahmer envisioned that directly behind his seat, on a shelf between the two
hanging skeletons would rest the shrunken skulls of several of his other victims
(Egger, 2002; Tithecott, 1999). Dahmer reasoned that the shrine of body parts
would enable him to feel connected to those he had killed, thereby sating his need
for belonging, something he had lacked throughout his entire life (Palermo,
2004). Some commentators note that Dahmer's fantasies consisted of a level of
power and control unlike any other they had ever experienced (Eggger, 2002;
Hickey, 2005; Holmes & Holmes, 2002a).

In the summer months prior to his final arrest in 1991, Jeffrey Dahmer was
killing at a rate of one victim per month (Flaherty, 1993). The frequency of these
slayings created a host of problems for him. For example, given the relatively
small size of his apartment, he soon found himself running out of room to store
the remains of his victims (Tithecott, 1999). Moreover, Dahmer devoted increased
amounts of time to his fantasies, cognitions, and impulses. These activities began
to interfere with his daily functioning (Holmes & Holmes, 2002a; Flaherty, 1993).
After 7 years of sustained employment, Dahmer was finally fired from his job at
the Ambrosia Chocolate Factory. He was also close to being evicted from his
apartment, as he was several months behind in rent payments. On July 22, 1991,
after a potential victim escaped, he was finally apprehended by local law enforcement authorities for the murder and mutilation of 17 young men (Hickey, 2001;
Flaherty, 1993; Tithecott, 1999).

## PARAPHILIC BEHAVIORS

Dahmer's early criminal history is indicative of paraphilic sexual offenses, particularly exhibitionism and public masturbation. In one instance of exhibitionism,
he exposed himself to several prepubescent boys while masturbating. Given that

the target audience for this display consisted of young boys, his paraphilic behavior would specifically be classified as hebephilia. This partialism includes a sexual interest in young children from puberty to adolescence (Holmes & Holmes, 2002a). Dahmer's subsequent arrest and court-ordered counseling for this incident seemed to have little to no effect in curbing Dahmer's increasingly aggressive sexual aberrations.

Investigators note that shortly following his first homicide, Dahmer was believed to have frequented local cemeteries (Martens & Palermo, 2005). Interestingly enough, he hoped to retrieve a corpse rather than to kill again (Egger, 2002; Hickey, 2005). Reviewers of Dahmer's biography corroborate this account (e.g., Palermo, 2004; Tithecott, 1999). In another display of paraphilia, Dahmer stole a mannequin from a local department store for the express purpose of acting out some of his fantasies. His grandmother, with whom he was living at the time, discovered the stolen mannequin after several weeks and made him discard it (Flaherty, 1993).

Following this incident, Dahmer's interests turned from the lifeless to the formerly living (Martens & Palermo, 2005; Palermo, 2004). He began scanning the newspaper obituaries for likely companions (Flaherty, 1993; Tithecott, 1999). After several unsuccessful reviews of the local obituary column, Dahmer identified someone that met his paraphilic interests: an 18-year-old male who had died in a car accident. Dahmer visited the funeral home, looked at the body, and decided that he liked what he saw. Following the funeral and burial, he took a shovel and a wheelbarrow to the cemetery in order to dig through the frozen ground (Flaherty, 1993). It proved to be an arduous process, and eventually (and reluctantly), he decided to give up the endeavor (Hickey, 2001).

Dahmer's experience with the stolen dummy and his attempt at retrieving a corpse both represent clear examples of paraphilic behaviors. Pygmalionism—sexual involvement with dolls, statues, or mannequins—is similar to necrophilia, in that the paraphiliac individual avoids rejection by having sexual contact with an inanimate object (i.e., dummy) or with a corpse (Hickey, 2005). With both forms of this behavior, he assumes total control over his environment, doing whatever he chooses to the object or body and then, finally, ridding himself of it.

Dahmer also experimented with vampirism. During his brief employment as a phlebotomist, he acted on one of his sexual fantasies and drank a vial of blood belonging to a young man to whom he had been attracted (Flaherty, 1993). Vampirism is a paraphilia in which sexual gratification is contingent upon smelling or drinking the blood of another person or an animal (Holmes & Holmes, 2002a).

As Dahmer's fantasies increased, the manifestation and progression of his paraphilias intensified, escalating toward the acute end of the paraphilic continuum. Indeed, the development of Dahmer's deviance transitioned from exhibitionism, pygmalionism, vampirism, to eventually, erotophonophilia. Dahmer's paraphilic tendencies consisted of such ancillary partialisms as anthropophagy, necrosadism, necrofetishism (collecting parts of corpses that are subsequently used for erotic stimulation and gratification), and necrophilia.

From the time of his first murder in 1978 to his final arrest on July 22, 1991, Dahmer's behavioral and criminal history reflects an array of paraphilic stimuli. Utilizing Abel's (1990) conceptualization of paraphilia as a spectrum of conduct ranging from mild to moderate to severe, Dahmer's paraphilia progressed and intensified accordingly. The transition from paraphiliac (i.e., exhibitionist) to erotophonophiliac (i.e., serial lust murderer) represents a profoundly chilling transformation.

Underscoring Dahmer's multiple homicides was the presence of paraphilia that functioned as motive, sustaining and driving his increasingly violent and sexualized fantasy system. As a component of the paraphilic process, Dahmer's fantasy system was replete with images of power, domination, and mutilation. Internal stimuli (e.g., feelings of aloneness, helplessness, hopelessness), in conjunction with social isolation, a troubled home life, and the ultimate need for sexual satisfaction, fueled Dahmer's violent desires, compelling him to commit 17 murders over the span of 13 years.

## SUMMARY AND CONCLUSION

Jeffrey Dahmer is perhaps one of the most sensationalized serial killers society has ever known (Egger, 2002). Upon his arrest in Milwaukee, Wisconsin, he entered the annals of America's most notorious sexual offenders' list (Holmes & Holmes, 2002a). He confessed to killing 17 men and was sentenced to 15 consecutive life terms, equivalent to 957 years in prison (Davis, 1998; Palermo, 2004). On November 28, 1994, while serving time at the Columbia Correctional Facility in Portage, Wisconsin, Dahmer was beaten to death by Christopher J. Scarver, another inmate serving time for murder (Hickey, 2001).

This chapter presented historical and biographical information sufficient to establish a portrait of Jeffrey Dahmer. The profile included a cataloging of important life themes consisting of such concerns as early childhood and adolescent development, early sexual identity and fantasy development, first victim and post-high school encounters, early criminal conduct, and employment history, as well as increasingly violent and acute paraphilic behaviors. Based on the presentation of this information, chronologically prepared and methodically sequenced, the case study of Jeffrey Dahmer serves an important and fundamental purpose of this book. His life narrative vividly captures the relationship between paraphilia, sexual homicide, and serial murder.

In the ensuing chapter, his case is analyzed more systematically. At issue are the respective explanatory properties emanating from the motivational model, the trauma control framework, and the integrative paraphilic typology. It remains to be seen where and how each organizing schema contributes to our overall understanding of erotophonophilia and those responsible for the commission of such acts.

# 6

# DAHMER, PARAPHILIA, AND LUST MURDER:

## TESTING THE MODELS

### OVERVIEW

The previous chapter presented both biographical and historical information taken from a variety of sources regarding the narrative of Jeffrey Dahmer. The methodological strategy informing this exercise was the instrumental case study approach. A useful profile of this serial sexual murderer was delineated based on data from several newspaper accounts, journal articles, and the Time Life volume on the compulsion to kill, as well as a number of monograph-length books. These data were organized and consolidated so that a developmental portrait was constructed that chronologically and systematically retold Dahmer's story. By cross-checking sources against other identified outlets, a relatively uncontested account of his varied life experiences from childhood to adolescence and adulthood was disclosed.

In order to assess the significance of these data, they must be examined within the context of the three conceptual typologies that form the basis of this volume's principal thesis. Additionally, given that the case study was presented instrumentally, it remains to be seen how the overall biographical and historical information enables us to comprehend the relationship, if any, that exists among paraphilia, sexual homicide, and serial murder. Thus, testing the explanatory properties of the motivational, trauma control, and integrated paraphilic models and exploring Dahmer's narrative, especially in terms of its capacity to more fully illuminate the linkages among several phenomena pivotal to an improved understanding of lust murder represent the substance of this chapter.

In order to address these relevant matters, the chapter is divided into four sections. The first three sections possess a somewhat comparable organization: the various components of the respective theoretical frameworks are applied to the case of Jeffrey Dahmer. Each typology contains several elements that are intrinsic to the operation of the other two. Thus, the ability of each model to explain the behavior of Dahmer will appear somewhat similar and a bit redundant. However, as will be evident in the subsequent analysis, each perspective yields important and distinct information not captured in the other two frameworks. These unique findings relate to an understanding of Dahmer's criminality as well as to the link between paraphilia and lust murder. As such, it is best to explore each model separately in the ensuing application work.

Accordingly, the Dahmer case is first examined in terms of the motivational model as developed by Burgess et al. (1986). Next, the Dahmer story is scrutinized based on the trauma control typology as conceived of by Hickey (1997, 2001). Then the case is reviewed following the insights of the integrated paraphilic framework. In each instance, Dahmer's developmental history, personality characteristics, and pre- and post-offense behavior are interpreted through the operating logic of the respective organizing schema.

In the final section of the chapter, targeted attention is directed toward the paraphilic process and its functioning as a motive underscoring erotophonophilia. The paraphilic continuum is a dimension of the integrated typology. Several noteworthy features of the process are explored in relation to the acts of Jeffrey Dahmer. Specifically, these elements include paraphilic stimuli and fantasies, orgasmic conditioning, facilitators, stressors, and the behavioral manifestations stemming from increasingly violent images. Here, too, where useful and appropriate, a recounting of important biographical and historical material associated with Dahmer's case is presented to substantiate the overall analysis.

## THE MOTIVATIONAL MODEL

Figure 6.1 specifies the fit between the Burgess et al. (1986) motivational model and the case of Jeffrey Dahmer. The elements of this five-phase typology were previously delineated in Chapter 3. In brief, these components include the following: ineffective social environment, formative development in childhood and adolescence, patterned responses, actions toward others and self, and feedback filter. Both the dynamic operation of these elements and the particular facets constituting them are delineated within the context of the Dahmer life narrative.

### INEFFECTIVE SOCIAL ENVIRONMENT

Phase one of the motivational model developed by Burgess et al. (1986) refers to the social environment the person inhabits and how various circumstances emanating from it can facilitate or impede his early childhood development. The elements of this phase specifically include essential formative dimensions such as the overall quality of the person's life within the family structure and emo-

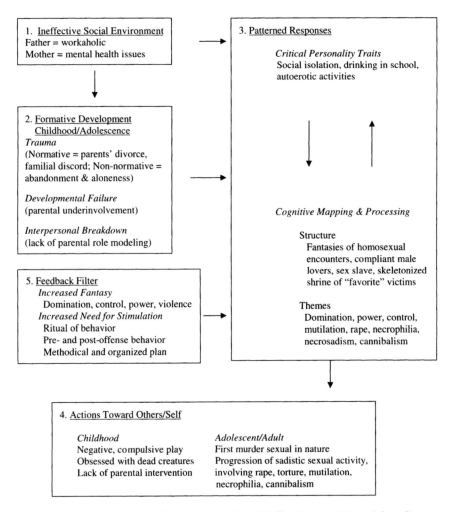

FIGURE 6.1   Motivational Model and the Case of Jeffrey Dahmer (Adapted from Burgess et al., 1986, p. 262; Ressler, Burgess, & Douglas, 1988, p. 70)

tional attachments established, attenuated, or severed between the child and the primary caregiver. An ineffective social environment and a lack of bonding with a parent or parental surrogate can contribute to the child's negative perception of reality, hinder the person's ability to establish prosocial relationships with others, and influence the individual's cognitive thought processes (including distortions) concerning sexuality.

According to the data, both of Dahmer's parents were underinvolved during his childhood and adolescence. Specifically, his mother was hospitalized for psychiatric reasons during his formative years, and his father was often absent because of work-related obligations. Once his brother David was born, Jeffrey had to compete with him for the sparse attention that increasingly (though parsimoniously) was available to his sibling. This information was corroborated by court documents produced during the divorce proceedings involving Dahmer's parents (Schwartz, 1992; Tithecott, 1999). Lionel and Joyce both claimed the other to be cruel and neglectful to Jeffrey and David, further creating a climate of disruption.

Jeffrey Dahmer's lack of emotional bonding with his parents was reflected in his inability to cultivate relationships with others his own age. Feelings of hopelessness, helplessness, isolation, and despair frequently engulfed his thoughts and informed his interactions. During this tumultuous and painful period, he struggled with his sexual orientation. Throughout adolescence, he perceived his homosexual inclination as morally bankrupt and professed shame for his fascination with young men.

## FORMATIVE EVENTS

According to Burgess et al. (1986), three distinctive elements influence a person's formative development. These factors include traumatic events, developmental failure, and interpersonal breakdown. Each of these elements is discussed below in relation to the story of Jeffrey Dahmer.

Following the motivational model, traumatic events are either *normative* or *non-normative* in orientation. Normative events include such things as divorce, illness, death, and, more generally, all factors analogous with typical lifespan development. Non-normative events consist of debilitating events or encounters such as psychological, physical, and sexual abuse. When trauma is experienced during an individual's formative development and is coupled with an ineffective social environment, the child/adolescent matures feeling unprotected and confused.

If the child is unable to constructively work through or otherwise resolve the deep-seated traumatization(s) that occurred, a perception of life's futility and vulnerability is reinforced. The impact of early childhood distress also influences developing thought patterns. Over time, these cognitions can emerge in the form of daydreams and fantasies. Indeed, imaginary constructions of self, others, and situations become an escape from a world in which the child increasingly feels powerless and without control.

In Jeffrey Dahmer's case, no history of physical abuse is substantiated within the available data sources. Moreover, whether or not he experienced sexual molestation remains uncertain; however, he did deny any memory of such conduct (Davis, 1998; Masters, 1993). To be clear, though, as a child he did suffer considerable non-normative emotional trauma. His psychological focus centered on an overwhelming fear of being abandoned and/or left alone (Martens & Palermo, 2005). Additionally, Dahmer experienced normative traumatization stemming from his parents' bitter relationship and eventual divorce. According to some experts, the troubled family environment to which he was consistently subjected significantly (and adversely) impacted his childhood and adolescent development (e.g., Egger, 2002; Hickey, 2001; Palermo, 2004).

Throughout his formative years, Jeffrey was privy to open displays of hostility that Joyce and Lionel Dahmer exhibited toward one another. These public demonstrations of marital discord consisted of incessant arguments and ongoing conflicts in which both participants were absorbed in their own needs rather than those of their children (Flaherty, 1993; Masters, 1993). A specific instance involved the manner in which the physical residence in which they lived was divided. Lionel and Joyce occupied separate areas in the home, and neither was permitted access to the other's living space without prior authorization.

Both the normative (i.e., parent's divorce) and the non-normative (e.g., psychological abandonment; feelings of isolation, helplessness, and despair) traumatizations sustained by Dahmer can be construed as developmental failures. In this context, these formative deficiencies contributed to his subsequent interpersonal breakdowns. According to Burgess et al. (1986), developmental failure occurs when there is a collapse within the relationship between the child and the primary care provider. Interpersonal breakdown takes place when the parent figure is unable or is ill-equipped to serve as an appropriate role model. A routine manifestation of interpersonal breakdown takes place when the parent exhibits a lack of sustained and meaningful participation in the child's evolving life. Both developmental failure and interpersonal breakdown are prominently featured in the case of Jeffrey Dahmer.

As previously specified, both of Dahmer's parents were so preoccupied with their own needs that they either displayed limited interest in or possessed insufficient psychological resources to care about the welfare of their children. Jeffrey's father often worked extended hours (particularly while he pursued his doctoral degree), and Jeffrey's mother struggled with depression, suicidal ideation, ongoing medication, and periodical psychiatric hospitalization (Egger, 2002; Masters, 1993).

Given these circumstances, Jeffrey's relationship with his parents was strained and most likely had deteriorated into a series of perfunctory interactions. This developmental failure significantly impeded his prospects for forming healthy attachments. When coupled with the marital conflict that pervaded the Dahmer residence, an absence of appropriate parental role modeling was evident. The interpersonal breakdown that Jeffrey Dahmer consequently experienced contributed to his social isolation and fueled his fantasy system.

## PATTERNED RESPONSES TO FORMATIVE DEVELOPMENT

According to Burgess et al.'s (1986) motivation model, two distinct elements characterize the patterned response phase: critical personality traits and cognitive mapping. The emergence of fantasies is a direct result of these interacting factors. Both elements specify how a person responds to or copes with early childhood formative events. This adaptation strategy further contributes to and influences the youth's ongoing psychological maturation.

An individual can possess either positive or negative personality traits. Positive traits stem from a developmental process in which the child develops feelings of trust and security in others, as well as a sense of individuation. Moreover, as Burgess et al. (1986) observed, when this healthy maturation process functions in concert with an effective social environment, the child develops both "competency and autonomy" (p. 264). As such, the presence of positive personality traits enables the youth to establish prosocial and meaningful relationships with others.

Conversely, when negative personality traits are formed through the course of the formative developmental process, problems occur. The child is unable to establish healthy attachments or foster emotional connections with others. A lack of self-esteem surrounding these deficiencies and a sense of interpersonal failure associated with the absence of constructive relationships are observed. The presence of both conditions increases the child's likelihood of social isolation. Social isolation facilitates reliance on fantasy and daydreaming. Imaginary configurations of self, others, and situations become a substitute for the human encounters the individual cannot forge.

Moreover, if his patterned responses are based on negative personality traits, the individual likely harbors a cynical view toward others and the culture or community from which the person feels profoundly rejected. What emerges is a genuine lack of regard for persons, places and institutions, vividly depicted in the severe criminality (i.e., violence) this profoundly detached person commits. When social isolation is coupled with deep-seated anger and hostility toward others and/or society, the interaction fosters aggressive fantasies. In the extreme, the individual relates only to others through the operation of this elaborate, sexually violent, image-based structure.

The development of fantasy and daydreaming is a patterned response or cognitive filtering system. The individual interprets new information and gives meaning to past events, but through the identified sorting process. When negative personality traits underscore the patterned response, certain destructive themes materialize. Examples of frequently featured themes linked to these imaginary constructions include power, control, domination, revenge, mutilation, rape, torture, and death.

Generally speaking, Jeffrey Dahmer's early personality development, behavioral characteristics, fantasy structure, and subsequent criminal history are all indicative of the negative personality trait component of the sexual homicide model. According to most investigators, Dahmer lacked friendships while growing up, failed to benefit from healthy relationships, drank alcohol heavily, and smoked marijuana frequently. Based on his own admission, Jeffrey experienced deep-seated feelings of frustration and emptiness that overwhelmed him and fueled his actions, especially given his fear of loneliness and abandonment (see Golman, 1991).

Dahmer's father indicated that his son kept mostly to himself as a child (Dahmer, 1994; Hickey, 1997). Consequently, it is reasonable to assume that this perceived interpersonal failure contributed significantly to Dahmer's social isolation. This retreat into a fantasy world, sustained by autoerotic activities, likely provided him with a sense of comfort and relief from the harsh realities of everyday life.

Mapping and processing patterned responses consists of both a cognitive structure and identifiable themes. The content of those themes representing Dahmer's fantasy system supports the presence of patterned responses based on negative personality traits. Similarly, the nature of his criminal behavior is consistent with this phase of the motivational model.

To illustrate, the composition of Dahmer's early imaginary constructions consisted of having sexual intercourse with other men. However, as his cynicism toward others grew, so, too, did the substance of his fantasies. As he continued to struggle with his sexual identity, his visions were focused on possessing an unconscious, totally compliant male lover who would never leave his side. Dahmer desired to control and dominate others. This desire for power was actualized through his serial murders.

Consistent with the Burgess et al. (1986) typology, there was a definite succession of violent eroticism within the composition of Dahmer's internal cognitions. Indeed, his fantasies escalated in intensity and consisted of such behaviors as necrosadism, necrophilia, sexual mutilation, and cannibalism. Moreover, his cognitions evolved from possessing a totally compliant, unconscious lover to controlling a lobotomized sex slave to erecting a skeletonized shrine of his "favorite" victims, who would forever be a part of his life. Here, too, the thematic presence of domination and power underscored the cognitive mapping dimensions of Dahmer's patterned responses.

## ACTIONS TOWARD OTHERS

This component of the motivational model specifically addresses the progression in fantasy from childhood to adolescence to adulthood, as well as the assorted behavioral manifestations of internal thought processes throughout this period. Burgess et al. (1986) intended this component to illustrate how the behavioral patterns of children, adolescents, and adults can be reflected in their cognitions. In the research informing the development of the motivational model, the subjects reported that the nature of their inner cognitions led them to be "preoccupied by troublesome, joyless thoughts of dominance over others" (Burgess et al., 1986, p. 266). Moreover, as the investigators noted, these thoughts materialized at various stages in the developmental process.

In childhood, these cognitions are often expressed through negative play with peers, cruelty toward animals, fire setting, property destruction, and a genuine lack of regard for others. In Jeffrey Dahmer's case, he spent his childhood compulsively fascinated by dead insects, animals, and other organisms. He collected, closely examined, and dissected their remains through various chemical experiments.

Burgess et al. (1986) noted that failure to intervene and eradicate early childhood expressions of violence serves as a catalyst for future abusive behavior. Additionally, they observed that children engaged in negative behaviors had a more difficult time establishing friendships than their nondestructive counterparts. Dahmer's parents were aware of the troubling ways in which their son amused himself. However, according to biographical accounts, no interventions were made to discourage him from collecting and dissecting the entrails of dead animals he found in the woods behind his home or on the side of the road. No efforts were made to deal with the souvenir collection of decaying animals and insects he stored in jars in the shed behind their home. Finally, no attempts were undertaken to address the animal cemetery he erected in their back yard.

As Jeffrey Dahmer matured into adolescence and adulthood, his behavioral patterns consisted of progressively more violent and repetitive impulses and actions. This trajectory in conduct is consistent with the rationale of the motivational model. Initially, these aggressive behaviors can include such things as burglary, arson, rape, and nonsexual murder. For the sexual homicide offender, they can evolve into rape, torture, mutilation, and necrophilia (Burgess et al., 1986, p. 266).

When Dahmer was 18, he committed his first murder, which was sexual in nature. However, the subsequent homicides he committed progressed in frequency and severity, and assumed a character consistent with that of the lust killer, featuring torture, mutilation, necrophilia, anthropophagy, and souvenir fetishism.

## FEEDBACK FILTER

The term *feedback filter* refers to the way in which an individual reacts to and evaluates his actions toward himself and others. Future behavior is contingent upon the way in which he responds to and assesses his surroundings. The individual justifies his actions, analyzes behavioral errors, "and makes mental corrections in order to preserve and protect the internal fantasy world, as well as to avoid restriction from the external environment" (Burgess et al., 1986, p. 267). Additionally, this component of the motivational model examines how the offender experiences an increased desire for stimulation, as well as an enhanced need for domination and control.

Dahmer's crimes were well organized and well rehearsed. His actions consisted of ritualized pre- and post-offense behavior. Initially, he would search for consenting partners. Next, he would invite a companion back to his home for drinks and conversation. Typically, the drink he gave his guest was laced with Halcion, a sleeping pill, which rendered his victim unconscious. Dahmer would then act out his fantasies by raping his comatose companion. His need for sexual arousal and stimulation would increase. Picquerism (sexual mutilation) and anthropophagy (cannibalism) fueled Dahmer's desires. Indeed, once apprehended, he reported to a treating psychiatrist that after his second murder he "became aroused when he slit open the abdomen of his victim, and examined the colors and textures of the entrails" (Flaherty, 1993, p. 19). Dahmer's subsequent murders were indicative of this increased arousal state, as seen from the sex acts he performed on his unconscious and/or lifeless victims.

With each new murder, Dahmer escaped suspicion, detection, and apprehension from authorities. As a result, the routine he constructed to satisfy his fantasies became more methodical and planned. To illustrate, he masqueraded as a photographer in search of male models who would pose nude for money (Hickey, 2001). He targeted young men, propositioned them, and brought them back to his apartment, where he gave them his special cocktail of tranquilizers and liquor. Once they were rendered unconscious, he raped them. This routine eventually included taking his victim's lives. Postmortem sexual experimentation, mutilation of the genitalia, cannibalism, and souvenir fetishisms were all part of Dahmer's lust murders. With each new homicidal act, Dahmer's fantasy system escalated in terms of arousal state, as well as his feelings of power, dominance, and control.

In Burgess et al.'s (1986) research sample, the sexual offenders were motivated to kill primarily by their way of thinking. The authors' findings also suggested that their subjects possessed an actively aggressive fantasy system developed during their formative years. This system was subsequently reinforced through increasingly violent thoughts, images, and impulses. The subjects of the study had become profoundly detached from the social rules, mores, and conventions of society, as exhibited by their cognitive mapping processes and their ongoing criminal conduct.

The comprehensive nature of the motivational model provides specific and dynamic information regarding the onset and progression of Jeffrey Dahmer's acts. Consistent with the Burgess et al. (1986) typology, Dahmer was a social introvert. He relied heavily on his fantasy system as an escape from the reality (i.e., feelings of abandonment, aloneness) he otherwise confronted. He also depended on his imaginary constructions of self, others, and situations for sexual reinforcement and excitement. As such, the motivational model represents a useful framework that explains how early environmental and developmental struggles, personality characteristics, and patterned responses interact to establish an offender responsible for murdering and mutilating 17 victims.

## THE TRAUMA CONTROL MODEL

Figure 6.2 delineates the relationship between the Hickey (1997, 2001) trauma control typology and the case of Jeffrey Dahmer. The components of this explanatory framework were described in Chapter 3. Overall, these components or elements consist of the following: predispositional factors, traumatic events and low self-esteem/fantasies, dissociation, trauma reinforcement, facilitators,

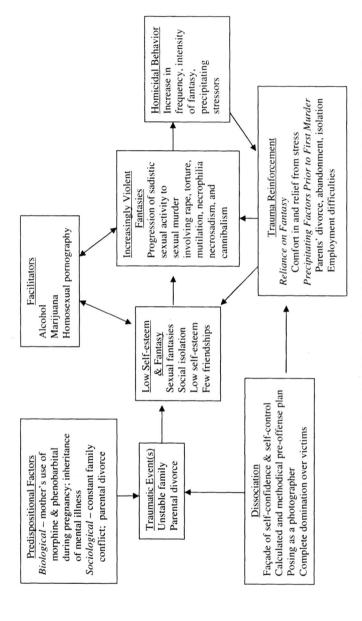

FIGURE 6.2   Trauma Control Model and the Case of Jeffrey Dahmer (Adapted from Hickey, 1997, p. 87)

increasingly violent fantasies, and homicidal behavior. The function of these discrete elements and their overall synergistic operation is specified within the context of the Dahmer life narrative.

## PREDISPOSITIONAL FACTORS

Hickey (1997) asserted that serial murderers possess certain predispositional factors that shape or otherwise impact their behavior. These factors or traits are biological, sociological, and psychological. They can function independent of or in conjunction with one another. An example of a biological factor is the extra Y chromosome syndrome exclusive to males, which can contribute in some circumstances to violent behavior. An illustration of a sociological factor is a dysfunctional home environment, which can influence some adolescents to engage in antisocial conduct during the formative years of their lives. An instance of a psychological factor is the presence of mental illness or certain personality disorders that can escalate and lead to aggressiveness and dangerousness.

Hickey (1997) examined several causal agents that might have influenced and contributed to Dahmer's homicidal actions. His efforts along these lines were corroborated by Jeffrey's father, Lionel. Together, they outlined a number of possible factors that, in combination, might have triggered Dahmer's urge to kill.

In his book, *A Father's Story* (1994), Lionel Dahmer postulated that Jeffrey's fetal and prenatal development might have been adversely affected. Specifically, his mother's use of phenobarbital and morphine during her pregnancy were noted. In addition to this biological account, another theory was linked to her psychiatric condition, that Jeffrey might have inherited some form of mental illness from his mother as well as some antisocial tendencies from his father.

Consistent with Hickey's (1997, 2001) thesis, additional predispositional factors could also account for the criminal behavior of Jeffrey Dahmer. An environmental and sociological explanation for his repeated displays of sexual violence could be traceable to the dysfunctional home life to which he was subjected throughout his formative years. Given that Lionel and Joyce were thoroughly unable to relate to one another, they divided up the house so that each of them could occupy their own private space. Moreover, there was continual marital discord between Dahmer's parents, and they eventually divorced during Jeffrey's senior year in high school. Information produced from court documents during the divorce proceedings further supported the presence of a destructive and unhealthy family environment. Specifically, the reports indicated that both Joyce and Lionel alleged that the other parent was extremely cruel and neglectful to both Dahmer and his younger brother, David (Schwartz, 1992).

Psychological documents corroborated emotional neglect and deprivation in Dahmer's childhood history (Egger, 2002; Hickey, 2001; Tithecott, 1999). Generally speaking, these reports indicated that Dahmer's parents assumed a peripheral role in his life. For example, during Jeffrey's formative development his mother was hospitalized for psychiatric reasons. His father was often absent from the home for long periods of time, attending to work-related responsibilities.

## TRAUMATIC EVENTS AND LOW
## SELF-ESTEEM/FANTASIES

These two components of the trauma control model address the negative effects of early traumatization on the developing child and adolescent, as well as the subsequent emergence of fantasy-based constructions of self, others, and situations. Low self-esteem, individual failure, and personal doubt are the direct results of these early debilitating experiences. Hickey's (1997) typology also stipulates that such traumas, especially when encountered during the formative years, are more likely to be exacerbated by social and environmental factors. In other words, trauma coupled with dysfunctional familial conditions compound the adverse effects and cripple the maturing individual's already diminished ego resources. Ongoing rejections from a parent or caregiver, as well as a frequently unstable and abusive home life, are the most common manifestations of these conditions.

After Dahmer's final arrest, he was subjected to a battery of psychological interviews and tests (e.g., Davis, 1998; Palermo, 2004). Based on the findings, there was no history of physical abuse and no evidence of sexual assault. However, as previously intimated in Chapter 5, these documents provided relevant information regarding Dahmer's troubled relationship with his parents. Specifically, they indicated that neither Lionel nor Joyce was involved in or engaged with their son's personal affairs.

While the available data are limited, they do not exclude emotional trauma. Indeed, lack of healthy and appropriate parental involvement is characteristic of psychological disturbance. Consistent with the trauma control model, this emotional suffering, coupled with the environmental stress of sustained family turmoil and parental neglect, help account for Jeffrey Dahmer's tendencies toward social isolation and fantasy development.

Hickey (1997) observed that when traumatic events are exacerbated by social and environmental factors, the child's and adolescent's developing experience of identity is adversely impacted. The degree, type, frequency, and duration of these traumatizations, as well as environmental conditions, can profoundly influence the individual's psycho-social maturation. Manifestations of these negative effects include a sense of personal failure, hopelessness, and helplessness. In the case of Jeffrey Dahmer, his emotional focus in life centered on a fear of being left alone or otherwise abandoned.

Biographical and historical accounts exploring Dahmer's early childhood and adolescent years demonstrate that he was socially isolated, suffered from low self-esteem, and relied heavily on fantasies and daydreams to compensate. He had few friends, no healthy sexual relationships, and mostly kept to himself. His fantasies became increasingly sexualized and violent. He later reported that it was at the time of his parents' divorce—admittedly an extremely tumultuous period in his life—that he harbored darker thoughts and more aggressive impulses. As he explained, "it was at this time when I began having fantasies of killing people; these fantasies overcame my feelings of frustration and emptiness" (Golman, 1991, p. A8).

## DISSOCIATION

When a child experiences a traumatic event and finds that he is unable to effectively work through the disturbance, he can eventually come to perceive his surroundings in a distorted way. Through the course of adolescent development, this imprecise and confused view of reality produces dissociative states of consciousness. As Hickey (1997, p. 88) noted, dissociation is an "effort to regain the psychological equilibrium taken from a person by people in authority, where the offender appears to construct masks, facades, or a veneer of self-confidence and self-control." Serial murderers yearn for others to believe that they are in control when, in fact, they are socially limited and morally inept. The illusory world that they create and inhabit becomes the only reality that sustains them.

Dahmer constructed a facade of self-assurance and self-discipline, and it functioned as a part of his pre-offense conduct. The persona he embodied reflected his ultimate need to control others by way of deceit and manipulation. Dahmer's pre-criminal behavior was routinized, calculated, and methodical. He approached potential victims while pretending to be a photographer, inviting them to pose nude for money. When he returned to his apartment with a guest, he would drug his companion, rendering the person unconscious, and would then rape his victim. He repeated this organized plan many times over. The severity of his acts progressed; eventually, he would assail his victims, conduct postmortem sexual experimentations with them, and mutilate their corpses.

Dahmer's capacity for murder was enhanced by his increasingly violent sexual fantasies, including the urge to control, harm, and dominate other people. This enabled him to gain some semblance of order over his own tormented and troubled life (Egger, 2002; Hickey, 1997; Palermo, 2004). Dahmer feared the thought of his victims leaving him, so he killed them by strangulation. This action further amplifies the chaos and turbulence that significantly pervaded Dahmer's life, along with an absence of equilibrium that he longed to experience.

## TRAUMA REINFORCERS

According to the trauma control typology, the psychological, physical, and/or sexual event encountered during the formative years of development has the potential to serve as a triggering mechanism. When this occurs, the individual lacks the capacity to cope with the stress that follows. Serial murderers possess an increased likelihood of internalizing a stressor, such as rejection from a significant other or a criticism from a work supervisor, because they do not have the requisite skills to constructively overcome the situation. The individual retreats into his psychological fantasy world, often embracing cynical and negative sentiments, until he finds comfort and relief in the images he fashions. Typically, these fantasies are of a sadistic and sexual nature.

Based on the historical and biographical data surrounding Dahmer's life, it is difficult to ascertain the precise situations in which he found himself confronted with and vulnerable to past traumatizations. Moreover, it is not clear what Dahmer may have regarded as a triggering mechanism. However, psychological reports as well as court documents produced from his parents' divorce indicate that Jeffrey suffered emotionally and psychologically both as a child and as an adolescent. Dahmer corroborated these accounts in his own remarks, describing deep-seated feelings of frustration, emptiness, and abandonment that were quelled only by thoughts of assailing other people. His desire to kill coincided with his mother and father's divorce. He murdered his first victim after high school graduation, which occurred around the same time.

Based on Hickey's (1997) analysis, there were various precipitating factors prior to Dahmer's initial slaying that, collectively, could be construed as a trauma reinforcer. Specifically, Jeffrey was abandoned by members of his family: his father resided at a nearby motel; his mother and brother moved out of the state (see Davis, 1998). Dahmer was completely alone and socially isolated during this period, especially given his employment difficulties. According to several investigators, the aloneness is precisely what he feared the most (e.g., Egger, 2002; Martens & Palermo, 2005; Masters, 1993). Thus, it follows that the events surrounding his abandonment likely triggered past feelings of unresolved trauma that, when relived, influenced his homicidal behavior.

## FACILITATORS

Following Hickey's (1997, 2001) trauma control model, it is common for serial murderers to immerse themselves in facilitating behaviors. Standard examples include alcohol, drugs, and pornography. When the offender relies on these facilitators, he experiences a state of dependency comparable to an addiction. In the case of pornography, the prolonged use of such material desensitizes the user. This practice further propels the individual into a state of escalation where the need for more deviant sexual imagery becomes increasingly evident. Alcohol and drugs decrease inhibitions; pornographic material fuels growing fantasies of violence, often resulting in the urge to behave deviously and/or criminally.

This component of the trauma control model is perhaps one of the most distinctive elements characterizing Dahmer's early behavioral problems. Based on the available biographical and historical data, there is a clear pattern of alcohol, drug, and pornography use throughout Dahmer's adolescence and adulthood. Classmates and teachers, aware that he attended class under the influence of liquor and marijuana, documented his substance abuse as early as high school

(Davis, 1998; Flaherty, 1993). Not surprisingly, this behavior impeded his ability to succeed in college and the Army. Dahmer's criminal record also reflects several alcohol-related offenses.

According to Hickey (1997, 2001), Dahmer turned to alcohol to relieve the pain of abandonment, feelings of low self-esteem, and his perceived sense of profound personal failure. He sought comfort in his imagined world, sustained by his steadfast reliance on homosexual pornography and the use of marijuana and liquor. Dependence on his fantasies and his facilitators became a habitual pattern of behavior for Dahmer (Egger, 2002; Palermo & Farkas, 2001).

## INCREASINGLY VIOLENT FANTASIES

The various components depicted within the trauma control model interact with one another and materialize into increasingly violent fantasies. Traumatic events occurring in the formative years of life can adversely impact the way in which the child perceives the world around him, as well as his evolving sense of self-worth. Living in a culture or community fraught with perceived social isolation and personal rejection catapults the child into a fantasy realm, an illusory haven, in which refuge is sought from the harsh realities of the external environment. When coupled with dissociation resulting from early trauma, as well as facilitating behaviors used to sustain his imaginary construction of self, others, and situations, the synergistic end result is an increase in violent fantasies that can grow in duration, frequency, and intensity.

Jeffrey Dahmer's life was indicative of the trauma control process as proposed by Hickey (1997). Family conflict and parental neglect left Dahmer feeling abandoned, rejected, and socially unskilled. He relied routinely and heavily on fantasy and daydreams to address his depleted self-esteem. The content of his early imaginary constructions focused on sexual intercourse with other men; over time, these fantasies progressed and included more aggressive and sadistic themes.

One of Dahmer's first elaborate and contrived fantasies consisting of homosexual and violent underpinnings was an attempt to fraternize with an attractive young jogger who frequently ran past his family's home. After contemplating the possibility of rejection, Dahmer's plan changed. His desire for this imagined runner became more violently sexual. He decided he would leap out from his hiding spot after the jogger passed, knock the runner on the head with a baseball bat, and drag his body into the woods, where he would have sexual intercourse with his unconscious victim.

During Dahmer's adolescent psychosocial development, he continually struggled with his sexual identity and obsessed over possessing a totally compliant male lover who would never leave his side. Dahmer's fantasies were fused with increasing eroticism and aggression, including deep-seated thoughts of violent intercourse, as well as the subsequent dismemberment and evisceration of his lover. Ultimately, Jeffrey Dahmer imagined that he would possess a sex slave that would never reject or abandon him. Necrosadistic and cannibalistic thoughts and impulses gradually became a part of his elaborate fantasy system.

## HOMICIDAL BEHAVIOR

According to the trauma control framework, each expression of murder generates new cognitions of injurious behavior. Moreover, each subsequent act of homicide is an attempt to fully satisfy and complete the perpetrator's sophisticated image-based constructions. Multiple murderers experience a sense of control over their own lives after taking the life of another (e.g., Holmes & Holmes, 2002a). Hickey (2001) noted the devastating effect of perceived personal failure or rejection from others and how these experiences function as catalysts (i.e., precipitating stressors) for future acts of violence and/or criminality.

When considering the events surrounding Dahmer's first murder, several factors could have operated as catalysts for his homicidal conduct. Certainly, his parents' divorce had an adverse and debilitating effect on him. Moreover, adjusting to his recent high school graduation, which followed on the heels of his parents' divorce, was both difficult and painful. Exacerbating this experience was his abandonment by family members; Dahmer was left all alone in the family home when he committed his first murder.

There is ample documentation that Dahmer had a paraphilic sexual encounter with his first victim postmortem. Moreover, this initial encounter proved to be very pleasurable for him—his most exhilarating fantasy to date had come true, and an attractive, helpless young man was completely available to him.

Dahmer's first murder enhanced his fantasy system and increased his need for more stimulation. His need for male companionship steadily progressed into a ravenous desire to experiment sexually with each new victim postmortem. In this way, Dahmer was able to have unfettered control over his own imagined sexual scenarios and to act on them without restraint.

Necrosadism and necrophilia became part of his homicidal ritual and, as his appetite for more bizarre and violent stimuli increased, so, too, did his behavior. Dahmer incorporated cannibalism and souvenir fetishism into his routine. He engaged in the latter by saving the remains of his victim's body parts so that he could masturbate and relive the experience within his imaginary construction. The goal of Dahmer's anthropophagy was fantasy based: By consuming his victims, they became part of him and made him more potent. His acts of cannibalism also enabled him to experience sustained arousal and, ultimately, orgasm.

Consequently, following the homicidal behavior component of the trauma control model, each subsequent act of murder committed by Dahmer was undertaken in an attempt to fully satisfy and complete his fantasy (Hickey, 1997). Each new paraphilic act (i.e., necrophilia, necrosadism, anthropophagy, and souvenir fetishism), as incorporated into Dahmer's conduct, was a vehicle to reify and complete his illusory system. Indeed, each murder resulted in an increased desire on Jeffrey Dahmer's part to actualize his fantasy.

## THE INTEGRATED PARAPHILIC MODEL

Figure 6.3 visually depicts the linkages between the integrated paraphilic model and the case of Jeffrey Dahmer. The elements of this explanatory framework were previously delineated in Chapter 4 and include the following: formative development (consisting of predispositional factors and traumatic events), low self-esteem, early fantasy and paraphilic development, the paraphilic process (including stimuli and fantasy as well as the orgasmic conditioning process and

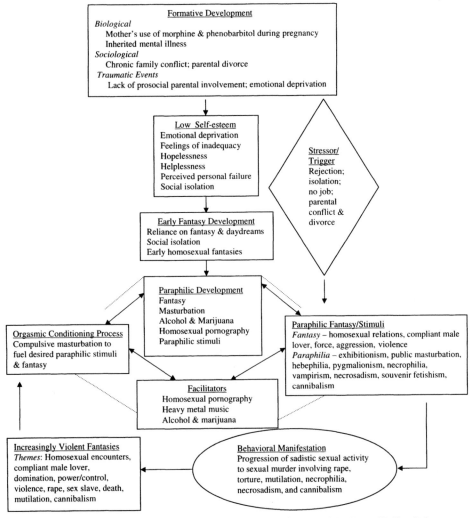

**FIGURE 6.3** Integrated Model On Paraphilia and Lust Murder and the Case of Jeffrey Dahmer. ◄——►, Paraphilic Process; ·········, Internal/External Stimulus Effect; ◄——, Feedback Loop (Reinforcer). (Adapted from Arrigo & Purcell, 2001, p. 20)

facilitators), stressors, behavioral manifestations, and increasingly violent fantasies. The operation of these elements and their specific components are described in this section, mindful of the Dahmer life narrative. Throughout the analysis, commentary on where and how this typology accounts for lust murder is provided. Although the paraphilic process is referenced here, the details of its function are more systematically reviewed in the final section of the chapter. The aim of the chapter's final section is to account for the crimes of lust murder as committed by Jeffrey Dahmer.

## FORMATIVE DEVELOPMENT

This dimension of the model functions as the foundation upon which the onset of paraphilic behaviors can be identified. In this instance, formative development specifically refers to childhood and early adolescent experiences. Consistent with the explanations provided by Burgess et al. (1986) and Hickey (1997, 2001), formative development significantly impacts the manner in which an individual appropriately and successfully encounters psychosocial adjustment throughout the lifecourse. There are two interdependent concepts that are essential features of the paraphiliac's maturation: predispositional factors and traumatic events.

### Predispositional Factors

As previously specified, sociological, biological, and psychological factors can function independently or jointly, especially as they influence the offender's behavior. However, regardless of the element constituting the person's formative development, the effect on the individual's maturation invariably is adverse, impeding prospects for future growth and prosocial conduct. A review of Dahmer's life consists of several likely debilitating factors.

Specifically, Jeffrey Dahmer experienced an interpersonal breakdown within his familial environment, which constituted a sociological predisposition as well as a developmental failure. Several accounts of Dahmer's childhood and adolescent maturation indicate that both parents were emotionally neglectful of and psychologically aloof toward him. The psychiatric condition of Joyce Dahmer and the workaholic tendencies of Lionel Dahmer, as delineated in various medical records and court documents, substantiate this position. In addition, their tumultuous marriage and bitter divorce represented key life events that, according to Dahmer's own account, profoundly and adversely affected him.

Moreover, several observations by Lionel Dahmer support the theory that a biological predisposition may have inclined his son to engage in repetitive acts of homicide. The alleged use of phenobarbitol and morphine during Joyce's pregnancy may have negatively affected Jeffrey's prenatal development. Additionally, a potential genetic predisposition toward aggression and violence is noted, given Joyce's persistent mental illness as well as Lionel's acute antisocial tendencies.

Theoretically, the presence of certain biological factors can influence the likelihood that antisocial conduct and criminal behavior will make themselves manifest (e.g., Giannengelo, 1996). Mindful of the integrated typology, certain biological factors can affect paraphilic activity, including the emergence of sexual sadism. The insights of Money (1990), Kafka (2003), Mednick, Moffitt, and Stack (1987), Moffitt, Lynam, and Silva (1994), and Raine (1993) in varying contexts confirm this position on the relationship between neuropsychology and violence.

Admittedly, it is difficult if not impossible to ascertain whether Dahmer had a biological predisposition toward paraphilic behavior. Interestingly, Joyce Dahmer unsuccessfully attempted to have her son's brain donated to science (Hickey, 2001). What remains unknown is whether certain pathways to Dahmer's limbic system were pathologically activated, simultaneously sending him messages to prey upon others and to do so in a sexually aggressive manner. This is how the paraphilia of sexual sadism operates in the mind of the offender (e.g., Bader, 2003; Canter & Wentinck, 2004; Canter et al., 2004; Money, 1990). The integrated model draws attention to these biological (as well as psychological and sociological) explanations.

**Traumatic Events**

Predisposing factors, such as the ones discussed above, coupled with traumatic events sustained in the formative years can devastate and impede an individual's future development. An inability to constructively confront and work through the debilitating event will likely overwhelm him, fostering profound feelings of self-doubt, despondency, and vulnerability. Ultimately, given their intensity, frequency, and duration, these sentiments can hinder the positive maturation of ego identity.

Research on lust murderers indicates that the formative years of psychological adjustment "are crucial to the personality structure and development of these offenders" (Hazelwood & Douglas, 1980, p. 21; see also Hickey, 2005). It is unusual for the lust murderer to come from a nurturing family environment free from abuse, alcoholism, drugs, or other factors that could cause considerable pain and suffering during childhood and adolescence (Money & Werlas, 1982; Simon, 1996). This critical formative period represents the phase during which positive bonds of attachment are established and nurtured or, conversely, strained and, in some cases, severed (e.g., Shipley & Arrigo, 2004).

There is little dispute that Jeffrey Dahmer was a lust murderer (Egger, 2002; Hickey, 2001). However, given the integrated paraphilic model, the question is: What was the nature of the emotional trauma he sustained during his formative development? Based on the available data, it appears that the lack of healthy parental involvement in his life, as well as the debilitating effects stemming from their marital discord and eventual divorce were catalytic traumatizations. Psychological documents, court reports, and other biographical information support the contention that Dahmer experienced emotional distress during this critical maturation phase.

As noted in both the trauma control typology and the motivational model, Lionel and Joyce Dahmer were peripheral figures in their son's life. Joyce's persistent and debilitating psychiatric condition and Lionel's frequent absenteeism and general aloofness indicate detached parenting styles. Complicating this pattern of neglect was the presence of Jeffrey's sibling, David. The infrequent and sparse parental nurturing that was available in the Dahmer household was increasingly extended to the younger son. There is clear and ample evidence suggesting that both parents were aware of Jeffrey's idiosyncratic and bizarre activities as a child (e.g., obsession with dissecting animals and insects; pet cemetery in the back yard); however, neither parent did anything to address these behaviors. Moreover, Jeffrey's father reported being unaware of his son's alcohol use during adolescence and his internal struggle regarding sexual orientation.

## LOW SELF-ESTEEM

The presence of traumatic events during the formative years of life does not guarantee emotional withdrawal and social isolation. Effectively resolving them creates a solid basis by which the maturing child cultivates a positive self-image and learns prosocial behavior. However, the dysfunctional social and psychological background of the paraphiliac mitigates this possibility (Abel et al., 1988; Douglas et al., 1995; Holmes, 1991; Holmes & Holmes, 2002a). Both the motivational model and the trauma control typology acknowledge the adverse consequences of traumatizations sustained during formative development. If these debilitating circumstances remain unresolved or otherwise go unaddressed, the emotional by-products that follow can be crippling. Devastating feelings of inadequacy, personal failure, and low self-esteem materialize.

Jeffrey Dahmer was unable to appropriately resolve and successfully confront his developmentally formative traumatizations. His inability to reconcile himself to these environmental setbacks and psychological disappointments fueled his growing emotional deprivation, adversely affecting his already fragile self-esteem. He became engulfed in feelings of frustration, aloneness, abandonment, and despondency. Consequently, he was ill-equipped to cultivate friendships and increasingly became socially isolative. In order to escape the immense pain stemming from these frightening feelings of rejection and helplessness, he cultivated an elaborate fantasy system.

## EARLY FANTASY AND PARAPHILIC DEVELOPMENT

A unique feature of the integrated framework is the conceptualization of a cyclical paraphilic process. Specifically, in this typology, several factors occur simultaneously, producing a synergistic effect. Social isolation arises concurrently with the early development of sexualized images, thereby activating or putting into motion the paraphilic system. Over time, this mobilization becomes entirely self-generating. Various fantasy-based constructions, along with compulsive masturbation, assorted facilitators, and paraphilic stimuli (e.g., fetishes, unusual objects, sadistic and erotic rituals), operate to sustain the paraphilic process.

Burgess et al. (1986) identified several personality characteristics within the patterned response component of the motivational model that were indicative of the paraphilic process as summarily described above. Among other things, these characteristics included social isolation, a preference for autoerotic activities, and fetishes. As others have noted, "the internal behaviors most [frequently] reported over the murderer's three developmental periods [include] daydreaming, compulsive masturbation, and isolation" (Ressler, Burgess, & Douglas, 1988, p. 30; see also Hickey, 2005).

Dahmer's early pattern of behavior is illustrative of the paraphilic process. He was socially isolated and relied on fantasy and daydreaming to quell feelings of hopelessness and helplessness. Initially, his imaginary constructions centered on a desire to have sexual intercourse with other men. These fantasies progressed and intensified to eventually include the possession of a totally compliant, unconscious lover, someone who would never leave Dahmer's side. Routine themes encompassing these aggressive cognitions and impulses consisted of death, mutilation, and disembowelment. Sustaining these early fantasies were various facilitators, such as a chronic reliance on alcohol and drugs, as well as a frequent use of homosexual pornographic material.

Several data sources confirm the paraphilic process as underscoring Dahmer's conduct. For example, Army associates recalled that Jeffrey typically would lie on his bunk all weekend while in the military, listening to heavy metal music while he drank liquor continuously until he passed out (Davis, 1998). Additionally, Dahmer reported a pattern of alcohol abuse, homosexual pornography, masturbation, and heavy metal music throughout his late adolescence and early adulthood (Flaherty, 1993, p. 14). Accounts such as these suggest that social isolation, sexually aggressive fantasy, and reliance on pornography, alcohol, and drugs essentially became a self-perpetuating process.

## THE PARAPHILIC CONTINUUM

In this final section of this chapter, the elements that constitute the paraphilic continuum or process are reviewed in relation to the case of Jeffrey Dahmer. These elements include paraphilic stimuli and fantasy, the orgasmic conditioning process, facilitators, stressors, behavioral manifestations, and increasingly violent fantasies. The context in which these facets of the integrated typology further account for erotophonophilia and those persons who would perpetrate such crimes are carefully delineated.

### PARAPHILIC STIMULI AND FANTASY

MacCulloch et al. (1983) examined the sadistic fantasies of several criminal offenders and found that the offenders had experienced significant difficulties in both their social and sexual relationships at a very early age. The Burgess et al.

(1986) motivational model, as well as Hickey's (1997, 2001) trauma control typology, further account for this. In their respective ways, these investigators indicated that a lack of social sexual bonding could produce feelings of inadequacy, driving a person into a world of fantasy and isolation. Over time, the images would become more violent and erotic, and fetishes, rituals, and unusual objects would be subsequently incorporated as stimuli.

The repetitive nature of the image-based construction furnishes a sense of personal power and general relief from the intra-psychic failures the individual painfully experiences. The felt sexual arousal, in conjunction with the sadistic fantasy, serves as reinforcement by means of classical conditioning. The presence of conditioning increases the habituation. The conditioning model proposed by MacCulloch et al. (1983) explained not only the strength and permanence of sadistic fantasies but also their progression from nonsexual to sexual. Given the above observations, the research undertaken by Burgess et al. (1986) and Hickey (1997, 2001) supports the notion that a paraphilic process of behavior underscores the activities of, respectively, the sexual homicide offender and the serial killer. We contend that this classical conditioning framework as a feature of the paraphilic continuum helps account for the behaviors of the lust murderer.

Dahmer was a social outcast known to possess few, if any, friends. He struggled considerably with his own sexual orientation, often feeling that homosexuality was unhealthy, deviant, and immoral. Dahmer's profound interpersonal struggle on this matter left him despondent. Indeed, he even contemplated suicide during that period in which he developed sexually aberrant fantasies (Hickey, 1997; Tithecott, 1999). Dahmer's inability to establish meaningful social and sexual bonds of attachment, coupled with his acute perception of failure, catapulted him into a world of fantasy. His pattern of cognitions and impulses is consistent with this specific element of the paraphilic model.

Moreover, Dahmer had an evolving array of sexually aberrant interests, which served as stimuli and fueled his increasingly violent fantasy system. In his case, several paraphilias were observed, including exhibitionism, public masturbation, hebephilia, pygmalionism, vampirism, necrophilia, necrosadism, anthropophagy, and souvenir fetishisms. Several biographical and historical reports substantiate Dahmer's use of sexually deviant behaviors in the commission of his crimes.

For example, early in his career offending, Jeffrey's target audience usually consisted of prepubescent males (i.e., hebephilia). Around this time, Dahmer also dabbled in exhibitionism; however, as his images amplified, so, too, did the intensity of his behavior. Eventually, his fantasies progressed from homosexual encounters to possessing a totally compliant male lover. In order to actualize this fantasy, Dahmer stole a mannequin from a nearby department store. The dummy satisfied his desires (i.e., pygmalionism). Moreover, during this period in Dahmer's sexual offending history, he wanted to have sex with the corpse of a young accident victim (i.e., necrophilia). Although Dahmer eventually realized the futility of exhuming the cadaver, his impulses on the matter were clear. As paraphilias, both pygmalionism and necrophilia are similar. The individual seeks to engage in these activities because they function as stimuli in which the avoidance of rejection is guaranteed, given the sexual contact with an inanimate object or a corpse (Hickey, 2005). Indeed, the paraphiliac individual assumes complete control and dominion over the situation and the parties involved. In this way, he is able to act out any dimension of his elaborate imaginary constructions.

The increasingly violent and sadistic evolution of Dahmer's paraphilias is also noted. As the themes of his fantasies escalated sadistically, so, too, did the nature and content of his partialisms. This progression is depicted in the repetitive acts of erotophonophilia he committed. Necrophilia, necrosadism, anthropophagy, and various displays of souvenir fetishisms (including vampirism) represented the sundry dimensions of Dahmer's lust murders.

## ORGASMIC CONDITIONING PROCESS

McGuire et al. (1965) recognized the role that masturbation assumed in the onset, formation, and maintenance of sexually deviant behaviors. These researchers proposed a conditioning theory to explain the function of masturbatory conduct among sexual offenders. They suggested that when a fantasy precedes an orgasm, the imaginary construction and stimulation the fantasy provides become a conditioned behavior. More specifically, any deliberate or situational sexual stimulation that regularly precedes an orgasm increasingly becomes erotically exhilarating. Indeed, intentional stimulation (i.e., compulsive masturbation that fuels the sadistic fantasy) prior to ejaculation is the process by which most sexual deviations are acquired (McGuire et al., 1965). Additional investigators, including Burgess et al. (1986), Canter et al. (2004), Giannangelo (1996), and Kafka (2003), similarly report the relevance of masturbation and fantasy in the orgasmic condition process for sexual offenders and its interactive role in sustaining paraphilias.

To illustrate, as previously reported in Chapter 3, Burgess et al. (1986) substantiated the importance of orgasmic conditioning in their assessment of sexual homicide offenders. These researchers found that compulsive masturbation was a significant characteristic in more than 50% of the subjects in their sample. Of these individuals, over 80% admitted to engaging in compulsive masturbation throughout their lives, commencing in childhood and progressing through adulthood. This activity of orgasmic conditioning fueled the subjects' increasingly violent and sexually aberrant behaviors.

The biographical and historical information concerning Dahmer's life narrative does not provide detailed accounts of his autoerotic activities. However, in one of his own remarks surrounding his compulsion to kill, Dahmer intimated that he did masturbate (Flaherty, 1993, p. 14) and, on some occasions, did so publicly (Davis, 1998). Still, there is scant material available on the frequency intensity, duration, and overall fantasy structure involving Dahmer's orgasmic conditioning process. However, noting the increasingly sadistic erotic imagery that he did employ as a basis upon which to act out his thoughts and impulses (having sex with a stranger; having sex with a person he met and then drugged; having sex with an unconscious and thus compliant lover; having sex with a corpse), it is logical to assume that orgasmic conditioning contributed to his paraphilic activities. Moreover, given the progressively violent nature of his sexual crimes (e.g., from exhibitionism to vampirism; from necrophilia to cannibalism), the orgasmic conditioning process is consistent with the conduct undertaken by such a lust murderer (see Hickey, 2005).

## FACILITATORS

The utilization of facilitators, including pornography, alcohol, and drugs, is a specific component of the paraphilic process. Both the trauma control model as well as the motivational typology examine these behaviors and explain how they are indicative of the serial murderer and sexual killer respectively. Additionally, Ressler et al. (1988) found that over half of the sexual homicide offenders within their research sample reported interests in pornography. Additional investigators have similarly identified the significant role that facilitators assume in the commission of serial and sexual murders (e.g., Egger, 2002; Douglas et al., 1995; Holmes & Holmes, 2002a; Palermo & Farkas, 2001; Schlesinger, 2003).

Dahmer had an extensive history of substance abuse as early as high school. His excessive reliance on alcohol interfered with his failed attempt at college and his brief stint in the military. For example, while in the Army, Dahmer observed that "alcohol abuse, homosexual pornography, masturbation, heavy metal music and a busy work schedule kept him out of serious trouble" (Flaherty, 1993, p. 14). Following his discharge from the military, Dahmer's cycle of self-perpetuating facilitative behavior continued. It became a part of (and essential to) sustaining his elaborate criminal acts.

Consistent with Hickey's (1997) analysis of serial killers, facilitators manifest themselves as addictions for the sexual deviant. Indeed, the paraphiliac individual becomes firmly entrenched in a cycle of habituation, experiencing both a dependency on and a craving for more of the stimulus. This activity of turning to facilitators (more intensely and more regularly) to fuel and sustain erotic desires is the process by which ultimate sexual satisfaction is realized for the offender.

Dahmer became dependent on the use of drugs and alcohol, as well as homosexual pornography and masturbation, to charge his paraphilic fantasies. Eventually, however, he became desensitized to their effects. To illustrate, after one of Dahmer's murders, he ate the flesh of his victim, drank heavily, and watched pornographic videos (Flaherty, 1993, p. 28), signifying just how immersed he had become in his cycle of self-perpetuating behavior. This conduct contributed to a pervasive paraphilic process that underscored his crimes of erotophonophilia.

Indeed, the facilitators of sexually explicit homosexual material, and drugs and alcohol were a part of his life dating back at least to adolescence and extending into adulthood (Schwartz, 1992; Hickey, 2005). They helped to activate and nurture his image-based fantasy system involving himself, others, and situations, illusory configurations that he could completely control. Eventually, the facilitators he employed became indispensable components of his elaborate masturbatory fantasies, and led him to kill repeatedly, to dissect his victims' bodies, to drink their blood, and to devour their flesh.

## STRESSORS

The integrative model proposes that when a stressor, either internal or external, occurs, the individual becomes unable to effectively deal with or otherwise resolve the conflict he confronts. Specifically, the stressor results in the person experiencing a momentary loss of control. These disturbing phenomena function as triggering mechanisms. They have the ability to resuscitate repressed negative feelings from the person's past that are linked to unsettled events or troubling concerns that were never addressed.

The triggering events or stressors then cycle back into the paraphilic continuum of behavior by way of a feedback loop. The stressors and what they signify (i.e., unresolved childhood trauma) are sustained by way of masturbation, facilitators, and fantasy. In some cases, the response to the disturbance may take the form of erotic and sadistic behavior. In extreme instances, the reaction to the triggering event can entail erotophonophilia.

According to the Burgess et al. (1986) typology, the manner in which the offender is motivated to respond to debilitating circumstances is largely based on his cognitive perceptions of the situation. These actions are developed as a result of the unresolved traumatic events sustained during the formative years of his life. When precipitating events occur through the course of adolescent development, the individual may experience a triggering mechanism, by which he relives and re-experiences the painful feelings associated with the early trauma (Hickey, 1997). As Hickey (2005) observed, these stressors make it essentially impossible for the traumatized person to deal effectively with routine conflict or strife that materializes later in life.

Dahmer's childhood and adolescent development were riddled with key debilitating events that likely had an adverse affect on him psychologically as well as socially. The lack of meaningful parental involvement and healthy attachments left him feeling isolated, abandoned, and rejected. Joyce and Lionel's failed marriage left him feeling frightened, troubled, and vulnerable. Jeffrey Dahmer's adolescent intra-psychic struggle with his sexual identity left him feeling deviant, immoral, and unworthy. Each of these events significantly impacted his fragile self-esteem (Egger, 2002; Masters, 1993; Tithecott, 1999).

Dahmer became socially isolative and withdrawn, possessing few friends and even more limited ego resources. He had a disastrous spell while enrolled in college, an alcohol-riddled stint while in the military, and several unsuccessful work-related experiences. These events were triggering mechanisms, reminding him (albeit unconsciously) of his unresolved childhood and adolescent traumatizations. When a person is unable to constructively work through stress, the individual seeks solace, relief, and comfort in fantasies or daydreams. Dahmer retreated into his imaginary world to quell the torment that he perceived.

## BEHAVIORAL MANIFESTATIONS AND INCREASINGLY VIOLENT FANTASIES

The feedback loop has the potential to escalate into behavioral manifestations, depending on whether or not the person is compelled to execute his fantasy system. By enacting the paraphilic images and stimuli, the individual attempts to satisfy, complete, and reify his internal illusions. Each time the behavior is inaugurated, the paraphiliac experiences sexual satisfaction, as well as an increased need for more stimulation. The behavior, whether criminal, deviant, or otherwise, acts as a reinforcer and sequences back into the fantasy system.

Both the motivational and trauma control models depict this process. The former focuses on the offender's need to evaluate his actions toward others and the self via a feedback filter (Burgess et al., 1986). The latter specifies how the fantasy life of the individual escalates, generating new images and sustaining existing ones (Hickey, 1997). As the person's fantasies become increasingly more violent, the paraphilic stimulus also progresses in intensity, duration, and frequency. This process can also be understood by utilizing the feedback loop, in which increased stimulation to sustain the allure of the image-based constructions is needed each time the fantasy is enacted.

Dahmer's criminal behavior followed this pattern. Each time he executed his illusion, his fantasies as well as his crimes became more severe in orientation and content. Some of his earliest imaginary configurations consisted of male companionship (whether with a living person or a mannequin) and homosexual curiosity. However, the thematic nature of his fantasies eventually escalated (e.g., possessing a totally compliant male lover; images of death, body mutilation, dismemberment, cannibalism). As Dahmer's violent sexual fantasies progressed, so, too, did the behavior on which he relied to actualize these images.

Dahmer's capacity for murder was enhanced by his increasingly violent sexual fantasies. Admittedly, his first murder in 1978 was sexual in nature; However, it took him until 1987 to kill again. Between these two murders, he was involved in several acts of lewd and lacivious conduct and public drunkeness. Within five years after his second murder in 1987, his killings became sadistically sexual, involving necrophilia, necrosadism, mutilation, cannibalism, and souvenir fetishism. During this time frame, Dahmer's fantasies continued to progress in intensity. Whether possessing a corpse to be used as a sex slave, saving the remains of his victims in order to construct fetishistic shrines, or consuming body parts in order to be a part of his victims and thereby increasing his potency, Dahmer wanted to be connected in some way to those whom he murdered. Feelings of dominance, power, and control, as well as an increased arousal state, fed back into his patterned responses and enhanced the details of his fantasy life.

## SUMMARY AND CONCLUSION

This chapter specifically examined the motivational model for sexual homicide, the trauma control typology for serial murder, and the integrative theoretical framework on paraphilia. In each instance, the central question was how the respective organizing schema accounted for the behavior of Jeffrey Dahmer. Moreover, the application of each model to the Dahmer narrative was intended to demonstrate how the various typologies possessed unique properties, as well as comparable features, that advanced our understanding of erotophonophilia.

Additionally, this chapter explored the paraphilic continuum, arguing that it functioned as an underlying motive in Dahmer's criminal behavior. It is worth noting that the integrative paraphilic process is a direct synthesis of the motivational model on sexual homicide as developed by Burgess et al. (1986) and the trauma control typology on serial homicide as conceived of by Hickey (1997). To help extend and deepen the analysis, the classic work of McGuire and colleagues (1965) as well as the insights of MacCulloch et al. (1983) were utilized. Each of these conceptual frameworks contributed to the integrated paraphilic model and the continuum that this theory argues underscores erotophonophilia.

In the ensuing chapter, a more systematic assessment of the three principal typologies examined in this volume and their respective explanations regarding the Dahmer case are provided. Points of similarity, dissimilarity, and uniqueness must be specified. By addressing these concerns, the extent to which any one of the typologies explains the onset, formation, and maintenance of lust murder is made more explicit. Moreover, by comparing the organizing schemas to one another based on points of convergence, divergence and distinctiveness, it is possible to ascertain which model possesses the most explanatory features. This activity is noteworthy, especially if clinical prediction, prevention, and treatment efforts are to have any reasonable chance of success. Additionally, this undertaking is significant if law enforcement profiling, tracking, and detection initiatives are to result in the apprehension of perpetrators of lust homicide.

# 7

## IN SEARCH OF MEANING:

### ON THEORY CONSTRUCTION AND MODEL BUILDING

### OVERVIEW

The preceding chapter explained how the motivational model on sexual homicide, the trauma control typology on serial murder, and the integrated framework on paraphilia could be usefully applied to the case of Jeffrey Dahmer. At issue in Chapter 6 was the extent to which the organizing schemas accounted for the emergence, progression, and maintenance of lust murder. There are discrete elements in each model that help to provide an in-depth analysis of Dahmer's psychological development, personality structure, and criminal behavior. However, it remains to be seen how the three frameworks compare with one another, especially with respect to erotophonophilia. Of particular interest here is a detailed explanation regarding Dahmer's extensive paraphilic history, sexually sadistic fantasy system, and repetitive acts of lust homicide. This chapter endeavors to address these very important concerns.

Accordingly, points of similarity and dissimilarity across the three typologies are identified and examined, as well as several unique features underpinning each model. In order to accomplish these tasks, the chapter is divided into four substantive sections. First, some general observations on the organizational approach that informs the ensuing comparative analysis are identified. This includes a number of comments that position the investigative undertaking within its appropriate criminological framework, as well as several remarks that explain and justify the proposed overall strategy. Second, areas of convergence across the three theories are explored. These similarities focus on important psychological, sociological, and behavioral themes or factors common to the three typologies. Third, several noteworthy points of divergence are enumerated. These include specific areas in which the models offer distinctive interpretations for shared themes. Third, novel features or unique qualities intrinsic to the motivational, trauma control, and integrative paraphilic frameworks are delineated. Specifying these qualitatively distinct elements is important to this volume's overall thesis on the paraphilic process as a system of behavior that critically underscores the crime of lust murder and those responsible for its serial commission.

## THE COMPARATIVE ANALYSIS: COMMENTS ON THE ORGANIZATIONAL APPROACH

Despite the various differences among and unique qualities within the three principal models of homicide considered throughout this book, they have funda-mental similarities. One area of correspondence is the implicit sociologically informed criminological perspective by which the typologies attempt to explain murder. As a general proposition, this approach to understanding crime and crim-inality examines the way in which various social structures (e.g., the institution of the family) and social processes (e.g., the presence or lack of parental attach-ments) interact to fashion delinquency and crime for individuals or groups (Arrigo, 2006). The associations formed through various relationships (including their frequency, duration, and intensity) are pivotal to explaining the onset and development of criminal behavior (Vold, Bernard, & Snipes, 2002). Given these connections, the social interaction that emerges essentially creates and transmits meaning for that particular individual or collective. Thus, the processes to which a person is (repeatedly) exposed significantly contribute to the type and severity of criminality that manifests itself (Cullen & Agnew, 2002; Lanier & Henry, 2004). This broad criminological perspective represents the organizational approach informing the comparative analysis that is delineated in this chapter. As such, it strategically situates the resulting commentary, especially in terms of pro-viding a systematic framework from which to describe how each theoretical model is similar, dissimilar, and unique.

Within the sub-discipline of criminology exists a vast array of social structure and process theories that could facilitate a more complete understanding of sexual, serial, and/or lust murder. To be sure, as described previously, the three typologies reviewed contain sociological, environmental, biological, and psy-chological variables that provide useful insights into the etiology and nature of homicide. This notwithstanding, a more thorough assessment of these phenom-ena warrants some consideration from within the specialty area of criminology. In part, this is because criminology is a field of academic inquiry that can help draw attention to the manner in which the identified typologies are compatible, divergent, and distinctive. Moreover, in order to more fully comprehend extreme forms of criminal behavior (e.g., erotophonophilia), one must examine delin-quency and crime from within various social and behavioral science perspectives (Arrigo, 2006). With these thoughts in mind, the criminological notions of *con-*

*tainment theory* and *self-concept* are reviewed in the proceeding analysis. As we contend, relying on these constructs provides a sensible consolidation schema from within which to assess the three primary models and their accounts of Jeffrey Dahmer's criminality.

Preliminarily, we note that the notion of containment theory within criminology has been appropriated for examining the causes of criminal behavior among delinquent youths (e.g., Vold, Bernard, & Snipes, 2002). Identified as a type of control theory in which the adolescent experiences a failure to bond (Lanier & Henry, 2004, pp. 183–184), the construct is linked to Bowlby's (1969, 1973) more psychodynamically animated attachment theory. In Bowlby's (1969) formulations, attention is directed to "the deleterious effects that children suffer when temporarily separated from their primary caretakers, typically the mother" (Shipley & Arrigo, 2004, p. 70). Indeed, as Bowlby (1969, xiii) observed, "the child's hunger for his mother's love is as great as his hunger for food [and without it] the child experiences a powerful sense of loss and anger."

Although Bowlby's (1969, 1973) insights initially applied to infants, subsequent formulations have traced the impact of attachment patterns and bonding styles in interpersonal relationships throughout various stages of adolescent and adult development (e.g., Arrigo & Griffin, 2004; Erickson, Sroufe, & Egeland, 1985; Grossman & Grossman, 1991; Levy & Blatt, 1999; Lewis & Feiring, 1991; Sroufe, 1983; Sroufe & Fleeson, 1996). What these and other studies repeatedly demonstrate is that an individual's likelihood for aggression and violence is a product of profound feelings of separation and loss (e.g., Main, 1995). In adulthood, this is particularly problematic, especially if the individual experienced a psychologically or sexually abusive caretaking history, leading to insecure attachments (Arrigo & Shipley, 2004; Cicchetti & Toth, 1995; Goldberg, 1991; Main, Kaplan, & Cassidy, 1985).

As linked to containment theory, the notion of attachment or bonding is significant. What is at issue is an individual's self-concept and sense of social identity. Learning not to commit a crime depends on the person's capacity to control his behavior. The successful acquisition of this ability is a function of a number of influencing factors, including the individual's routine interaction and ongoing communication with significant others. The extent to which these processes are appropriately and constructively in place (especially with parental figures, as well as with peers and other agents of socialization) is the degree to which his healthy development and ongoing maturation is secured. Moreover, these stabilizing features of development critically impact personality, motivation, cognitive schemas, beliefs, perceptions, feelings, attitudes, values, inhibitions, and self-control (Barlow, 1993; Cullen & Agnew, 2002). If prosocial bonds are not in place, the absence of containment and the presence of criminality are increasingly assured.

One of the first theorists interested in the relationship between self-concept and containment theory, specifically applied to criminality, was Walter Reckless ([1950], 1961, 1973; Reckless, Dinitz, & Murray, 1956; Reckless & Dinitz,

1967). Reckless examined the notion of delinquency in the context of a push-and-pull system. Pushes signify the pressures and strains of the environment. Examples include adverse living conditions, poverty, the lack of legitimate opportunities, and family problems. Pulls refer to the inducements and/or demands of peers. Examples consist of breaking the law, harming others, and abusing animals. To stave off delinquency (and crime), Reckless (1961) argued, both internal and external controls had to be in place. External controls are what he identified as instances of outer containment, such as parental involvement and affection, as well as adherence to school discipline and rules. Internal controls are what he termed instances of inner containment and involved healthy ego development, an internalized sense of guilt for wrongdoing, and a positive self-concept. The interaction among these dynamic forces produce varying degrees of conformity and/or delinquency in an individual. To illustrate, a positive self-image and a secure social identity could be amplified by external approval from parental figures, thereby solidifying the individual's bond to conventional or orthodox behavior (Lanier & Henry, 2004). If the individual's self-concept was fragmented or under-developed stemming from unresolved family dysfunction, internal or psychic pushes such as hostility, bio-psychological impairments, impulsivity, and aggressiveness could materialize and manifest themselves externally through acute criminal behavior.

To date, the application of containment theory and its link to the notion of self-concept have not been systematically examined in relation to sexual homicide, serial murder, and/or lust killing. As such, relying on these criminological concepts for general classification guidance (i.e., points of similarity, dissimilarity, and uniqueness) may appear somewhat misguided and/or premature. Notwithstanding, the theory of containment and its connection to the self-concept construct are germane to the overall operation of the three typologies as delineated within this volume. Accordingly, in what follows, additional details on these criminological notions are provided where appropriate and useful, particularly in regard to how the models can be usefully contrasted based on these organizational constructs. However, before turning to these matters, some summary observations on the proposed strategy informing the comparative analysis are warranted.

As a point of departure, we note that Table 7.1 succinctly specifies the manner in which the three typologies are similar, dissimilar, and unique. This categorization emerges from the assessment each theoretical model provided in regard to the Jeffrey Dahmer case. These individual assessments were developed and chronicled in Chapter 6. Similarities located across the three models represent reccurring themes. In other words, psychological states, sociological conditions, biological processes, or other related ecological phenomena stationed within each typology represent important (and shared) conceptualizations regarding the etiology and/or development of serial, sadistic, and sexual homicide. Along these lines, several themes and emerging sub-themes are specified within this analysis: sociological and environmental factors, traumatic events, dissociation, low self-esteem and fantasy, increasingly violent fantasies, power and control, and stressors.

The comparative analysis also considers points of divergence across the respective typologies. These differences can best be understood by the way in which a particular theme is examined, based on a distinct theoretical position or orientation. Interestingly, the motivational, trauma control, and integrative typologies investigate similar issues in several instances; however, each has a different interpretation for the factor or circumstance in question. These areas of divergence help to distinguish the three models, especially as they conceptually account for the crime of erotophonophilia.

Finally, the comparative analysis identifies the unique facets or the distinct features of each theory. These are inherent qualitative differences prevalent in one typology but not the others. Identifying the exclusive features of each model is significant. In the context of this volume's focus on the paraphilic process and the psychology of lust murder, this activity draws attention to each model's capacity to more (or less) completely address these fundamental issues.

Reliance on the analytic framework of comparing theoretical models based on points of convergence, divergence, and distinctiveness has been employed in a number of criminological and psychological contexts. For example, Arrigo (1999) utilized this strategy when examining the way in which different critical criminological theories account for the relationship between social and criminal justice (see also Arrigo, 2000). Elsewhere, he appropriated this same thematic-driven approach in an effort to develop a multidisciplinary and integrative perspective for understanding crime (Arrigo, 2005). Finally, in the realm of psychology and law, Arrigo (2004) employed this comparative strategy when developing a critically informed psychological jurisprudence. In each of these instances, disparate theories were evaluated in terms of their similarities, dissimilarities, and unique properties.

Admittedly, the previous contexts in which the analytic strategy of comparing and contrasting criminological (and psychological) theories may be of some limited utility to the present endeavor. After all, social justice, an integrated multidisciplinary perspective for understanding crime, and psychological jurisprudence are not the same as comprehending homicide or lust murder. This observation notwithstanding, Arrigo's (1999) methodology seems quite serviceable. Indeed, it signifies one sensible consolidation approach by which to investigate, albeit somewhat provisionally, a plethora of conceptually charged matters, including those found in legal and criminological psychology. His strategy provides a solid and workable foundation such that the principal theoretical models examined within this study can be scrutinized for consistency, variation, and novelty.

Accordingly, in the remaining portions of this chapter, Arrigo's (1999, 2000, 2004, 2005) methodology fundamentally underscores the ensuing analysis. This includes a review of the similarities found across the models as well as how examining these resemblances help account for the criminal behavior of Jeffrey

**TABLE 7.1**   A Comparative Analysis of Murder Typologies and the Case of Jeffrey Dahmer

| | Sexual Homicide (Motivational Model) | Serial Murder (Trauma Control Model) | Paraphilia and Lust Murder (Integrative Model) |
|---|---|---|---|
| **SIMILARITIES** Sociological and Environmental | 1. *Ineffective social environment* (Parental apathy toward and underinvolvement in children's lives) | 1. *Sociological predisposition* (Sustained and intense family conflict; parental divorce) | 1. *Formative development–predispositional factors* (Parental self-absorption, conflict, and divorce) |
| *Sub-theme* Traumatic Events and/or Stressors | 2. *Formative events* (Dysfunctional parenting styles; parental conflict and divorce) | 2. *Traumatic events* (Emotional deprivation; disregard and rejection from primary caregiver) | 2. *Formative development–traumatic events* (Profound sense of separation, loss, and abandonment stemming from parental emotional abuse) |
| Dissociation | 1. *Ineffective social environment* (The child's perception of trauma that occurs early in his development can adversely affect his sense of reality. These negative appraisals contribute to cognitive distortions regarding sexuality) | 1. *Dissociation* (Perceptions of trauma occurring in early development can negatively affect the child's appraisal of self and others. These adverse perceptions can produce dissociative states of consciousness) | 1. *Low self-esteem–early fantasy development* (Dysfunctional family conditions and traumatic events foster personal doubt and low self-esteem; resentment toward others and the external world are harbored; escape into a fantasy world follows and functions as a coping strategy; dissociation quells pain of reality) |

| | | | |
|---|---|---|---|
| *Sub-theme* <br> Low Self-esteem and Fantasy | 2. *Patterned responses* <br><br> (Negative personality traits; cynicism toward society; disdain toward others; fantasy/daydreams; power, control, and domination) | 2. *Low self-esteem/fantasies* <br><br> (Anger and hostility; sustained social isolation; violent imagery; power over others) | 2. *Low self-esteem and early fantasy development* <br><br> (Personal failure; social detachment; emotional deprivation; low self-esteem; aggressive images; power and control) |
| *Increasingly Violent Fantasies* | 1. *Actions toward self and others* <br><br> (Negative and repetitive play; obsession with dead animals, insects; sexual progression of sadistic activity, e.g., rape, murder, torture, mutilation, necrophilia, cannibalism) | 1. *Increasingly violent fantasy* <br><br> (Synergistic effect linked to traumatic events, social isolation, low self-esteem, fantasy, dissociation and facilitators; reclaim power and regain control through serial murder) | 1. *Increasingly violent fantasy* <br><br> (Emphasis on the paraphilic process as system of behavior; repetitive reliance on sexually aberrant stimuli and fantasies, e.g., fetishes, rituals; imagined paraphilias progressively intensify, e.g., homosexual encounters, serial rape, necrophilia, cannibalism; restoration of psychic balance) |
| *Sub-theme* <br> Power and Control | | | 1. *Stressor/Trigger* <br><br> (The stressor cycles back into the paraphilic systemic process sustained by masturbation, facilitators, and violent fantasies; the trigger explains the offender's lack of control and need to dominate others) |
| Stressor and Triggers | 1. *Precipitating stressors* <br><br> (Conflict with both males and females; birth of a child; physical injury; legal and employment problems; stress from death) | 1. *Trauma reinforcers* <br><br> (Rejection and criticism both trigger and reinforce past traumatizations and the psychological discomfort and pain associated with them) | |
| *DIFFERENCES* <br> Facilitators | 1. *Critical personality traits* <br><br> (Implied in the Burgess et al. model and includes the use of alcohol, drugs, and sexually explicit material; linked to the critical personality traits of the sexual murder) | 1. *Facilitators* <br><br> (Explicitly identified in the Hickey typology and includes pornography, alcohol, and drugs; sustained use fosters dependency and desensitization, leading to compulsivity) | 1. *Facilitators* <br><br> (Explicitly identified in the integrated framework and includes the use of alcohol, drugs, and pornography; necessary to the paraphilic process; understood as a system of behavior; facilitators help to sustain the cycle of sexualized violence) |

*(continues)*

TABLE 7.1   (*continued*)

| | Sexual Homicide (Motivational Model) | Serial Murder (Trauma Control Model) | Paraphilia and Lust Murder (Integrative Model) |
|---|---|---|---|
| Progression of Violent Fantasy and Behavior | 1. *Lifespan perspective* (Childhood, i.e., cruelty to animals, adolescence, i.e., drug use, nonsexual murder, and adulthood, i.e., sexual murder; behaviors signify increasing levels/types of sexualized violence) | 1. *Adult psychosocial view* (Synergistic effect of adverse development during childhood coupled with perceived sense of personal failure leads to fantasies that are welcomed escapes; by incorporating facilitators, fantasies increase in their sexualized and aggressive content; in adulthood, they lead to violent behavior, e.g., rape, torture, mutilation) | 1. *Feedback loop* (Erotic deviance and violence escalate by way of a feedback loop; when sexual arousal and/or orgasm are not achieved through images, increasing levels of sadistic violence are employed; the progressively violent conduct, e.g., sexual murder, necrophilia, cannibalism, functions as a reinforcer that cycles back into the paraphilic system of behavior, including the complex fantasy system itself) |
| *UNIQUENESSES* Investigatory Focus | 1. (Sexual murder focus; based on law enforcement and behavioral science profiling insights; emphasis on critical personality traits, cognitive processing activities, and motivation) | 1. (Serial murder focus; concern for victims; first to provide empirical research on the subject; emphasis on traumatizations and their control) | 1. (Lust murder focus; emphasis on the etiology of paraphilia understood to be a systemic process that intensifies and manifests itself through criminal conduct; identifies the role of increasingly aberrant or sexual deviance in the commission of violent serial crime) |
| *Model's Orientation* | 1. (Cognitive and psychosocial approach) | 1. (Psychological and sociological predispositional events approach) | 1. (Paraphilic behavioral systems approach) |

Dahmer. Moreover, the dissimilarities of each typology are discussed, especially as they pertain to the case at hand. Finally, the distinctive features of each model are enumerated. We contend that attention to this matter demonstrates how the integrative framework for paraphilia and lust murder provides a more inclusive and robust conceptual appreciation for the sexual dynamics that underscored Dahmer's repetitive acts of erotophonophilia.

## SIMILARITIES AMONG THE MODELS

As a point of departure, we note that many of the external and internal factors identified within Reckless's ([1950], 1961, 1973; Reckless & Dinitz, 1967) containment theory are consistent with factors inherent in each of the theoretical models delineated on murder. For example, both sociological and environmental concerns are noteworthy themes subsequently identified within the analysis of similarities among the homicide typologies. Specifically, sustained family discord and unresolved traumatic life events (e.g., emotional abuse) contribute to the etiology of murder. These push factors profoundly interact with internal dynamics (e.g., the development of low self-esteem, aggressiveness, fantasy). In accordance with Reckless's containment and control formulations, exploring the push (and pull) features identified within each model might be of considerable utility when accounting for the phenomenon of homicide. When linked to the notions of self-concept, social identity, and criminality, the emergence and progression of serial, sexual, and lust murder appear somewhat correlated with a sociologically informed criminology. This is an approach in which the social structure and process features of Dahmer's behavior, interaction, and personality could be subjected to further, more sustained scrutiny.

It is worth noting that there are considerably more similarities than dissimilarities intrinsic to the motivational model developed by Burgess et al. (1986) and the trauma control typology conceived of by Hickey (1997). This is not surprising. As stipulated previously, the seeming comparability and apparent assimilation between these two frameworks was pivotal to why the frameworks were selected in the first place; indeed, this is how the proposed integrative model on paraphilia and lust murder was constructed. In this respect, there are numerous themes or likenesses across the three models that are relatively constant and stable. The likenesses identified within the ensuing analysis signify building blocks, making it possible to more comprehensively explain the phenomenon of erotophonophilia. In a number of instances, the shared themes help to establish a sequence of events whose manifestation is dependent on the likeness that preceded it.

To illustrate the presence of this sequential relationship, consider the connection between adverse environmental factors and the subsequent onset of low self-esteem and fantasy. Each model offers some commentary on this phenomenon. The presence of a fractured social identity (or poor self-concept as articulated in containment theory) stems from such factors as family discord and dysfunctional parenting. In other words, sociological and environmental hardships negatively affect the developing child. Low self-esteem surfaces, and reliance on fantasy and daydreaming develops to escape the harsh realities of everyday life. Clearly, then, the identification of sequential associations is itself an organizational similarity that exists across the three typologies. With these preliminary comments in mind, we now turn to the specific thematic likenesses that inform each of the identified theoretical models on murder.

## SOCIOLOGICAL AND ENVIRONMENTAL THEMES

Sociological and environmental points of convergence are clearly discernible within each theoretical model. Closely linked to this broader commonality is the emergent sub-theme of traumatic events. Stressful life circumstances consist of the debilitating and detrimental effects such occurrences have on the child's psychological development, especially when sustained early on in his life.

Within Burgess et al.'s (1986) sexual homicide typology and Hickey's (1997, 2001) serial murder model, the investigators recognized the significance of social and environmental factors, particularly in terms of their impact on the formative maturation of the child. More specifically, these researchers noted how certain conditions or circumstances occurring during this period of psychological growth could impede, rather than foster, prosocial and healthy development. Given the importance of this organizing theme, some summary observations on how these two frameworks similarly appropriate it in their conceptualizations on murder are warranted.

In the motivational model, the quality of the relationship between the child and the primary care provider was identified as fundamental. A severe breakdown in this bond (e.g., apathetic and/or dysfunctional parenting styles) could acutely influence the way in which the developing child perceived the world, including the ability (or lack thereof) to cultivate positive and meaningful relationships with others.

In the trauma control typology, environmental failure (e.g., sustained and intense family conflict) was identified as an important marker for a sociological predisposition to engage in criminal behavior. As Hickey (1997) asserted, if stressors or traumatizations (e.g., perceived emotional deprivation stemming from parental apathy and neglect; loss and separation following parental divorce) manifested themselves during a child's formative development, they were likely to be exacerbated by the social and environmental circumstances that remained unresolved. Similar to Burgess et al. (1986), Hickey (1997) also recognized how a negative relationship between the child and the primary caregiver could have a profoundly devastating effect on the individual's future development.

The integrative typology regarding paraphilia and lust murder postulates that aberrant behaviors manifesting as sexual deviance originated from unresolved or inappropriately addressed traumatic events occurring during the impressionable period of early adolescence. The largely dysfunctional environmental background of the paraphiliac individual (e.g., parental self-absorption, conflict, divorce) exacerbated a general breakdown within the formative years of childhood and adolescent development (e.g., profound sense of separation, loss, and abandonment). More specifically, research on lust murderers indicates that the early years of psychological adjustment "are crucial to the personality structure and development of these offenders" (Hazelwood & Douglas, 1980, p. 21; see also Hickey, 2005). It is highly unusual for the erotophonophiliac to come from a nurturing family environment free from abuse, alcoholism, drug abuse, or other factors that could result in significant childhood pain and suffering (Arrigo & Purcell, 2001; Money & Werlas, 1982; Schlesinger, 2003; Simon, 1996).

As previously stated, each model regards the presence of an ineffective social environment as a pivotal traumatic circumstance. In the context of the comparative analysis, the emergence of such traumatizations collectively represents a noteworthy sub-theme operating across the three typologies. As such, some global comments regarding this similarity are necessary.

The formative events component of the motivational model specifies three factors akin to stressors or traumatizations. These include the debilitating circumstance or condition itself, developmental failures, and interpersonal breakdowns. The trauma control typology interprets traumatic events to consist of an unstable and abusive home environment. Common manifestations of these traumas include the child experiencing a genuine sense of disregard and rejection from his primary care provider. The integrative model on lust murder indicates that traumatizations are an essential feature of the paraphiliac individual's formative development. Traumatizations or stressors include sexual, physical, and emotional abuse.

## THE THEME OF DISSOCIATION

When a child encounters traumatic circumstances that foster developmental failures and interpersonal breakdowns during his formative phase of development, there is a loss of control. The inability to constructively confront, work through, and resolve the trauma or stressor hinders the child's ability to resist the external or internal pushes (and pulls) that sustain his felt sense of debilitation, helplessness, injury, and hopelessness. In an attempt to regain control and contain the delinquency and criminality, the child often experiences some form of dissociation from the actual event. Dissociation functions as a means of escaping the experience itself. It also represents one (constructive) way in which the youth endeavors to make sense of the event.

Each theoretical model acknowledges the significant role of dissociation, particularly as a means to escape the disturbance operating within the home environment. Each typology explains how this activity is an adaptive or coping strategy that enables the person to make sense of stressful events. The sexual homicide model developed by Burgess et al. (1986) and the serial murder typology delineated by Hickey (1997) intimated that controlling or abating trauma through dissociation influences the child's perception of self as well as perceptions of others. Specifically, Burgess et al. (1986) asserted that ineffective social bonds within the child's early environmental and family circumstances contributed to the individual's negative appraisal of reality and cognitive distortions regarding sexuality. Hickey (1997) observed that as the child matured, these distorted perceptions of self, others, and situations could produce dissociative states of consciousness. This notion of an altered consciousness or a reconstituted (imagined) reality is expressly depicted within the dissociation construct of Hickey's (1997, 2001) trauma control framework.

Consistent with this theme of dissociation, the integrative model examines how early traumatic events, which materialize as a consequence of dysfunctional environmental and sociological circumstances (e.g., family turmoil), foster profound feelings of self-doubt and low self-esteem. As such, the developing child regards himself as a personal failure and harbors resentment toward the world in which he lives. In order to cope with these profoundly debilitating sentiments, the adolescent retreats into a make-believe world of fantasies and daydreams and escapes the brutality of everyday existence. Turning inward represents an inventive, adaptive strategy in which the individual removes and insulates himself (i.e., dissociates) from the harshness of external reality. Over time, in the absence of resolving such traumatic events, sexualized fantasies emerge within the maturing child's psyche.

The manifestation of low self-esteem and fantasy are sub-themes linked to the presence of dissociation as specified across the three typologies. Specifically, the emergence of early childhood sexual imagery and daydreaming, in conjunction with a poor self-concept or social identity, stems from the impact of traumatic events the maturing child encounters. These stressors are traceable to problematic sociological and environmental (i.e., familial) circumstances and conditions. The following observations explain the likeness of low self-esteem and fantasy as functioning within the three models on murder.

Interpersonal inadequacies, including low self-esteem and lack of self-worth, are dimensions of personality that can significantly contribute to how the child relates to others. Following the motivation model, the patterned response component addresses the onset and maintenance of these deficiencies vis-à-vis the child's failure to establish positive social relationships. Moreover, as Burgess et al. (1986) explained, the presence of negative personality traits in conjunction with a cynical view of society and a contemptuous outlook toward others acts as a catalytic generator for fantasy and daydream. Consistent with this perspective, Hickey (1997) suggested that anger and hostility, combined with sustained social isolation, interact to form violent imagery. The integrative typology also accounts for the phenomenon of low self-esteem and fantasy, especially in the context of its manifestation and effects early in an individual's psychosocial development. A profound sense of personal failure and social detachment stemming from deep-seated emotional deprivations fuel his debilitated ego, thereby giving rise to low self-esteem and aggressive fantasies. Indeed, research on paraphiliacs indicates that imaginary constructions of self, others, and situations are an integral component to facilitating sexualized and violent deviance (e.g., Hickey, 2005; Kafka, 2003; MacCulloch et al., 1983; McGuire et al., 1965; Prentky et al., 1989; Reinhardt, 1957; Schlesinger, 2003).

In each of the models, fantasy principally functions as a means of escape. In this respect, then, the individual's retreat into an internal reality is similar to the process of dissociation: this is how the distressed individual attempts to regain some semblance of control over his life. In these instances, personal scenarios, typically involving power over and subjugation of others, are manufactured. Fantasy represents a stand-in for the social relationships the individual is unable or ill-equipped to form. The issues of power and control as conditioning the individual's cognitions, impulses, and actions is an emergent sub-theme linked to the manifestation of increasingly violent fantasies. As such, violently aggressive (and eroticized) imagery is the next similarity discussed in this chapter.

### THE THEME OF VIOLENT FANTASIES

The presence of increasingly violent fantasies is a common denominator across the three models. This similarity accounts for the sub-theme of power and control within the three murder typologies. Given the very close relationship between these two likenesses, they will be examined somewhat in tandem.

The motivational framework specifically addresses the way in which the behavioral patterns of children, adolescents, and adults reflect their internal or cognitive schemas. These behavioral patterns can manifest themselves at any point within the lifespan of that individual. Typically, they become more violent over time, given the degree to which the person comes to rely on the mechanism of escape or retreat as a coping strategy. Examples of such behavioral patterns in childhood and adolescence include repetitive and negative play (e.g., obsession with dead animals and insects; animal cemetery in Dahmer's backyard). The more imaginary constructions are depended on to quell low self-esteem or a deflated self-concept, the more intense the fantasies. As such, violent and sadistic images, cognitions, impulses, desires, and behaviors are likely to steadily emerge and/or progress.

The trauma control model similarly denotes an increasingly violent fantasy component. This feature is influenced by the other elements depicted within Hickey's (1997, 2001) serial murder typology. He examined how traumatic events, coupled with social isolation, could induce fantasies and daydreams. In addition to other contributing factors, including dissociation and facilitating behaviors, Hickey (1997) noted a synergistic effect. Ultimately, this effect gave way to an increase in fantasy that had the capacity to grow in duration, frequency, and intensity.

The integrated model concurs with the presence of increasingly violent fantasies as contributing to serial, sexual murder, and, most especially, lust murder.

In this model, the paraphilic process as a system of behavior is emphasized, including the repetitive reliance on sexually aberrant stimuli and fantasies (e.g., fetishes, rituals, erotically charged objects). When the individual successfully actualizes the sadistic and aggressive fantasy, increasingly violent imagery is necessary in order to achieve subsequent arousal or sustain sexual gratification.

As previously noted, power, control, and domination represent important subthemes that impact the emergence of low self-esteem and fantasy. They also affect the presence of progressively more violent images. Behaviors indicative of these intensifying themes can include rape, torture, mutilation, necrophilia, and cannibalism. Based on an assessment of the three typologies investigated within this volume, serial, sexual, and lust murderers all have the potential to engage in the above-mentioned behaviors.

Traceable to early childhood traumatic events, the notions of domination, subjugation, and/or perverse authority are further related to the dysfunctional or troubled social environment the child routinely encounters. More specifically, an inability to constructively confront, adjust to, or otherwise work through the early trauma leaves the developing child feeling out of control or not in charge of his life. Following the three identified typologies on murder, the individual may elect to compensate for the absence of personal power experienced throughout the course of maturation by attempting to regulate those around him.

Noting that this lack of control can materialize at any point during the lifespan, Burgess et al. (1986) illustrated how it occurs through the actions-toward-self-and-others component of their model. As they explained, these behaviors (i.e., sexual progression of sadistic behaviors) increase in severity, especially as the individual psychosocially develops. Hickey (1997) similarly addressed the issue of control within his research. As he observed, stressors within the life of the offender can serve to remind him of an absence of authority over his very existence. When this occurs, the offender ultimately takes the life of another (e.g., serial murder, necrophilia, cannibalism) to reclaim power, regain control, and reconstitute reality. The integrated typology focuses on the issue of power and control through the paraphilic process, as understood to be a system of intensifying behaviors. The progression in imagined sexualized violence (e.g., possessing a compliant lover, serial rape, creating a sex slave, necrophilia, postmortem mutilation, cannibalism) signifies acts of sadistic power over others designed to restore the individual's sense of psychic disequilibrium stemming from the absence of personal control.

## THE THEME OF STRESSORS AND/OR TRIGGERING MECHANISMS

Each theoretical model identifies stressors or triggers as antecedents to the actual commission of offender behavior. The motivational model specified a series of precipitating stressors as accounting for sexual homicide. These antecedent stressors were identified as occurring immediately prior to the murder and consisted of the following factors: conflict with both males and females, parental conflict, financial stress, marital problems, birth of a child, physical injury, legal and employment problems, and stress from a death (Ressler et al., 1988, pp. 45–46).

Hickey's (1997, 2001) trauma control typology specifically designated a trauma reinforcer component as activating serial murder. He noted that unresolved childhood stresses or traumatizations could trigger the commission of future acts of violence. More specifically, when the individual experienced either a form of rejection from an intimate or a criticism from a superior, that person was unable to constructively work through the disappointment, pain, embarrassment, and others emotions linked to the event. Thus, the circumstance itself functioned to trigger and reinforce the psychological discomfort associated with the initial trauma, rekindling not only the past traumatization but also the frustration and anxiety connected with its failed resolution. The individual would retreat into his internalized and imagined fantasy world, seeking relief from the lack of control he profoundly relived. Given the absence of closure on the initial traumatization and following the manifestation of the triggering event, the individual would act out the violent images of sexual control and domination that increasingly engulfed his consciousness by taking the life of another.

The integrative model regarding paraphilia and lust murder similarly relies on the notion of a stressor or trigger when accounting for serial and sexual homicide. Adopting Hickey's (1997) trauma reinforcer position, the synthetic typology focuses on how the individual copes with the reinforcer. In this context, the stressor or trigger cycles back into the paraphilic systemic process vis-à-vis a feedback loop. Sexually deviant behavior is sustained within the cycle by use of masturbation and facilitators (e.g., alcohol, drugs, pornography), as well as by the intricate and often violent fantasy system. The trigger essentially explains the lack of control the perpetrator experiences over his reality, as well as his need to dominate others through paraphilic behavior. As previously suggested, in the extreme the response to the stressor may manifest itself in sadistic offending, such as erotophonophilia.

## POINTS OF SIMILARITY, CONTAINMENT THEORY, AND SELF-CONCEPT

The various themes described in the preceding commentary resonate with Reckless's ([1950], 1961, 1973) position on external and internal pushes, particularly in relation to social identity, ego development, and self-concept (see also Reckless, Dinitz, & Murray, 1956; Reckless & Dinitz, 1967). Each theory demonstrates the veracity of this statement. Indeed, as specified at the outset of this section, homicidal behavior can be profoundly influenced by parental pushes (e.g., family discord, apathetic parenting) that lead to attenuated and even severed attachments. When bonding styles include the child's perceived abandonment and/or rejection, inner containment is likely to consist of low self-esteem and an underdeveloped sense of social identity. If internalized, these sentiments can manifest themselves through impulsive, aggressive, and violent cognitions.

Moreover, following a social process and structure orientation to criminology, these conditions, if left unsettled or unchecked, have the capacity to render the individual despondent, helpless, and out of control. As a consequence, various forms of deviance (e.g., obsessions with animals and insects, including their evisceration; sex with mannequins and corpses), delinquency (e.g., chronic alcoholism; marijuana use; and adolescent pranks), and criminality (e.g., serial and sexual homicide; torture, cannibalism) are likely to surface. Consistent with the motivational, trauma control, and integrated models, the presence of these conditions can be further amplified by turning to the insights of a more sociologically informed criminology.

## DIFFERENCES AMONG THE MODELS

When accounting for an organizational theme that is dissimilarly examined by the three models in question, it is useful to consider how the respective typologies interpret that discrete phenomenon. In other words, a difference can best be understood by the way in which it is defined through the operation of the conceptual framework under review. Both the motivational and trauma control typologies investigate similar elements; however, what varies is how these factors are construed by the model in question. For purposes of this section's inquiry regarding points of divergence, both the role of facilitators and the progression of violent fantasy and behavior are discussed. Additionally, the relationship between these areas of dissimilarity and their more criminological roots are specified. In particular, several summary observations on how Reckless's ([1950], 1973) containment theory and self-concept notion further our regard for the three typologies and their assessment of murder based on noteworthy themes of difference are enumerated.

### THE THEME OF FACILITATORS

The critical role of alcohol, drugs, and pornography in the commission of murder is one area in which the models offer mostly dissimilar interpretations. Understood as facilitators that sustain or otherwise contribute to the offender's increasingly aggressive and sexualized fantasy system, reliance on such behavior is pivotal to the operation of each typology. Again, how facilitators are interpreted within the functioning of each model is what creates a point of dissimilarity among the theories.

Although not explicitly identified as a central feature of their typology, Burgess et al. (1986) did identify, at least implicitly, the significance of facilitators in the behavior of the sexual murderer. Specifically, in a follow-up article based on the original sample data, the authors commented on the role of facilitators. As the investigators noted, over half of the subjects reported an interest in or the use of pornography. Moreover, 81% of the sexual homicide offenders indicated "interests in fetishism, voyeurism, and masturbation" as linked to such facilitative conduct (Ressler et al., 1988, p. 25). These observations are telling, especially in relation to the initial research that was undertaken and the critical personality traits of the assailants. In short, while Burgess et al. (1986) did not stipulate that use of alcohol, drugs, and/or pornography functioned as a conceptual facet of their motivational model, subsequent research by these same investigators confirmed that such behavior was positively correlated with the sexual murderer.

The trauma control model developed by Hickey (1997, 2001) included the presence of facilitators as a distinct component that underscored the overall operation of his repetitive homicide framework. Indeed, as he explained, the individual's continual use of alcohol and drugs, as well as his appropriation of sexually explicit material, could over time desensitize him. Moreover, Hickey (1997) noted that if immersed in these various facilitating behaviors, the person might experience addiction, dependency, and an intense desire for more stimuli. In the trauma control typology, reliance on facilitators could become intensely compulsive.

Similar to the trauma control model, the integrative framework on lust murder identifies the role of facilitators as a pivotal dimension of the typology's general operation. Indeed, the synthetic theory specifies the use of facilitators as an essential organizational component of the model. However, unlike the trauma control framework, the integrative schema specifies that the use of drugs, alcohol, and/or pornography is necessary to the paraphilic process as a system of behavior. In short, what makes facilitators so significant to the functioning of the integrative model is that they help to sustain the cycle of sexualized violence on which the offender compulsively relies in order to maintain arousal and achieve orgasm.

Facilitators are thematically important to each typology; however, the manner in which they are invoked is dissimilar. The motivational model tacitly acknowledges their significance in the context of understanding sexual homicide, but they are not depicted as an essential component of the Burgess et al. (1986) framework. The trauma control typology stipulates that alcohol, drugs, and/or pornography are an important conceptual feature of serial murder. However, Hickey's (1997, 2001) organizational schema focuses chiefly on the addictive and desensitization dynamics that inform the repetitive act of homicide for the assailant. Finally, the integrative typology extends and deepens Hickey's observations. Alcohol, drugs, and/or pornography are compulsively appropriated by the offender and, over time, the desire for increasing levels and/or types of stimulation are needed for sexual excitement, especially as the offender becomes accustomed to relying on them. However, facilitators also help to fuel the paraphilic process, demonstrating how the process itself represents a system of increasingly aggressive and erotic fantasies that lead to criminal behavior, including lust murder. Thus, each typology (varyingly) acknowledges the role of facilitators and differentially accounts for their significance.

## PROGRESSION OF VIOLENT FANTASY AND BEHAVIOR

The role of increasingly violent fantasy and homicidal behavior was previously identified as a similarity that informed the operation of each model. However, this theme can be further evaluated based on the conceptual orientation by which the respective typologies interpret it. The motivational framework focuses on a lifespan perspective. The trauma control schema employs an adult psychosocial approach. The integrative typology incorporates the insights of both based on the operation of a feedback loop. These points of dissimilarity are briefly enumerated below.

The Burgess et al. (1986) model investigated the potential manifestation of behavior, criminal or otherwise, from within childhood, adolescence, and adulthood. When aggressive (and sexualized) images materialize and result in criminal behavior, they manifest themselves in a progressively more serious manner. Examples of this escalation in childhood include cruelty to animals and setting fires. Instances of this intensification in adolescence consist of assault, drug use, and nonsexual murder. Illustrations of this likely amplification in adulthood encompass such offenses as sexual murder.

The notion of actions toward others is implied within the Hickey (1997, 2001) framework. This is particularly evident in the increasingly violent fantasy component of his model, as well as in the homicidal behavioral dimension. Hickey (1997) focused on the synergistic effect of adverse development during the formative years of life and the perceived sense of personal failure that subsequently emerged in the child or adolescent. Moreover, he explained how fantasy became a welcome escape as the individual incorporated alcohol, drugs, and/or pornographic material into his retreatist routine, thereby fueling (and sustaining) the existing imaginary constructions of himself, others, and situations. Consequently, increasingly aggressive fantasies would surface. As Hickey (1997) noted, they could grow in duration, frequency, and intensity. In the trauma control schema, behavioral manifestations of such progressively violent images include rape, torture, and mutilation. Unlike the motivational model developed by Burgess et al. (1986), Hickey's (1997) typology neglected to account for the presence of these criminal actions within childhood and adolescent development. Instead, he principally focused on violent, erotic fantasies and their behavioral manifestation in adulthood.

Contributing to the differentiation of the motivational and trauma control models on the shared theme of progressively violent fantasy and their behavioral manifestation is the type of criminal conduct specified by the respective investigators. As delineated in Chapter 3, Burgess et al. (1986) examined deviant childhood behaviors as well as other nonfatal actions. Hickey (1997, 2001) exclusively considered the crime of serial murder. Although this distinction is not a direct product of the particular perspective informing the researchers' inquiries, it is a dissimilarity underscoring the assessment of this theme as undertaken by these investigators.

The integrative model builds on and consolidates the insights of the motivational and trauma control frameworks. It exclusively addresses the paraphilic process as a system of behavior that progresses by way of intensified images that are increasingly violent and sexual. The feedback loop is utilized to illustrate how erotic deviance can escalate in severity along a continuum from noncriminal to criminal. Once the fantasy system itself and the behavior of the perpetrator are executed, an increased need for greater stimulation materializes. As the gravity of the behavior increases (e.g., rape, sexual murder, mutilation, necrophilia, cannibalism), the conduct functions as a reinforcer that sequences back into the complex fantasy system. This overall process accounts for an increase in aggressive and sadistic sexual imagery as well as the progression in violent criminal behavior.

## POINTS OF DISSIMILARITY, CONTAINMENT THEORY, AND SELF-CONCEPT

The two points of dissimilarity discussed within the previous subsection can be further amplified by turning to Reckless's ([1950], 1961, 1973) containment theory as well as his observations on self-concept and social identity, specifically in relation to criminality. At issue here are the conditions under which the person fails to learn how to control deviant, delinquent, and criminal inclinations. Generally speaking, facilitators, the progression of fantasy, and increasingly violent behavior function as tangible expressions of how an individual interprets, knowingly or otherwise, the detrimental pushes stemming from the harmful actions of family members (e.g., parental conflict, perceived abandonment). These identifiable, external expressions of trauma and neglect give rise to the absence of inner controls in which the adolescent (or adult) struggles to establish a positive self-image and healthy ego identity. Thus, the internalized and psychically debilitating stress that builds up, traceable to family pushes and their external manifestation, makes the containment of deviance, delinquency, and crime increasingly problematic.

A reliance on pornography, alcohol, and drugs further signifies that these external indicators or coping strategies stem from poor inner containment (i.e., low self-esteem, poor social identity). Excessive dependence on such outward behavior magnifies the intense feelings of despondency, helplessness, and isolation that the individual harbors, given the profound sense of parental detachment that overwhelms him. Over time, if effective bonding is not restored, this immersion in facilitative behaviors becomes addictive. The negative pushes from family discord prevent prosocial attachments, the absence of inner containment fosters arrested ego development, the use of illicit substances or sexually explicit material steadily progresses, the procurement of appropriate bonding styles is thwarted, and the likelihood of delinquent or criminal conduct is almost assured.

The presence of increasingly violent fantasies and aggressive behavior follows a similar trajectory. Not learning self-control, given external pushes that include parental neglect and rejection as well as inner pushes steeped in perceived personal failure, means that containment will become progressively unlikely. A reliance on sexually explicit and sadistic imagery represents an effort to restore psychic equilibrium through controlling others. Over time, when such imaginary constructions of self, others, and situations are insufficient to foster containment, behavioral manifestations surface. The absence of control, linked to such external push factors as adverse living conditions, becomes internalized. The individual's sense of self-esteem and social identity become increasingly fragile. Low self-esteem, aggressiveness, and hostility surface and represent outward expressions of failed inner containment. The reliance on fantasy functions as an internal wish to restore psychosocial balance, inner control, and positive bonds of attachment. Themes of power, domination, and authority are externalized expressions of this unspoken but felt sentiment. These internalized dynamics become embedded in the individual's developing personality, perceptions of reality, and behavioral motivations.

Jeffrey Dahmer was predisposed to the effects of various environmental factors in his formative development that constituted environmental pushes. Ongoing marital strife between his parents, as well as a genuine lack of bonding with his mother and father, were critical life events that negatively and deeply influenced Dahmer's sense of outlook toward the world. As external manifestations of these environmental pushes, their impact on his maturation was enormous. These traumatizations interfered with his ability to cultivate positive and healthy relationships with others throughout the course of his life. In other words, having failed to learn how to bond effectively and appropriately, his internalized self-appraisal was riddled with personal doubt, disregard for others, and disdain for social conventions.

In order to escape the hopelessness affiliated with the lack of attachment he felt and the inner turmoil that engulfed him, a steady reliance on fantasies and daydreaming surfaced. Dahmer's imagined world became a reality that he could control. His fantasy life became a substitute for the human interaction he simply was unable to form. However, when his imaginary realm, fueled by facilitators, no longer fostered inner containment, a steady increase in the severity of his delinquency and then his criminality materialized.

## UNIQUE FEATURES AMONG THE MODELS

Unique themes or qualitatively distinct characteristics that set each model apart from the others are discernible. These features are intrinsic to the particular typology of the particular models and can be further illuminated by incorporating Reckless's ([1950], 1973; see also Reckless & Dinitz, 1967) insights on containment theory, self-concept, and criminality. Along these lines, two distinctive elements are specified: the investigatory focus and the model's orientation.

Admittedly, because the three typologies collectively include some statement on both of these themes, one could reasonably argue that they are shared matters that are differentially interpreted by the architects of the framework under review. In other words, the theory's focus and the typology's approach ostensibly represent point of convergence. However, given their fundamental significance to the distinctive operation of the particular model in question, it is more appropriate to regard these elements as inherently and qualitatively unique properties. These matters are summarily discussed below.

## INVESTIGATORY FOCUS

There are several unique features to the motivational model on sexual homicide. Principally, this typology investigates sexual murder from a law enforcement and behavioral science perspective. The development of this approach, as well as the subsequent body of research on sexual killing (e.g., Ressler et al., 1988; Douglas et al., 1995; Holmes & Holmes, 2002b), was the first law enforcement-oriented behavioral science criminal personality (and profile) research project (Depue, 1986; Egger, 2002; Holmes & Holmes, 2002a). Burgess et al. (1986) chose to focus the model on the critical personality traits as well as the cognitive processing activities of the offender. They hypothesized that these variables functioned as motivating factors in the commission of sexual homicide.

Moreover, the original research was intended to elicit specific information regarding each assailant's developmental history, physical and personality characteristics, modus operandi, pre- and post-offense behavior, victim selection process, and use of manipulation and control in the criminal event, as well as techniques employed to successfully evade detection, apprehension, prosecution, and confinement (Depue, 1986). Thus, the comprehensive nature of the original (and subsequent) sexual homicide investigations coupled with the creation of a motivational explanatory framework distinguishes this model from all other theoretical competitors.

The trauma control model proposed by Hickey (1997, 2001) specifically investigates the phenomenon of serial homicide in relation to adults. Hickey's (1997, 2005) research emphasizes the devastating effects of this behavior on victims. He was the first social scientist to conduct empirical inquiries on serial homicide within the United States, identifying the fundamental psychosocial underpinnings (i.e., trauma and control) of this form of murder.

The unique aspect of the integrative model is that it attempts to explain the etiology of paraphilia as a systemic process that progresses over time and manifests itself through criminal behavior. Additionally, the model identifies the role of increasingly aberrant, sadistic, and violent deviance as a motive in sexual crimes. This is particularly the case for the lust murderer. The other models fail to locate or otherwise specify the phenomenon of erotophonophilia in their respective explanatory frameworks.

## THE MODEL'S ORIENTATION

Each model adopts a unique theoretical orientation when accounting for murder. The sexual homicide model adopts a cognitive psychosocial approach when examining the motivations of the offender, including an assessment of personality traits and thought-based distortions. The trauma control typology identifies certain psychological and sociological factors/events that contribute to the emergence and maintenance of serial murder, in which a cycle of self-perpetuating behavior materializes (e.g., violent fantasy, violent offending, the use of facilitating agents). The integrative model for sexual deviance and lust murder assimilates the other two frameworks and appropriates a paraphilic behavioral systems approach. This schema acknowledges that aberrant sexual behavior can become a self-sustaining process leading to extreme forms of criminal conduct (e.g., erotophonophilia).

## POINTS OF UNIQUENESS, CONTAINMENT THEORY, AND SELF-CONCEPT

Despite the various foci and orientations of the three theoretical models, each investigates the phenomenon of murder. Thus, the question is: How can the unique properties of the respective typologies be advanced through a sociologically informed criminology? Comparable to the previous assessments concerning points of convergence and divergence across the conceptual frameworks, the notion of containment, self-concept, and social identity are useful to answer the above question.

The sexual homicide model focuses on how personality characteristics and cognitive factors motivate an individual to engage in murder. According to Reckless et al. (1956), the development of such personality factors as well as an individual's thought processes can and do contribute to delinquent and criminal behavior. As indicators of poor self-concept and fragile ego identity, manifesting these factors reflects the absence of inner containment. This failure in control can intensify in severity, especially given the presence (or lack thereof) of prosocial bonds of attachment. More specifically, critical personality traits and internal thought processes, as well as perceptions, beliefs, and motivations, can contribute to sexual homicide. Facilitating this are discrete push factors that underscore the person's evolving sense of self, particularly during childhood and adolescence (i.e., formative development). External expressions of this include a dysfunctional home environment (e.g., family discord, parental neglect), that pull the individual away from the normative social order, giving rise to low levels of inner containment.

The trauma control model also draws attention to the impact of family pushes that foster low self-esteem. Adverse traumatic events sustained during childhood and left unresolved during adolescence can be devastating. Indeed, stress-inducing experiences contribute to the social identity of the offender (Reckless

[1950], 1973; Reckless & Dinitz, 1967) and ultimately affect his ability to control behavior. These events or circumstances as expressions of deficient parental attachments erode the inner containment that would otherwise reduce, impede, or prevent his inclination to perform delinquent and/or criminal acts. Violent, sexualized fantasies, as well as the cyclical (and habitual) use of alcohol, drugs, and pornography are external indicators of absent self-restraint.

The trauma control typology and the motivational model both yield essential information relative to Jeffrey Dahmer's dysfunctional background, interpersonal struggles, fantasy development, and criminal behavior. However, these theoretical frameworks fail to explain Dahmer's pathological use of paraphilic stimuli, as well as how these behaviors become a self-generating process. Understanding these issues is crucial to a proper assessment of lust murder. Moreover, Burgess et al. (1986) and Hickey (1997, 2001) neglected to account for the potential sequencing of sexually deviant or aberrant behaviors, as well as their criminal manifestation. Portions of Chapter 6 systematically accounted for these various phenomena. Elaborating on the unique features of the integrated typology, based on insights derived from containment theory and Reckless's (1961) appropriation of self-concept, is useful (see also Reckless et al., 1956).

According to the integrative framework, paraphilias originate within the formative years of psychological growth and maturation. Traumatic events sustained within early childhood and adolescence are comparable to external push factors, especially if emanating from consistent family strife (Reckless et al., 1956). The nature and quality of the social relationships encountered during formative development (e.g., rejection from parents, lack of attachments) contribute to an individual's overall sense of meaning regarding himself and others. Consequently, adverse external factors sustained by the individual essentially create and transmit a negative appraisal.

Internal dynamics operate similarly to environmental stressors when establishing social structure and meaning for a person. If inner containment is low, given the individual's perceived personal failure, negative assessments of others, and cynicism toward society, social controls will not likely be secured. Instead, he is likely to succumb to his deep-seated sense of disequilibrium and disorder. Retreat into fantasy—aggressive, sadistic, and/or violent though it may be—signifies the deployment of an adaptive coping strategy designed to stave off a total breakdown in control. The use of facilitators (e.g., alcohol, drugs, sexually explicit material) can have a calming effect, provided they contain the delinquent or criminal conduct. In that case, they become part of a fixed cycle in which self-perpetuating behaviors (e.g., fantasies fueled by facilitators used for sexual excitement and orgasm) inhibit violent impulses. However, when these mechanisms no longer keep in check the individual's cognitively distorted schemas, inner containment breaks down entirely. In other words, when the use of facilitators, paraphilic stimuli and fantasy, and orgasmic conditioning fail, then the self-control that would otherwise hinder criminality is no longer possible. This lack of inhibition is sustained through the synthetic model's reliance on a feedback loop, which reinforces the sexually deviant behavior (as imagined and as enacted) such that it is sequenced into the overall process. As the need for greater sexual stimulation and gratification increases, the fantasy system and the manifestation of violent behavior escalate in severity and intensity. Again, this is because self-control is lacking, inner containment is altogether thwarted, and the impact of debilitating pulls on the individual (e.g., family neglect) is acute.

## SUMMARY AND CONCLUSION

This chapter carefully considered how the motivational, trauma control, and integrative typologies created meaning with respect to the case of Jeffrey Dahmer and the sexual and repetitive homicides he committed. Along these lines, noteworthy points of similarity, dissimilarity and uniqueness were all enumerated. Underscoring this analysis was the extent to which each theoretical framework accounted for the phenomenon of lust murder and those persons responsible for its serial commission. Informing this methodical review were the contributions of a social structure and process approach to criminology. Specifically, the relevance of containment theory, self-concept, and social identity were all brought to bear on the explanatory properties of the respective typologies and the delinquent and criminal conduct of Jeffrey Dahmer.

As the work undertaken in this chapter reveals, each theory offers useful information on the crime of erotophonophilia. However, the integrative model, in its attempt to assimilate and extend the contributions of the motivational and trauma control conceptual schemas, yields considerably more expository utility. This is especially the case when noting how paraphilia functions as a motive underpinning the crime of lust murder. Moreover, this is particularly significant when identifying how sexually deviant behaviors operate systemically. resulting in increasingly violent fantasies and conduct that, in the extreme, gives way to serial acts of erotophonophilia.

It remains to be seen where and how the synthetic framework can be sensibly applied in particular instances or settings. As the subsequent chapter reveals, the specialty areas of law enforcement administration and management, forensic psychology, and social and public policy are three practical domains that could realistically appropriate the synthetic model's theoretical insights in a myriad of training, treatment, and programmatic contexts. Accordingly, with these observations in mind and recognizing the certainly speculative and clearly provisional nature of this exercise, the ensuing comments endeavor to move the debate on the psychology of lust murder into the realm of much needed reform, change, and progress.

# 8

# IMPLICATIONS AND CONCLUSIONS

## OVERVIEW

This book has examined the psychology of lust murder, mindful of the role of paraphilia in the serial commission of this crime. Along these lines, two well-established theories (the motivational model and the trauma control typology) were delineated. By assimilating these theories, an integrated conceptual framework was proposed.

The previous chapter systematically explored each of these three models, arguing that they possess similarities, dissimilarities, and unique properties. We asserted that this consolidation and organizing strategy facilitated a more thorough assessment of the particular explanatory properties the individual typologies embodied, especially in relation to erotophonophilia and the criminal behavior exhibited by Jeffrey Dahmer. Moreover, by turning to the contributions of a sociologically informed criminology, a deeper understanding the frameworks themselves and the offense of lust murder was provided. The theory of containment, the notion of self-concept, and the phenomenon of social identity were all brought to bear on the psychology of lust murder.

Based on the overall analysis, the integrated typology demonstrates how paraphilias function as a process of increasingly sadistic and sexualized fantasies that over time lead to violent criminal conduct. As a coordinated system of progressively intense and severe behavior, aberrant sexuality both underscores the commission of and operates as motive in the serial act of erotophonophilia. The case of Jeffrey Dahmer, as methodically examined in this volume, amply demonstrates the veracity of these conclusions.

This chapter provisionally explores and tentatively considers the implications stemming from the book's position on the salience of the integrated typology. As a general proposition, the explanatory (and predictive) dimensions of the synthetic framework raise a host of questions germane to justice administration and management, criminal and clinical psychology, and law and public policy. Commentary on these matters is useful, especially since it moves the debate on the crime of lust murder from mere theoretical speculation and model building to one of sensible action and cogent programmatic reform. Indeed, some of the more obvious implications stemming from the integrated typology relate to police profiling and training, clinical intervention for and treatment of sexual offenders, and legislative initiatives regarding violent serial and sexual criminals.

Specifically, within the field of law enforcement, the synthetic framework could aid federal and state police personnel in the identification, detection, and apprehension of offenders. Moreover, in the context of officer field training, the typology usefully draws attention to the underdeveloped though increasingly complex domain of crime scene investigation. In the realm of treatment, the integrated model reasonably extends clinical knowledge relative to the profoundly debilitating adverse effects traceable to unresolved childhood trauma. This includes practical insight on the emergence, progression, and maintenance of dysfunctional behavior, especially when it assumes the form of sexually charged violence. In the domain of public policy, forensic psychologists, familiar with the etiology and development of erotophonophilia, can provide accurate and prudent programmatic information relative to the risk assessment and management of paraphilic individuals. This is particularly pertinent to state and federal legislation that affects the rights of violent sexual offenders, including such matters as civil commitment and community notification statutes, as well as general institutional changes in correctional and mental health hospital planning.

The above concerns are all discussed in the remaining pages of this volume. However, we note that the issue of treatment is particularly problematic in the case of the paraphiliac individual generally and, more specifically, the lust murderer. As Liebert (1985) noted, erotophonophiliacs "may be able to maintain effective facades as impostors, imitating normal people, but they are not normal enough to tolerate the intensive bonding demands for meaningful psychotherapy" (p. 197). Moreover, the public's perception regarding repeat sexual offenders raises serious questions about prospects for successfully managing them in institutional (e.g., penal, psychiatric) environs. As Hickey (2005) noted, society's continued frustration in dealing with dangerous sex offenders has led to a growing ostracism of these individuals. Commenting on this social trend, he stated: "Unfortunately, although the intent [behind this collective behavior] may be good, such an approach will do little to deter someone who wishes to act out his deviant sexual fantasies" (Hickey, 1997, p. 270).

Given the concerns linked to treatment, some comments on psychology's capacity to intervene with profoundly disturbed offenders are warranted. The most compelling literature on this matter includes the research on psychopathy and criminality. Interestingly, the personality structure and behavioral patterns of the psychopath are, in several important respects, consistent with what we know about the lust murderer. Thus, it follows that detailing the research on psychopathy may further our understanding of the phenomenon of erotophonophilia and those responsible for its serial commission.

Accordingly, this chapter is divided into four substantive parts. First, the extant literature on psychopathy is summarized. Where useful and appropriate, several connections to the integrated typology and the crime of lust murder are provided. Second, the practical implications that emerge from the synthetic framework are specified. Again, given the exploratory and theoretical nature of this book, these remarks can only be described as provisional and speculative at best. Third, the generalizability of the integrated typology is explored. Arguably, lessons learned from the paraphilic framework can be sensibly applied to other lust murderers. Several tentative observations along these lines are offered. Fourth, the thesis of this volume is reconsidered, noting the purpose of each substantive chapter. This includes a synopsis of major points raised throughout the text as well as how these points were addressed in the respective chapters.

## PSYCHOPATHY, CRIME, AND LUST MURDER: A PRELIMINARY REVIEW

While a detailed presentation of the history and evolution of psychopathy is beyond the scope of this chapter, some background information is warranted. The present-day construct of psychopathy has evolved from several hundred years of clinical (and criminological) inquiry by American and European behavioral and social scientists (Arrigo & Shipley, 2001; Berrios, 1996; Millon, Simonsen, & Birket-Smith, 1998). As noted by Millon et al. (1998), "psychopathy was the first personality disorder recognized by psychiatry. The concept has a long historical and practitioner tradition, and in the last decade a growing body of research has supported its validity" (p. 28).

As a psychological construct, psychopathy has developed into an empirically measurable syndrome (Hare, 1991) and has become increasingly significant within the field of criminal justice. For example, empirical evidence exploring the correlation between psychopathy and crime has been consistently demonstrated by studies examining both juvenile delinquent (e.g., Forth & Mailloux, 2000; Frick, Barry, & Bodin, 2000; O'Neill, Lidz, & Heilbrun, 2003) and adult offender (e.g., Heilbrun et al., 1998; Poythress, Edens, & Lilienfeld, 1998) populations. The significance of psychopathy as a predictor for recidivism in general, and for violence in particular, also is well established (e.g., Dolan & Doyle, 2000; Hart & Hare, 1998; Salekin, Rogers, & Sewell, 1996; Serin, 1991; Hemphill, Hare, & Wong, 1998; Yarvis, 1995). Such empirically sound and convincing evidence supports the assertion that "psychopaths are difficult to ignore [and] are involved in many of today's most serious problems" (Gacono, 2000a, p. xix).

Cleckley is credited with developing the modern clinical construct of psychopathy in his work *The Mask of Sanity* (1941). As summarized by Hart and Hare (1998), Cleckley's conceptualization of the psychopath was descriptive: "Interpersonally, psychopaths are grandiose, arrogant, callous, superficial, and manipulative; affectively, they are short-tempered, unable to form strong emotional bonds with others, and lacking in empathy, guilt, or remorse; and behaviorally, they are irresponsible, impulsive, and prone to violate social and legal norms and expectations" (p. 25).

In responding to criticism that existing diagnostic criteria neglected persistent personality traits, Hare (1980) developed the Psychopathy Checklist (PCL), followed by revised versions in 1991 and 2003 to operationalize the concept of psychopathy, largely based on Cleckley's original model (Arrigo & Shipley, 2001; Shipley & Arrigo, 2004). To ensure accurate diagnosis, the PCL-R requires expert observer (i.e., clinical) ratings based on a semi-structured interview, a review of case history material (e.g., interviews with family members and employers, criminal and psychiatric records), and supplemental behavioral observations (Hare, 2001). Specific scoring criteria are used to rate each of 20 items according to the extent to which they apply to a given individual. Today, the PCL-R stands as the only instrument with demonstrated reliability and validity used to operationalize psychopathy in adults (Bodholt, Richards, & Gacono, 2000; Hare, 1991, 1996, 1998; Kosson, Smith, & Newman, 1990; Salekin, Rogers, & Sewell, 1997; Schroeder, Schroeder, & Hare, 1983; Siegel, 1998).

The clinical assessment of psychopathy is achieved through an examination of several trait and behavioral criteria. Among the 20 behaviors and traits assessed by the PCL-R are a grandiose sense of self-worth, glib and superficial charm, pathological lying, manipulativeness, lack of remorse or guilt, need for stimulation, impulsivity, promiscuous sexual behavior, early behavior problems, callousness, lack of empathy, and criminal versatility (Hare, 2003). Utilizing these defining criteria, the PCL-R enables an evaluation of psychopathy from a 2-factor perspective. Described by Meloy (1992) as aggressive narcissism, Factor 1 constitutes those items on the PCL-R that indicate egocentricity and a callous and remorseless disregard for the rights or feelings of others (Hare, 2003). Factor 2, described in terms of a chronically unstable and antisocial lifestyle, is characterized by an irresponsible, impulsive, thrill-seeking, and antisocial lifestyle (Hare, 2003). Clearly, when recalling the phenomenon of erotophonophilia and the integrated typology used to explain it, several of these PCL-R personality and behavioral items were prominently featured in the specific lust murder case of Jeffrey Dahmer.

Research indicates that even in childhood, psychopaths are impulsive, aggressive, and emotionally isolated, and that their craving for excitement is curtailed neither by social norms nor by conscience (Bender, 1947; Cleckley, 1941; Hare & Cox, 1978; Klinteberg, Humble, & Schalling, 1992). Meloy (1992) and Stone (1998) suggest that a significant factor involved in the psychopath's predisposition to aggressive behavior is the lack of attachment or affective bonding with others. The unique combination of antisocial traits and impulsive/aggressive behavior is the foundation for assertions that psychopaths are ideal candidates for perpetrating predatory violence (Meloy, 1992). In sum, the psychopath's empathy deficit, egocentricity, grandiosity, sense of entitlement, impulsivity, general lack of behavioral inhibitions, and need for power and control produce a proclivity for asocial, antisocial, and criminal acts (Hare, 1998).

Meloy (1992) suggests that psychopaths are inclined toward criminal and predatory violence for several reasons. First, the inability to empathize with victims allows the individuals harmed to be devalued. Second, the aggressive tendencies of the psychopath combined with the individual's detachment from the experience of others are predictors of cruel interpersonal exchanges. Third, the psychopath's ability to detach from others increases the likelihood that victims will be treated much like an object in a private ritual. As a result, the reactions of psychopaths to the damage they have inflicted upon individuals or society in general "are more likely to be cool indifference, a sense of power, pleasure, or smug satisfaction than regret or concern for what they have done" (Hare, 2001, p. 11).

The development of psychopathy is explained by a wide variety of cognitive, psychodynamic, behavioral, and biological models (Comer, 1995). For example, childhood abuse, neglect, and the witnessing of violence are factors identified by many researchers as central to the development of violent, antisocial behavior, including traits associated with psychopathy (Widom, 1997). Likewise, the American Psychiatric Association's Diagnostic and Statistical Manual of Mental Disorders IV-TR (2000) suggests that child abuse or neglect can increase the likelihood that conduct disorder during adolescence may develop into psychopathy during adulthood (Shipley & Arrigo, 2004). Psychodynamic theorists assert that psychopathy is caused by a failure of the "superego," that is, the part of the psyche that constitutes the "moral precepts of our minds as well as our ideal aspirations" (Brenner, 1973, p. 35; Comer, 1995). According to this perspective, the individual does not develop an adequate conscience, resulting in poor behavioral controls that can have deleterious consequences later in life (Widom, 1997). Behavioral theorists contend that adaptively effective coping styles within abusive homes (e.g., desensitizing oneself against feelings, exhibiting manipulative behavior in order to get what is needed) leave the individual ill equipped for prosocial adult relationships and activities. Other studies suggest that biological factors are associated with the development of psychopathy. For example, the autonomic and central nervous systems of persons with psychopathy have been found to respond more slowly than those without the disorder (Comer, 1995; Raine, 1998).

Notwithstanding their apparent differences, explanations for the development of psychopathy are not mutually exclusive (Shipley & Arrigo, 2004). Lykken's (1995) findings support the notion that these individuals experience less anxiety than others and are therefore less likely to learn socially acceptable behaviors that, in others, develop from a desire to avoid the anxiety created by others' disapproval. Some researchers suggest that psychopaths cannot learn from feelings of anxiety or empathy because they do not experience these sentiments (Comer, 1995). Importantly, there is a wide range of individual and behavioral differences among psychopathic subjects, and many clinicians and researchers agree that contemporary measures of the disorder identify a heterogeneous cohort (e.g., see Blackburn, 1998; Gacono, 1998; Gunn, 1998; Steuerwald & Kosson, 2000).

In general, the variety of individual and societal contexts in which psychopathy exists is virtually unlimited (e.g., see Hare, 1998, p. 196). Despite the challenges presented in identifying psychopathy among a heterogeneous population, understanding the value of accurately assessing it is crucial within institutions, hospitals, and correctional facilities (Gacono, 2000). In the context of lust murder, this is particularly important, given the severity and serial nature of the crimes committed. However, accurate assessments are problematic for two fundamental reasons.

First, there exists some confusion regarding diagnoses for psychopathy and other closely related psychological constructs. For example, antisocial personality disorder (ASPD) and sociopathy are erroneously used as synonyms for psychopathy, notwithstanding the wealth of published literature that differentiates psychopathy as a qualitatively and quantitatively unique construct from these other disorders (Arrigo & Shipley, 2001). While an examination of the distinction between psychopathy and other diagnoses (i.e., ASPD) is well beyond the scope of this section, the differences are important and other scholars have discussed them at considerable length (e.g., see Gacono et al., 2000; Millon et al., 1998). For purposes of this section, the term "psychopathy" is used only when appropriate, mindful of its distinctive character from other psychiatric conditions or constructs.

A second factor that makes the diagnosis of psychopathy difficult is the behavior of the individual. The deceptive nature of psychopathic subjects often complicates diagnoses and requires the use of pertinent independent historical information for thorough assessment (Meloy & Gacono, 2000). Because a goal of the psychopathic patient is usually to gain a more dominant position in relation to his (or her) environment, whether a person, an institution, or a legal proceeding (Meloy, 1992), the forensic psychologist is vulnerable to gross manipulation in a treatment setting. In light of the aforementioned challenges to accurate assessments, the use of trained clinicians and formal diagnostic protocols are prerequisites for any application of the PCL-R or its variants. Importantly, PCL-R evaluation findings should be integrated with other personality and risk assessment data (Gacono, 2000).

A strong association between psychopathic diagnoses and violence in males has been demonstrated by a number of researchers. Findings observed by Hare (1993) suggest that while psychopaths constitute approximately 1% of the general population, they are responsible for more than 50% of all serious crimes committed. However, many psychopaths operate on the fringes of legality, successfully avoiding contact with the criminal justice apparatus while manipulating the system and other people to achieve their own needs (Cleckley, 1982; Meloy, 1992). Therefore, as a matter of convenience and practicality, considerable research on the relationship between psychopathy and violence involves an examination of offender populations in correctional custody and their respective recidivism rates following release.

To illustrate, in their meta-analytic review of 18 empirical studies investigating the relationship between the PCL-R and violent and nonviolent recidivism among prison releasees, Salekin, Rogers, and Sewell (1996) concluded that the ability of the PCL-R to predict violence was unparalleled in the literature on the assessment of dangerousness. Harris, Rice, and Quinsey (1993) found that the PCL-R was the single most important predictor of violent recidivism among 618 offenders released from a maximum-security unit and pretrial assessment center. Other studies present similarly supportive findings for the predictive and explanatory capabilities of the PCL-R in relation to violent and recidivistic outcomes (e.g., Harris, Rice, & Cormier, 1991; Harris, Rice, & Lalumiere, 2001; Hart, Kropp, & Hare, 1988; Hemphill, Hare, & Wong, 1998; Rice, 1997; Serin, Peters, & Barbaree, 1990).

To be clear, studies of psychopathic individuals have not been limited to correctional populations. Psychopathy research has expanded to include industrial and organizational (I-O) psychology (Babiak, 1995, 2000; Gustafson & Ritzer, 1995), the study of the behavior and interaction of people within work settings. As Babiak (2000) noted, non-institutionalized psychopaths are known for their ability to elude detection, therefore representing a more difficult population to investigate. Babiak (2000) reported the summary findings of six longitudinal I-O studies conducted within six corporate organizations. Using the PCL-R as an assessment instrument, several individuals scored above the cutoff for psychopathy. Interestingly, those identified as psychopathic scored high on Factor 1 (the aggressive narcissism component) and moderate on Factor 2 (the antisocial personality component) (Babiak, 2000). When interpreting these findings, Babiak (p. 180) observed that "they displayed the personality traits ascribed to psychopaths without exhibiting antisocial acts or a lifestyle typical of criminal psychopaths [that] would have attracted the formal attention of society." One of the psychopath's distinct "career phases" noted in the I-O psychology literature is the manipulation phase, in which the psychopath enjoys playing the role of "puppet master" (Babiak, 2000). This individual creates a false image of himself as an ideal employee based on his own sense of loyalty and competence, and constantly seeks recognition from power holders and support and adulation from others (Babiak, 2000).

Although decidedly beyond the parameters of the present investigation, the relationship among psychopathy, crime, and lust murder is worth noting. A more systematic exploration on this matter could prove salient, especially with respect to either specifying or clarifying the operation of several personality and behavioral dynamics informing the proposed integrated typology. This could be particularly useful given that an individual's reliance on aberrant sexuality, whether through ongoing fantasy or ritualistic behavior, involves the appropriation of traits and actions consistent with what we know about psychopathy. For example, the erotophonophiliac's penchant for impulsivity, disdain toward others, lack of attachments, use of manipulation, reliance on violence, and desire for control, power, and domination are all prominent personality and behavioral criteria specified by the PCL-R. Moreover, in terms of the case of Jeffrey Dahmer, these factors manifested themselves repeatedly (see Chapter 5 for more detail). However, what is not clear is precisely how these characteristics fit within the psychopathic profile as delineated by those who study this phenomenon or employ the Psychopathy Checklist-Revised.

It may very well be that the onset, progression, and maintenance of paraphilia are best explained through the synthetic framework. Then, too, it may be that the emergence of the lust murderer is best personified in the model's systematic assessment of the paraphilia-erotophonophilia relationship. However, what psycho-diagnostically accounts for both could be the entrenched (and underlying) psychopathic inclinations of the sexual offender. Clearly, these matters warrant more detailed attention. We submit that future investigators of psychopathy, crime, and lust murder would do well to carefully examine and thoughtfully consider them.

## THE INTEGRATIVE TYPOLOGY: SPECULATIVE AND PROVISIONAL IMPLICATIONS

In this section, several very conditional implications stemming from the conceptually animated commentary on paraphilia and lust murder are delineated. These remarks draw attention to the integrative model's capacity to move sensibly beyond mere theoretical conjecture and model building to the realm of everyday practice. Along these lines, three distinct, though related, domains of practical inquiry are briefly considered: police administration and management, criminal and clinical psychology, and law and public policy.

### LAW ENFORCEMENT ADMINISTRATION AND MANAGEMENT

The nature of the paraphilic process, as a dynamic system of behaviors, is both unique and complex. However, the typology we propose draws specific attention to its key components (e.g., formative development, low self-esteem, stressors, fantasy, facilitators). Understanding these components and the manner in which they manifest themselves will enable police personnel to profile offenders with greater precision, erudition, and alacrity. We submit that this degree of familiarity with the phenomenon of lust murder will significantly contribute to the future effectiveness of crime scene analysis in the field.

Hickey (1997) contends that the "strength of [criminal] profiling will come as a result of interagency and interdisciplinary cooperation" (p. 257). Law enforcement officials—working in concert with forensic psychologists, criminologists, and others well versed in the thought patterns, personality predispositions, and behavioral manifestations of the paraphilic offender—will make tracking and detection of lust murderers easier and more exacting. From our perspective, the integrative conceptual model provides a useful blueprint, identifying many of these intricate and underlying characteristics.

Finally, training in the police academy and in the field is essential for the future administration of justice in the area of policing sex crimes (Douglas et al., 1995; Holmes & Holmes, 2002a). It is imperative that officers be exposed to the psychological dynamics of persons who commit sadistic sexual offenses, including erotophonophilia. As such, law enforcement personnel need practical training regarding the processes by which they can positively and accurately identify sexual homicides involving an underlying paraphilic motive.

To illustrate, police officers need instruction in how to correlate certain paraphilias (e.g., piquerism, flagellationism) with particular sexual offenses (e.g., lust murder). They need to learn about the likely personality predispositions, the fantasy systems, the cognitive distortions, and the behavioral characteristics employed by persons who commit these acts of repetitive homicide. In short, law enforcement personnel, whether entering the academy or working the streets, need to be acquainted with the kind of sex offender they might confront in the course of their field duties. An important feature of this training is information that is timely, accessible, and useful. We maintain that the integrated paraphilic typology considerably advances the research on this most troubling of phenomena in ways not previously suggested. Moreover, the elements of the model are clearly portable and easily transferable to a training environment or to a classroom setting. Accordingly, we submit that, in conjunction with what we already know about sexual homicide and serial killers, the synthetic model offers considerable utility for those engaged in both the order-maintenance and the protect-and-serve functions.

A valuable resource for facilitating the flow of information across geographic areas or jurisdictional boundaries is the National Center for the Analysis of Violent Crime (NCAVC). This organization serves as a clearinghouse and resource for law enforcement agencies involved in "unusual, bizarre, or particularly vicious or repetitive violent crimes" (Brooks, Devenie, Green, Hart, & Moore, 1987, p. 41; see also Douglas et al., 1992; Palermo & Kocsis, 2005). Given the nature of this organization and the likely implications of the integrated model for ongoing law enforcement work, specifying the various divisions of this multipurpose governmental unit is warranted.

The National Center for the Analysis of Violent Crime was established in 1984. It is a law enforcement–oriented behavioral science and computerized resource center that consolidates research, training, and operational support functions

(Brooks et al., 1987). NCAVC consists of four programs: Research and Development; Training; Profiling and Consultation; and Violent Criminal Apprehension (VICAP). Each of these programs is summarily described below.

The research and development (R&D) division focuses on violent crime and criminals. Its subjects include murderers, rapists, and child molesters; the victims of such assailants; and various crime scenes in which these offenses occur. The law enforcement perspective is highly valued in these inquiries, especially since policing is central to the investigations. The aim of the R&D unit is to gain insight relative to the offender's personality characteristics and behavioral motivations, as well as to examine how such offenders successfully evade identification, apprehension, prosecution, and incarceration. Additionally, the R&D division conducts ongoing qualitative research regarding various types of violent offenders. This research provides additional information, including programmatic recommendations, that impacts law enforcement investigative techniques and other "best practice" solutions in policing.

The training component of NCAVC provides ongoing education and guidance to the criminal justice community. Federal, state, and local agencies, as well as other selected professions within the broader behavioral science field, benefit from continual instruction it offers. In part, the training helps orient its various constituencies to NCAVC's array of resources. In addition, the training division makes available crime prevention and citizen awareness information, benefiting justice agencies and ancillary organizations.

The profiling and consultation program of NCAVC offers criminal profiling and conferring services to various criminal justice groups or departments. These NCAVC employees are experienced behavioral science consultants working in the field of criminal investigation and profiling. As experts, they conduct detailed analyses of violent crimes on a case-by-case basis. Their goal is to establish useful offender portraits or profiles that can aid law enforcement agencies and other branches of local, state, and federal government invested in the tracking and apprehension of unknown (and violent) assailants. The criminal portrait facilitates the investigation by narrowing the focus to the *most likely* suspect. Conferring services are only available in the event of serial and exceptional cases. The specific services offered by this unit include tactical planning, case strategies, information disclosures (e.g., search warrant updates), personality assessments, interviewing techniques, and prosecutorial coaching (e.g., how to interview and/or cross-examine violent criminals).

The Violent Crime Apprehension Program (VICAP) functions as a nationwide clearinghouse designed to collect, collate, and analyze specific crimes that are violent in nature (Howlett, Hanfland, & Ressler, 1986). VICAP reviews reports submitted by law enforcement agencies that meet the following criteria: (a) solved or unsolved homicides or attempted murders—of specific interest are abductions, random or motiveless offenses, sexually oriented crimes, or those offenses known or suspected to be serial in nature; (b) missing persons, in which the evidence indicates the presence of foul play and where the person in question has yet to be located; and (c) unidentified dead bodies, in which the cause of death is known or suspected to be homicide.

The main objective of VICAP is to recognize similar patterns across individual cases of violent criminality that are submitted to the division by various law enforcement agencies nationwide. When a law enforcement unit consults with VICAP, the division endeavors to provide that agency with the information necessary to initiate a coordinated multi-agency investigation. This inquiry, undertaken and coordinated by VICAP, is designed to facilitate the identification, tracking, and apprehension of the perpetrator. The identification of patterned likenesses (i.e., similarities) entails the analysis of modus operandi as well as the assessment of such crime scene factors as victim selection, physical evidence, suspect description, and suspect behavior exhibited before, during, or after the crime's occurrence.

The integrated paraphilic paradigm has considerable utility with respect to each of the four programs that constitute the National Center for the Analysis of Violent Crime. Given the types of assistance NCAVC provides, reliance on the synthetic model will assist law enforcement authorities in the appropriate collection, classification, and distribution of investigatory information pertinent to the apprehension of sadistic sexual killers. Here, too, multi-agency partnerships, trans-state task forces, inter-jurisdictional agreements, and cross-disciplinary collaborations can expedite and consolidate the acquisition of data necessary to capture an offender. Whether in the context of research and development, training and education, profiling and consultation, or data assessment and analysis, the integrated framework on paraphilia enables NCAVC and law enforcement personnel to more comprehensively address the crime of lust murder and those responsible for its serial commission.

## CRIMINAL AND CLINICAL PSYCHOLOGY

Until relatively recently, the treatment of the paraphilic individual has been a mostly neglected area in psychiatric medicine (Kafka, 2003; Protter & Travin, 1987; Schlesinger, 2003). The competent treatment of sexually aberrant conduct involves a specific focus requiring extensive training (Abel & Osborne, 1992, p. 302; see also Hickey, 2005). Consequently, it is vital that forensic clinicians possess the requisite skills to discern and recognize paraphilic behavior; to comprehend the scientific literature regarding its onset, progression, and maintenance; and to evaluate the effectiveness and appropriateness of specific treatment strategies.

The paraphilic process, as a system of cyclical and self-generating conduct, is rooted in the formative years of pre-adolescent development. Thus, practicing forensic clinicians must recognize the etiology and sequencing of this disorder in specific instances. The synthetic typology suggests a process constituted by several notable markers (e.g., low self-esteem, fantasy, facilitators). One facet of clinical treatment is prevention. The key to prevention is identifying risk factors that produce the erotophonophiliac or lust murderer (Hickey, 2005; Holmes & Holmes, 2002b; Money, 1990; Schlesinger, 2003).

As previously suggested, lust murder is composed of several interdependent paraphilias. Their interactive and combinatory effects result in erotically animated fantasies, including aggressive, violent, and sadomasochistic imagery (Arrigo & Purcell, 2001). Preventive treatment begins with skillful assessment and diagnostic work that competently screens for paraphilic indicators in particular cases. To date, no diagnostic instruments exist that accomplish this objective. The extant research also demonstrates that no unifying theory has emerged regarding the onset of paraphilia. As such, no single therapeutic approach has proven itself to be successful in the treatment of paraphiliac individuals. However, the integrative model is suggestive for the future development of appropriate evaluation tools, given the seamless manner in which it conceptually consolidates the relevant sexual homicide and serial murder typologies.

Notwithstanding Liebert's (1985) cautionary comments, the paraphilic cycle specifies key access points that mobilize and sustain the process. If intervention breakthroughs are to be realized, carefully derailing an offender's investment in this dysfunctional cycle of thought, fantasy, and behavior is both necessary and prudent. For example, forensic mental health experts must examine more closely the manner in which paraphilic stimuli and impulses are linked to drugs, pornography, and/or alcohol for particular individuals. Treating clinicians must assess more systematically why increasingly violent images compel some but not others to enact their sadistic fantasies through sexual murder. These and other similar treatment questions are largely unexamined in the relevant literature; however, the nature of the proposed synthetic typology intimates that more sustained clinical analysis along these lines is sorely needed.

Moreover, the skilled clinician must gather detailed information that will assist in the overall assessment and treatment process. Such factors as the age of onset for paraphilia, the gender of the assailant's victims, the frequency of the paraphiliac individual's misconduct, the level of aggression during the commission of a criminal act, and the number and type of erotic fantasies that involve sexually aberrant behavior are crucial components impacting proper assessment, diagnosis, and treatment (Abel & Osborne, 1992, p. 303). Collecting and analyzing these types of data, although somewhat idiosyncratic, will yield a rich source of information from which to explore available treatment options, thereby increasing prospects for effective (and timely) clinical intervention.

Finally, determining the conditions under which a person is unlikely to re-offend and is unlikely to pose a risk to society is largely a clinical judgment. Threat assessment instruments that specifically take into account erotophonophilia are non-existent. Risk assessment in this field represents a unique challenge for forensic mental health clinicians. The integrative paraphilic typology indicates that triggering mechanisms or stressors linked to latent childhood trauma can ignite the mutually interdependent process of sadistic and erotic fantasy construction, facilitators, and orgasmic conditioning. Indeed, the integrative schema intimates that these stressors are trauma reinforcers (Hickey, 2001) that feed the paraphilic process. Thus, precisely determining an individual's proclivity for future violent sexual acts may very well hinge on accurately assessing the offender's present coping skills. The better the mental health specialist is at evaluating how the individual manages rejection, humiliation, disappointment, or ostracism, for example, the more definitive the clinician's threat assessment determination will likely be.

Research in the area of risk or threat assessment points out that the type of sexual offense committed is related to the probability of recidivism, and that those offenders with multiple paraphilias are at an increased risk of re-offending (McGrath, 1991, p. 334; see also Hickey, 2005). Investigators have identified various factors that can help determine the likelihood of sexual re-offending. These factors include a prior criminal record, sexual arousal patterns, impulsivity, alcohol abuse, use of force, lack of social supports, and traumatizing environmental events (e.g., Arrigo, 2006; Douglas et al., 1995; McGrath, 1991; Palermo & Farkas, 2001).

Several of the risk factors mentioned above are indicative of paraphilic offending, as illustrated within the integrative typology. These particular factors or components include multiple paraphilias, use of force, alcohol abuse, and lack of social supports. These risk factors are succinctly described below and then subsequently linked to the need for more risk assessment initiatives undertaken by criminal and clinical psychologists.

The presence of multiple forms of sexual deviance, when coupled with increasingly violent fantasies, is a determining factor for re-offending in the synthetic schema. When looking at the use of force, research indicates that those assailants who rely on force when committing their crimes recidivate at a higher rate than those who do not (Hickey, 2005). This is especially the case for those attackers whose sexual arousal is fused with aggression and/or sadism (Groth & Birnbaum, 1979; Hazelwood, Reboussin, & Warren, 1989; Simon, 1996; Schlesinger, 2003).

Moreover, the paraphilic process as specified within the integrated typology recognizes how certain facilitating behaviors (e.g., use of alcohol, drugs, and pornography) have an influencing effect that sustains and contributes to the manifestation of sadistic sexual offending. Investigators note that sexual aggression and alcohol are closely associated (McGrath, 1991). Alcohol has an inhibitory impact relative to social controls while at the same time increasing sexual arousal. Mindful of this relationship, "there is no suggestion that alcohol causes sexual aggression; rather, [the suggestion is that] alcohol . . . facilitate[s] a preexisting inclination to sexual aggression" (Crowe & George, 1989, p. 384).

Lastly, the social support factor identified within the research indicates that offenders who do not have a stable, supportive social network, either by choice or circumstance, are at a higher risk for re-offense than their counterparts with strong, healthy, and supportive ties (Hickey, 2001; McGrath, 1991). Paraphiliac individuals are typically regarded as loners and isolates, lacking the ability to engage in meaningful, prosocial relationships. As described in the synthetic framework, this is principally due to some form of trauma sustained within the formative years of development. The traumatic event, when linked to the absence of positive parental attachment, fosters feelings of inadequacy. This inclines the individual to retreat into fantasy and daydreaming. These avenues of escape eventually become substitutes for the human relationships the person cannot fashion.

Precisely determining an individual's tendency toward future violent sexual deviance may very well hinge on the accurate assessment of discrete risk factors such as those identified above, as well as others not directly addressed within the scope of this volume. To be clear, however, the integrative typology suggests that several of these risk factors (e.g., the offender's present social support network, past sexual offense history, use of force and violence, type and number of paraphilias, compulsion to rely on drugs and alcohol) are all indicative of sexually deviant offenders, specifically lust murderers. Consequently, criminal and clinical psychologists would do well to pursue the development of risk assessment instruments and/or strategies along these underdeveloped, though certainly worthwhile, investigatory lines.

## LAW AND PUBLIC POLICY

It is difficult to say with any degree of precision whether the psychological treatment of sex offenders in general can curb their behavior (e.g., Brown, 2005; Geffner, Crumpton Franey, Geffner, & Falconer, 2004; Prendergast, 2003). The notion of clinical treatment is particularly problematic in the instance of paraphilia and, more specifically, erotophonophilia (Hickey, 2005). Complicating these matters are a number of very serious questions stemming from the public's outrage over a rehabilitative intervention model for these offenders (Egger, 2002; Holmes & Holmes, 2002b). Concerns for tax dollars poorly spent, the efficacy of treatment, and the protection of the offender's constitutional rights over the safety and welfare of society reflect the public's sentiments (e.g., Arrigo, 2006; Janus, 2000; Pratt, 2000; Simon, 2000; Zevitz & Farkus, 2000).

Perhaps most disturbing (and frustrating) is the absence of agreement regarding what fundamentally works, especially with respect to re-offense (Doren, 2002). Commenting on this dilemma, Palermo and Farkas (2001, p. 150) noted the following:

> Overall, there is critical debate and little consistency in the conclusions drawn from the research on sex offender treatment and recidivism. Existing studies of the effectiveness of treatment produce mixed results with a wide variety of recidivism rates found in the literature. Although some studies claim a decrease in recidivism rates for sex crimes and non-sex crimes, many studies indicate substantial recidivism rates for sex crimes and non-sex crimes. . . .

Given the lack of consensus on how best to clinically address the behavioral problems posed by these most violent of offenders, it comes as no surprise that the treatment status of and the planning recommendations regarding the lust murderer are extraordinarily problematic (Hickey, 2005). This is particularly the case when civil commitment statutes and community notification practices are employed following a sex offender's release from prison. Although these outcomes are far from likely in the instance of erotophonophiliacs, especially since the gravity of the offense and the repetitive nature of the criminal conduct mitigate this possibility, both of these options raise troubling questions about the appropriate role of law and public policy in the process. Mindful of the integrated typology on paraphilia, some cursory observations concerning the framework's capacity to assist legislatures, courts, and, consequently, treatment facilities (e.g., penal, psychiatric) are tentatively enumerated below.

The present legislative trend is to marginalize the status of sex offenders and, in the process, to regard them as less than fully human. While this strategy may make for good politics, it is a far cry from establishing sound policy (e.g., Walker, 2006). Framing the debate much like a "war" in which innocent victims are subject to devastating assault by evil, predatory, and callous offenders does nothing but inflame emotions at the expense of promoting reasoned judgment. The synthetic typology provides a useful blueprint of sorts for accessing the world of the lust murderer. This blueprint, although far from complete, could be a basis by which politicians undertook the task of meaningfully and thoughtfully balancing (perhaps even coalescing) the need for public safety with the offender's need for therapeutic treatment. These concerns are not mutually exclusive, and the theoretical model on paraphilia substantially helps to clarify much of the confusion surrounding the phenomena of sexual, serial, and lust homicide.

Coupled with legislative reform and the context in which it could occur is the legal status of sex offenders in the wake of *Kansas v. Hendricks* (1997). In this case, the United States Supreme Court ruled that a sex offender could be "confined indefinitely without treatment in the interests of public safety" (Palermo & Farkas, 2001, p. 151). Courts rely on scientific knowledge derived from sound behavioral and social scientific inquiry to interpret the law. The proposed integrative framework on paraphilia specifies an interpretive model that could be subjected to theory testing. Arguably, if prudently initiated, the ethical and moral dilemma implied in the *Hendrick* decision (i.e., should the mental health system be used to warehouse rather than treat patients if such confinement serves the public good?), could be obviated altogether. Moreover, the reactionary and punitive posture of the legislature could be sensibly curtailed if relevant data were made available that furthered society's understanding of the sexual homicide offender and the nature of his repetitive crimes. In order to realize these worthwhile ends, it is necessary to engage in relevant theory construction and model building. The proposed explanatory model enables legislators to more completely comprehend the dynamic features of erotophonophilia. Indeed, this may very well be the first step to developing correctional and treatment policy that is as efficacious as it is effective.

As previously discussed, the prognosis for treatment is not good. Moreover, public support for rehabilitation (generally) is declining. However, understanding the paraphilic process and system of behavior could reveal more of the psychological complexities of these killers than previously recognized. Mindful of the core elements of the integrated conceptual schema, these features might be significant for ongoing correctional and psychiatric programming.

For example, the framework could facilitate better threat assessment and general management practices within institutional settings. Familiarity with the operation of the paraphilic process (e.g., the role of early childhood traumatizations, self-esteem, fantasy, facilitators, triggering mechanisms, orgasmic conditioning) in specific cases might help to prevent additional violence while the offender remained confined (Adson, 1992). This degree of working knowledge regarding the theoretical facets of the framework would likely serve the interests of prison and hospital staff and administrators, as well as those confined. This is especially important since psychopathic sex offenders do not appear amenable to treatment (Craissati, 2004; Laws, Hudson, & Ward, 2000; Spencer, 1999), and the connections between this type of assailant and the lust murder are readily apparent (for example, see the section on psychopathy described earlier in this chapter).

Finally, societal attempts to counteract the problems posed by violent sexual offenders recently have intensified (Pratt, 2000), consistent with existing efforts at penal punitiveness (Garland, 2002). Civil commitment statutes and community notification and registration practices following incarceration aptly illustrate this point. In the instance of a serial lust killer, release from custody is most assuredly not likely, unless the person is found not guilty by reason of insanity. Under that circumstance, the person would receive psychiatric treatment at a mental health facility until such time as the symptoms giving rise to the murderous conduct are held in check or otherwise neutralized (see, e.g., Arrigo, 2002; Steadman et al., 1993). If intervention and treatment are effective, custodial release and community re-entry follow (Buchanan, 2002; Fisher, 2002; Hodgins & Janson, 2002; Landsberg, Rock, Berg, & Smiley, 2002). However, for our purposes, the question remains whether the integrated model can assist lawmakers, as well as correctional and mental health hospital administrators, especially as they assess the culture of control that informs present-day policy.

The synthetic schema provides a sensible way to account for the role of paraphilia in the commission of serial sexual homicides. It demonstrates how aberrant sexuality that both intensifies and increases over time functions as an underlying motive in the crime of lust murder. Thus, the model enables the penal and psychiatric systems to reconsider whether the varied practices of containment and the stigma that attaches to it are the best defenses against the potential harms perpetrated by erotophonophiliacs. In other words, the integrated typology contributes to the policy debate on whether existing laws concerning sex offenders are merely punitive, rather than therapeutic, adversely affecting prospects for treatment and, in the end, woefully failing to promote the safety and welfare of the public.

## GENERALIZING FROM THE INTEGRATIVE TYPOLOGY

Generalizing from the integrative typology is not an easy or straightforward exercise. The most troubling reason for this is the reliance on a data set of one (i.e., Jeffrey Dahmer). The Dahmer case study, while certainly provocative and replete with elements that amplify the utility of the paraphilic framework, does not, in and of itself, fundamentally legitimize the theoretical model. At best, the application of the model to the case draws attention to potentially worthwhile areas of explanation regarding the psychology of lust murder that warrant more detailed assessment and more systematic testing. Thus, with these thoughts in mind, the analysis entertained throughout this volume must be considered suggestive and exploratory.

This notwithstanding, the presentation of Dahmer's life story and the application of the integrated typology to his personal narrative demonstrate several linkages between paraphilia and lust murder not previously identified in the extant literature on sexual homicide and serial murder. And, to be clear, this is the purpose of an instrumental case study inquiry (see Chapter 5 for more on the project's method, including strengths and limits of the approach). In this respect, the case makes possible certain generalizations to which the case itself is bound. These generalizations were developed in Chapter 7, and featured an assessment of similarities, dissimilarities, and unique facets pertinent to the three theoretical schemas reviewed. The work that entails the application of the integrated model to several other noted serial sexual offenders whose personality structures and ritualistic behaviors could benefit from the sort of scrutiny undertaken in this volume.

So, who are these assailants, how would these inquiries unfold, and what lessons could be gleaned from these sorts of analyses? In recent years, examples of such offenders include John Wayne Gacy, Theodore Robert Bundy, Henry Lee Lucas, and the BTK killer, Dennis Rader. This is not an exhaustive cataloging. However, in each instance, the question is: What explanatory (and predictive) properties does the synthetic paraphilic framework embody that are not specified in the motivational and trauma control typologies? In other words, the capacity to generalize from the synthetic schema necessitates that the model demonstrates how it would adequately (if not comprehensively) account for the onset, progression, and maintenance of paraphilia among other sexual offenders whose conduct, when fully disclosed, rose to the level of repetitive murder. Moreover, the context in which aberrant sexuality functioned as an underlying motive in the serial commission of the assailants' respective killing sprees would need to be thoughtfully accounted for as well.

To date, what we do know about each of these offenders is quite chilling. Gacy was responsible for the deaths of 33 boys and young men (Sullivan & Maiken, 1983). Bundy was considered the culprit in the slayings of 17 women (Winn & Merrill, 1980). Law enforcement authorities linked Henry Lee Lucas to the homicides of no less than 100 individuals (Hickey, 2003; Newton, 2000). And Rader was convicted of the murders of 10 people. Although noted in varying degrees, early childhood traumatizations, flawed or attenuated parental attachments, reliance on fantasy and daydreaming, the use of facilitators, the presence of cognitive distortions, the susceptibility to deviant sexuality (e.g., fetishes, perversions), and the manifestation of increasing displays of erotic violence (both imagined and acted on) were dimensions of the patterned thoughts, impulses, and behaviors of these attackers.

In order to more fully grasp the potential significance of the proposed integrated typology and offer more global observations about the model's capacity to explain the phenomenon of lust murder, these and other similar cases must be systematically examined. Although this particular task is decidedly beyond the scope of the present section as it would entail the development of a more complete personality profile for each of the assailants mentioned above, the need for this undertaking as a basis to reasonably assess the generalizability of the proposed model is critical. Summarizing what we know about each assailant's personal history (i.e., social and familial), specifying the nature of their criminal actions, and outlining the sense of self-concept they exhibited would require careful and detailed attention. The data elicited from these case study investigations would then need to be situated within the three theoretical models addressed throughout this book. Pivotal to this enterprise would be an evaluation of the role of paraphilia as a systemic process of increasing violence that functioned as the motive underpinning the homicides each assailant committed. Undertaking this research task would most assuredly advance our overall understanding of the integrated paraphilic model, the framework's capacity to account for the phenomenon of lust murder, and those additional offenders who have engaged in its serial commission.

## SUMMARY AND CONCLUSIONS

This chapter spotlighted a number of implications that emerge from the proposed integrated typology and the psychology of lust murder, mindful of the theoretical nature of the overall project. In order to situate these implications within their appropriate context, several comments on the phenomenon of psychopathy were provided. As this analysis revealed, the relationship between this disorder and erotophonophilia are quite apparent, especially in terms of the personality and behavioral criteria as specified by the PCL-R. Indeed, the aggressive narcissism and antisocial lifestyle factors of this instrument, when reviewed in the instance of Jeffrey Dahmer, indicate that he exhibited traits consistent with the psychopathic (sexual) offender. As this section concluded, future researchers would do well to explore the connections between this psychiatric condition and the phenomenon of lust murder, given the elements that constitute the synthetic schema.

Additionally, this chapter described a number of implications stemming from the targeted analysis as developed throughout the volume. Although certainly provisional, these observations were designed to move beyond mere theoretical speculation to the realm of everyday practice. In particular, remarks linked to police administration and management, criminal and clinical psychology, and law and public policy were featured. In each instance, the contributions of the integrated model to the routine work of various professionals were showcased. In the field of policing, this included profiling, tracking, and apprehension efforts, as well as crime scene investigative training in the police academy and on the job. In the area of forensic mental health, this entailed future research, clinical treatment and prevention, evaluations and diagnostics, and risk/threat assessments. In the domain of social and public policy, this consisted of a legislative reframing of the issue, better efforts at balancing the public's concern for safety versus the offender's need for therapeutic (and efficacious) treatment, and the management of offenders in correctional facilities, psychiatric hospitals, and community environments.

Finally, this chapter revisited the psychology of lust murder and the integrated paraphilic framework, arguing that the model's generalizability was, in part, a function of how the instrumental case study method operates and what it endeavors to specify. More particularly, the capacity of the synthetic typology to demonstrate useful explanatory and predictive qualities was linked to its applicability in other high-profile and well documented cases of serial sexual homicide. Several examples of such individuals were identified, a number of suggestions for how these related investigations could unfold were delineated, and future inquiries based on these targeted assessments were encouraged.

This book examined the unique and complex phenomenon of paraphilia, especially as it relates to the crime of lust murder and those responsible for its serial commission. As described in Chapter 1, the literature on lust murder is somewhat sparse, and the phenomenon of erotophonophilia is typically classified with all sexual and serial homicides. However, as we explained at the outset of our investigation, lust murder is a distinct subcategory of both forms of killing. Indeed, as initially argued, underscoring the crime of erotophonophilia is a series of aberrant or deviant expressions of erotic behavior. These paraphilias, when actualized beyond mere fantasy, give rise to progressively violent conduct, functioning as underlying motive in the commission of these offenses. In order to better situate the proposed analysis, a brief review of sexual homicide and serial murder was supplied. At issue here was the need for a more comprehensive theoretical framework that adequately explained the presence of paraphilia, especially since it was mostly implied—rather than expressly accounted for—in the principal typologies on the subject.

In Chapter 2, the phenomena of paraphilia and lust murder were systematically reviewed. By way of strategically accessing these constructs, attention was first directed toward the relevant research on sexuality. This construct was placed on a continuum ranging from normal to abnormal to pathological. Additionally, the notion of aberrant sexuality was examined. This included the provision of a working definition as well as an assessment of the phenomenon's etiology. On this latter point, the role of fantasy, aggression, and sexuality were highlighted, noting especially how such experiences inform or otherwise contribute to violent paraphilic behaviors. The chapter concluded by specifying what we know about erotophonophilia, including FBI typologies for the lust murderer (i.e., organized nonsocial and disorganized asocial offenders), the profile of these killers, and the types of crimes these assailants commit.

Chapter 3 methodically canvassed the existing research on sexual homicide and serial murder. In particular, the motivational model developed by Burgess et al. (1986) and the trauma control typology constructed by Hickey (1997, 2000) were featured. Additionally, the classical conditioning framework proposed by MacCulloch (1983) and the sadistic murderer schema articulated by Brittain (1970) were incorporated into the overall analysis. Important cognitive, psychological, social, and biological facets underscore the operation of erotophonophilia. As such, specifying these elements, built around relevant models, was pivotal to our theoretical enterprise on paraphilia and lust murder. The chapter concluded by identifying the limits of the classical conditioning, motivational, and trauma control typologies. This exercise was undertaken precisely because it set the stage for the conceptualization of the integrated typology as developed in the subsequent chapter.

Chapter 4 thoroughly explored the integrative model, noting that it represented an assimilation of the pertinent factors contained in the sexual homicide, the serial murder, and the related ancillary typologies. Fundamental to this task was the realization that aberrant sexuality both informs the behavior of the lust murderer and functions as a motive. To position the ensuing commentary, pertinent research calling for the creation of a synthetic framework was summarized. This was followed by several observations on the elements of the paraphilic model itself. Next, the operation of the integrated typology was described, especially in relation to the offense of erotophonophilia. The chapter concluded by delineating the limits of the proposed synthetic schema. Along these lines, several observations linked to increasing the model's overall explanatory and predictive properties were identified.

Chapter 5 presented the case of Jeffrey Dahmer. Dahmer was convicted of the slayings of 17 young men; they were raped and mutilated both pre- and post-mortem. In order to access the case and the context in which it was subjected to review, several methodological concerns were specified. These matters principally related to the instrumental case study approach, including several remarks justifying the selection of the qualitative strategy as well as a number of observations regarding the data that was collected. Both historical and biographical information concerning Jeffrey Dahmer's life was delineated. This material was sequenced chronologically, beginning with Dahmer's early childhood development, moving through his aggressive and violent fantasies to his criminal encounters, and concluding with his paraphilic behaviors. In this respect, a workable and sensible profile for the lust murderer, Jeffrey Dahmer, was constructed.

Chapter 6 emphasized the testing of relevant models that were the source of examination throughout this volume. To accomplish this goal, the data described in Chapter 5 was linked to the Dahmer case. At issue was the extent to which the sexual homicide model, the trauma control typology, and the integrated framework comprehensively accounted for the onset, progression, sequencing, and maintenance of paraphilia, given the serial commission of Dahmer's killings. To address these matters, each organizational schema was applied to the Dahmer case separately. Although this created some overlap and redundancy in explanation, the respective frameworks captured important points not otherwise specified or completely explained in the other models.

Chapter 7 examined and discussed the findings. As an organizational strategy, thematic points of similarity and dissimilarity across the typologies were featured. Moreover, the distinctive facets of each framework were delineated. To address these matters, comments on the comparative approach were enumerated. This included some general remarks regarding the utility of employing a sociological criminology (i.e., social structure and process theories, containment/control criminology, attachment/bonding styles, self-concept and social identity) for guidance, as well as some global observations about the overall analytic and consolidation framework. Next, areas of convergence were specified, consisting of themes consistently found across the three typologies. This was followed by an assessment of points of divergence. The work undertaken here entailed the identification of different interpretations for shared themes located across the three theories. Finally, novel features or unique qualities intrinsic to a particular typology were specified. Mindful of the volume's general thesis on sexual deviance and lust murder, the paraphilic continuum or process, as a system of progressively intense and severe behavior, was identified as essential to the analysis of Jeffrey Dahmer's life narrative. This process includes aberrant sexual stimuli and fantasies, orgasmic conditioning, facilitators, stressors, and the manifestation of increasingly violent conduct stemming from aggressive imagery. In short, the paraphilic continuum, so integral to the operation of the integrated model, was acknowledged as the underlying motive that gave rise to Dahmer's criminally sadistic behavior. This conclusion was not borne out or otherwise accounted for when relying on either the motivational or trauma control typologies.

As the summary portion of this section explained, Chapter 8 reviewed the implications stemming from the overall analysis on the psychology of lust murder. Although certainly provisional and clearly speculative, a number of important comments linked to psychopathy and sexual offending (i.e., murder), police administration and management, criminal and clinical psychology, and law and public policy were described. Moreover, the capacity to generalize from the analysis of the Dahmer case, given the synthetic schema on paraphilia, was delineated. On this score, attention was directed toward the limits of the theoretical work undertaken throughout this book. The application of the integrated model to other instances of serial sexual homicide was highly recommended.

This book has addressed a mostly misunderstood and largely neglected psychological phenomenon. Building on the contributions of other social and behavioral scientists, refinement in theory development and model making were chiefly emphasized. Although far from complete, the direction suggested by this volume—especially in terms of future research, programming, and policy—cannot be ignored or dismissed. Indeed, if our capacity to understand the etiology of erotophonophilia is to expand in any appreciable way, then a sensible organizational framework that consolidates the existing theory-based work must first be undertaken. *The Psychology of Lust Murder* substantially fills this gap in the extant literature. As such, the text considerably moves the debate on aberrant sexuality, erotophonophilia, and those responsible for its serial commission that much farther in the realm of science and theory. The challenge ahead is to transform the insights generated from the integrated typology into discrete, testable hypotheses. If thoughtfully conceived and soundly executed, this timely endeavor could shed even greater light on the crime of murder, particularly when expressed sadistically, sexually, and serially. This is a challenge that homicide researchers would do well to seriously consider and steadfastly pursue.

# REFERENCES

Abel, G. G., Becker, J. V., Cunningham-Rather, J., Mittleman, M., & Rouleau, J. L. (1988). Multiple paraphilic diagnoses among sex offenders. *Bulletin of the American Academy of Psychiatry and the Law, 16,* 153–168.

Abel, G. G., & Osborne, C. (1992). The paraphilias: The extent and nature of sexually deviant criminal behavior. *Psychiatric Clinics of North America, 15,* 675–687.

Adson, P. R. (1992). Treatment of paraphilias and related disorders. *Psychiatric Annals, 22,* 299–300.

Ainsworth, M. D. S., Blehar, M. C., Waters, E., & Wall, S. (1978). *Patterns of attachment: A psychological study of the strange situation.* Hillsdale, NJ: Erlbaum.

American Psychiatric Association. (1994). *The diagnostic and statistical manual of mental disorders* (4th ed.). Washington, DC: Author.

American Psychiatric Association. (2000). *The diagnostic and statistical manual of mental disorders revised* (5th ed.). Washington, DC: Author.

Arrigo, B. A. (1999). *Social justice, criminal justice: The maturation of critical theory in law, crime, and deviance.* Belmont, CA: Wadsworth.

Arrigo, B. A. (2000). Social justice and critical criminology: On integrating knowledge. *Contemporary Justice Review, 3,* 7–37.

Arrigo, B. A. (2002). *Punishing the mentally ill: A critical analysis of law and psychiatry.* Albany, NY: State University of New York Press.

Arrigo, B. A. (Ed.). (2004). *Psychological jurisprudence: Critical explorations in law, crime, and society.* Albany, NY: SUNY Press.

Arrigo, B. A. (2005). Conclusion: Towards an interdisciplinary understanding of crime. In S. Guarino & J. Trevino (Eds.), *Understanding crime: A multidisciplinary approach* (pp. 41–60). Cincinnati, OH: LexisNexus-Anderson.

Arrigo, B. A. (2006). *Criminal behavior: A systems approach.* Upper Saddle River, NJ: Prentice Hall.

Arrigo, B. A., & Griffin, A. (2004). Serial murder and the case of Aileen Wuornos: Attachment theory, psychopathy, and predatory aggression. *Behavioral Sciences and the Law, 22,* 375–393.

Arrigo, B. A., & Purcell, C. E. (2001). Explaining paraphilias and lust murder: An integrated model. *International Journal of Offender Therapy and Comparative Criminology, 45,* 6–31.

Arrigo, B. A., & Shipley, S. L. (2001). The confusion over psychopathy (I): Historical considerations. *International Journal of Offender Therapy and Comparative Criminology, 45,* 325–344.

Asher, S. R., & Coie, J. D. (Eds.). (1990). *Peer rejection in childhood.* Cambridge, MA: Cambridge University Press.

Babiak, P. (1995). When psychopaths go to work: A case study of an industrial psychopath. *Applied Psychology: An International Review, 44,* 171–188.

Babiak, P. (2000). Psychopathic manipulation at work. In C. B. Gacono (Ed.), *The clinical and forensic assessment of psychopathy: A practitioner's guide* (pp. 287–311). Mahwah, NJ: Erlbaum.

Bader, M. J. (2003). *Arousal: The secret logic of sexual fantasies.* New York: St. Martin's Griffin.

Bancroft, J. (1985). *Deviant sexual behavior.* New York: Oxford University Press.

Barclay, A. (1973). Sexual fantasies in men and women. *Medical Aspects of Human Sexuality, 7,* 204–216.

Barlow, H. D. (1993). *Introduction to criminology* (6th ed.). New York: Harper Collins.

Becker, J. V., & Abel, G. G. (1977). The treatment of victims of sexual assault. *Quarterly Journal of Corrections, 1,* 38–42.

Bender, L. (1947). Psychopathic behavior disorders in children. In R. Lindner & R. Seliger (Eds.), *Handbook of Correctional Psychology.* New York: Philosophical Library.

Berrios, G. E. (1996). *The history of mental symptoms: Descriptive psychopathology since the nineteenth century.* Cambridge: Cambridge University Press.

Blackburn, R. (1998). Psychopathy and the contribution of personality to violence. In T. Millon, E. Simonsen, M. Birket-Smith, & R. D. Davis (Eds.), *Psychopathy: Antisocial, criminal, and violent behavior* (pp. 50–68). New York: Guilford.

Bodholt, R. H., Richards, H. R., & Gacono, C. B. (2000). Assessing psychopathy in adults: The psychopathy checklist—revised and screening version. In C. B. Gacono (Ed.), *The clinical and forensic assessment of psychopathy: A practitioner's guide* (pp. 55–86). Mahwah, NJ: Erlbaum.

Bowlby, J. (1969). *Attachment and loss: Vol. 1. Attachment.* New York: Basic Books.

Bowlby, J. (1973). *Attachment and loss: Vol. 2. Separation: Anxiety and anger.* New York: Basic Books.

Brenner, C. (1973). *An elementary textbook on psychoanalysis* (Rev. ed.). New York: International Universities Press.

Brittain, R. P. (1970). The sadistic murderer. *Medicine, Science, and the Law, 10,* 198–207.

Bromberg, W., & Coyle, E. (1974, April). Rape!: A compulsion to destroy. *Medical Insight,* 21–22, 24–25.

Brooks, P. R., Devenie, M. J., Green, T. J., Hart, B. C., & Moore, M. C. (1987, June). Serial murder: A criminal justice response. *Police Chief,* 40–44.

Brown, S. (2005). *Treating sex offenders: An introduction to sex offender treatment programs.* Cullompton, Devon, UK: Willan Publishing.

Buchanan, A. (Ed.). (2002). *Care of the mentally disordered offender in the community.* New York: Oxford University Press.

Burgess, A. W., Hartman, C. R., Ressler, R. K., Douglas, J. E., & McCormack, A. (1986). Sexual homicide: A motivational model. *Journal of Interpersonal Violence, 13,* 251–272.

Cafasso, L. L., Camic, P. M., and Rhodes, J. E. (2001). *Middle school examined and altered by teacher-directed intervention assessed through qualitative and quantitative methodologies.* Paper presented at the annual meeting of the National Middle School Association, Washington, DC.

Cameron, D., & Frazer, E. (1988). *The lust to kill: A feminist investigation of sexual murder.* New York: New York University Press.

Canter, D. V., Alison, L. J., Alison, E., & Wentink, N. (2004). The organized/disorganized typology of serial murder: Myth or model? *Psychology, Public Policy and the Law, 10,* 293–320.

Canter, D. V., & Wentink, N. (2004). An empirical test of Holmes and Holmes's serial murder typology. *Criminal Justice and Behavior, 31,* 315–489.

Chodorow, N. J. (1994). *Femininities, masculinities, sexualities: Freud and beyond.* Lexington, KY: University of Kentucky Press.

Cicchetti, D., & Toth, S. L. (1995). Child maltreatment and attachment organization. In S. Goldberg, R. Muir, & J. Kerr (Eds.), *Attachment theory: Social, developmental, and clinical perspectives* (pp. 271–308). Hillsdale, NJ: The Analytic Press.

Claussen-Rodgers, N., & Arrigo, B. A. (2005). *Police corruption and psychological testing: A strategy for pre-employment screening.* Durham, NC: Carolina Academic Press.

Cleckley, H. (1941). *The mask of sanity (1st ed.).* St. Louis: Mosby.

Cleveland, M. (2002). *Pure freedom: Breaking the addiction to pornography.* Bemidiji, MN: Focus Publishing.

Cohen, M. L., Garofalo, R. F., Boucher, R., & Seghorn, T. (1971). The psychology of rapists. *Seminars in Psychiatry, 3,* 307–327.

Comer, R. J. (1995). *Abnormal psychology* (2nd ed.). New York: Freeman.

Craissati, J. (2004). *Managing high risk sex offenders in the community: A psychological approach.* London: Routledge.

Creswell, J. W. (1998). *Qualitative inquiry and research design: Choosing among five traditions.* Thousand Oaks, CA: Sage Publications.

Crowe, L. C., & George, W. H. (1989). Alcohol and human sexuality: Review and integration. *Psychological Bulletin, 105,* 374–386.

Cullen, F. T., & Agnew, R. (2002). *Criminological theory past to present: Essential readings* (2nd ed.). Los Angeles, CA: Roxbury Press.

Dahmer, L. (1994). *A father's story.* New York: Morrow.

Danto, B. (1982). A psychiatric view of those who kill. In J. Bruhns, K. Bruhns, & H. Austin (Eds.), *The human side of homicide* (pp. 3–20). New York: Columbia University Press.

Davis, J. A. (1998, January–February). Profile of a predator: A psychological autopsy of an American serial killer. *The Forensic Examiner,* 28–33.

Davis, J. A. (2002). Voyeurism: A criminal precursor and diagnostic indicator to a much larger predatory problem in our community. In R. Holmes & S. Holmes (Eds.), *Current perspectives on sex crimes* (pp. 73–84). Thousand Oaks, CA: Sage.

DeHart, D. D., & Mahoney, J. M. (1994). The serial murderer's motivations: An interdisciplinary review. *Omega, 29,* 29–45.

Depue, R. L. (1986, December). An American response to an era of violence. *FBI Law Enforcement Bulletin,* 2–8.

DeRiver, J. P. (1949). *The sexual criminal: A psychoanalytic study.* Springfield, IL: Thomas.

DeRiver, J. P. (1956). *Crime and the sexual psychopath.* Springfield, IL: Thomas.

Dietz, P., Hazelwood, R., & Warren, J. (1996). The sexually sadistic serial killer. *Journal of Forensic Sciences, 41,* 970–974.

Dolan, M., & Doyle, M. (2000). Violence risk prediction: Clinical and actuarial measures and the role of the Psychopathy Checklist. *British Journal of Psychiatry, 177,* 303–311.

Doren, D. M. (2002). *Evaluating sex offenders.* Thousand Oaks, CA: Sage.

Douglas, J. E., Burgess, A. W., Burgess, A. G., & Ressler, R. K. (1992). *Crime classification model: A standard system for investigating and classifying violent crimes.* Lexington, MA: Lexington Books.

Douglas, J. E., Burgess, A. W., & Ressler, R. K. (1995). *Sexual homicide: Patterns and motives.* New York: The Free Press.

Egger, S. A. (1990). *Serial murder: An elusive phenomenon.* Westport, CT: Greenwood.

Egger, S. A. (2002). *The killers among us: An examination of serial murder and its investigation* (2nd ed.). Upper Saddle River, NJ: Prentice-Hall.

Erickson, M., Sroufe, L., & Egeland, B. (1985). The relationship between quality of attachment and behavior problems in preschool in a high-risk sample. In I. Bretherton & E. Waters (Eds.), *Growing points of attachment theory and research: Monographs of the Society for Research in Child Development, 50,* 147–166.

Eth, S., & Pynoos, R. S. (1985). Developmental perspective on psychic trauma in childhood. In C. R. Figley (ed.), *Trauma and Its Wake: The Study and Treatment of Post-Traumatic Stress Disorder* (pp. 36–52). New York: Brunner/Mazel.

Fisher, W. H. (2002). *Community based interventions for criminal offenders with severe mental illness.* Greenwich, CT: JAI Press.

Flaherty, T. H. (Ed.). (1993). *True crime, compulsion to kill.* Alexandria, VA: Time Life Books.

Forth, A. E., & Mailloux, D. L. (2000). Psychopathy in youth: What do we know? In C. B. Gacono (Ed.), *The clinical and forensic assessment of psychopathy: A practitioner's guide* (pp. 25–54). Mahwah, NJ: Erlbaum.

Freud, S. (2000). *Three essays of the theory of sexuality* (Rev. ed.). New York: Basic Books.

Frick, P. J., Barry, C. T., & Bodin, S. D. (2000). Applying the concept of psychopathy to children: Implications for the assessment of youth. In C. B. Gacono (Ed.), *The clinical and forensic assessment of psychopathy: A practitioner's guide* (pp. 3–24). Mahwah, NJ: Erlbaum.

Gacono, C. B. (1998). The use of the PCL-R and Rorschach in treatment planning with ASPD patients. *International Journal of Offender Therapy and Comparative Criminology, 42,* 47–55.

Gacono, C. B. (Ed.). (2000a). *The clinical and forensic assessment of psychopathy: A practitioner's guide.* Mahwah, NJ: Erlbaum.

Gacono, C. B. (2000b). Suggestions for implementation and use of the psychopathy checklists in forensic and clinical practice. In C. B. Gacono (Ed.), *The clinical and forensic assessment of psychopathy: A practitioner's guide* (pp. 175–201). Mahwah, NJ: Erlbaum.

Gacono, C. B., Nieberding, R., Owen, A., Rubel, J., & Bodholdt, R. (2000). Treating juvenile and adult offenders with conduct disorder, antisocial, and psychopathic personalities. In J. Ashford, B. Sales, & W. Reid (Eds.), *Treating clients with special needs.* Washington, D.C.: American Psychological Association.

Garland, D. (2002). *The culture of control: Crime and social order in contemporary society.* Chicago: University of Chicago Press.

Geffner, R., Crumpton Franey, K., Geffner, T., & Falconer, R. (2004). *Identifying and treating sex offenders: Current approaches, research, and techniques.* Binghamton, NY: Haworth Press.

George, W. H., & Marlat, A. G. (1989). Introduction. In D. R. Laws (Ed.), *Relapse prevention with sex offenders* (pp. 1–13). New York: Guilford Press.

Giannangelo, S. J. (1996). *The psychopathology of serial murder: A theory of violence.* Westport, CT: Praeger.

Glenn, H. S., & Nelsen, J. (2001). *Raising self reliant children in a self indulgent world: Seven building blocks for developing capable young people.* Three Rivers, MI: Three Rivers Press.

Goldberg, S. (1991). Recent developments in attachment theory and research. *Canadian Journal of Psychiatry, 36,* 393–400.

Golman, D. (1991, August 7). Clues to a dark nurturing ground for one serial killer. *The New York Times,* A8.

Graney, D. J., & Arrigo, B. A. (2002). *The power serial rapist: A criminology-victimology typology of female victim selection.* Springfield, IL: Charles C Thomas.

Greenlinger, V., & Bryne, D. (1987). Coercive sexual fantasies of college men as predictors of self-reported likelihood to rape and over sexual aggression. *Journal of Sex Research, 23,* 1–11.

Grossman, K. E., & Grossman, K. (1991). Attachment quality as an organizer of emotional and behavioral responses in a longitudinal perspective. In C. M. Parkes, J. Stevenson-Hinde, & P. Harris (Eds.), *Attachment across the life cycle* (pp. 93–114). London: Tavistock/Routledge.

Groth, A., & Birnbaum, H. (1979). *Men who rape: The psychology of the offender.* New York: Plenum.

Groth, A. N., Burgess, A. W., & Holmstrom, L. L. (1977). Rape, power, anger, and sexuality. *American Journal of Psychiatry, 134,* 1239–1243.

Grubin, D. (1994). Sexual murder. *British Journal of Psychiatry, 165,* 624–629.

Gunn, J. (1998). Psychopathy: An elusive concept with moral overtones. In T. Millon, E. Simonsen, M. Birket-Smith, & R. D. Davis (Eds.), *Psychopathy: Antisocial, criminal, and violent behavior* (pp. 32–39). New York: Guilford.

Guntrip, H. (1971). *Psychoanalytic theory, therapy, and the self.* New York: Basic Books.

Gustafson, S. B., & Ritzer, D. R. (1995). The dark side of normal: A psychopathy-linked pattern called aberrant self-promotion. *European Journal of Personality, 9,* 147–183.

Guttmacher, M. S., & Weihofen, H. (1952). *Psychiatry and the law.* New York: Norton.

Hare, R. D. (1980). A research scale for the assessment of psychopathy in criminal populations. *Personality and Individual Differences, 1,* 111–119.

Hare, R. D. (1991). *The Hare Psychopathy Checklist—Revised.* Toronto: Multi-Health Systems.

Hare, R. D. (1993). *Without conscience: The disturbing world of the psychopaths among us.* New York: Pocket Books.

Hare, R. D. (1996). Psychopathy and antisocial personality disorder: A case of diagnostic confusion. *Psychiatric Times, 13,* 39–40.

Hare, R. D. (1998). Psychopaths and their nature: Implications for the mental health and criminal justice systems. In T. Millon, E. Simonsen, M. Birket-Smith, & R. Davis (Eds.), *Psychopathy: Antisocial, criminal and violent behavior* (pp. 188–212). New York: Guilford.

Hare, R. D. (2001). Psychopaths and their nature: Some implications for understanding human predatory violence. In A. Raine & J. Sanmartin (Eds.), *Violence and psychopathy* (pp. 5–34). New York: Kluwer.

Hare, R. D. (2003). *The Hare Psychopathy Checklist—Revised* (2nd ed.). Toronto: Multi-Health Systems.

Hare, R. D., & Cox, D. N. (1978). Clinical and empirical conceptions of psychopathy and the selection of subjects for research. In R. D. Hare & D. Schalling (Eds.), *Psychopathic Behaviour.* Chichester, UK: John Wiley & Sons.

Harris, G. T., Rice, M. E., & Cormier, C. A. (1991). Psychopathy and violent recidivism. *Law and Human Behavior, 15,* 625–637.

Harris, G. T., Rice, M. E., & Lalumiere, M. (2001). Criminal violence: The roles of psychopathy, neurodevelopmental insults, and antisocial parenting. *Criminal Justice and Behavior, 28,* 402–426.

Harris, G. T., Rice, M. E., & Quinsey, V. L. (1993). Violent recidivism of mentally disordered offenders: The development of a statistical prediction instrument. *Criminal Justice and Behavior, 20,* 315–335.

Hart, S. D., & Hare, R. D. (1998a). Association between psychopathy and narcissism: Theoretical views and empirical evidence. In E. F. Ronningstam (Ed.), *Disorders of narcissism: Diagnostic, clinical, and empirical implications* (pp. 415–436). Washington, DC: American Psychiatric Press.

Hart, S. D., & Hare, R. D. (1998b). Psychopathy: Assessment and association with criminal conduct. In D. M. Stoff, J. Breiling, & J. D. Maser (Eds.), *Handbook of antisocial behavior* (pp. 22–35). New York: Wiley.

Hart, S. D., Kropp, P. R., & Hare, R. D. (1998). Performance of psychopaths following conditional release from prison. *Journal of Consulting and Clinical Psychology, 56,* 227–232.

Hazelwood, R. R., & Douglas, J. D. (1980, April). The lust murderer. *FBI Law Enforcement Bulletin,* 18–22.

Hazelwood, R. R. (2001). *Practical Aspects of Rape Investigation: A Multidisciplinary Approach* (3rd ed.). Boca Raton, FL: CRC Press.

Hazelwood, R. R., Reboussin, R., & Warren, J. (1989). Serial rape: Correlates of increased aggression and the relationship of offender pleasure to victim resistance. *Journal of Interpersonal Violence, 4,* 65–78.

Heilbrun, K., Hart, S., Hare, R., Gustafson, D., Nunez, C., & White, A. (1998). Inpatient and post-discharge aggression in mentally disordered offenders: The role of psychopathy. *Journal of Interpersonal Violence, 13,* 513–527.

Hemphill, J. F., Hare, R. D., & Wong, S. (1998). Psychopathy and recidivism: A review. *Legal and Criminological Psychology, 2,* 141–172.

Hendrix, H., Hunt, H. L., Hannah, M. T., Luguet, W., & Mason, R. C. (2005). *Imago relationship therapy: Perspectives on theory.* San Francisco, CA: Jossey-Bass.

Hensley, C., & Tewsbury, R. (Eds.). (2003). *Sexual deviance: A reader.* New York: L. Rienner Publishers.

Herdt, G. (2005). *The Sambia: Ritual, sexuality, and change in Papua.* Belmont, CA: Wadsworth.

Hickey, E. (1985, March). *Serial murderers: Profiles in psychopathology.* Paper presented at the annual meeting of the Academy of Criminal Justice Sciences, Las Vegas, NV.

Hickey, E. (1986). The female serial murderer. *Journal of Police and Criminal Psychology, 2,* 72–81.

Hickey, E. (1990a). The etiology of victimization in serial murder. In S. Egger (Ed.), *Serial murder: An elusive phenomenon* (pp. 53–71). New York: Praeger.

Hickey, E. (1990b). Missing and murdered children in America. In A. R. Roberts (Ed.), *Helping crime victims: Research, policy, and practice* (pp. 158–185). Newbury Park, CA: Sage.

Hickey, E. (1991). *Serial murderers and their victims.* Belmont, CA: Wadsworth.

Hickey, E. (1996, January). *Preliminary findings in profiling juvenile firesetters.* Paper presented at the annual meeting of the California Association of Arson Investigators, Fresno, CA.

Hickey, E. (1997). *Serial murderers and their victims* (2nd ed.). Belmont, CA: Wadsworth.

Hickey, E. (2001). *Serial murderers and their victims* (3rd ed.). Belmont, CA: Wadsworth.

Hickey, E. (Ed.). (2003). *Encyclopedia of murder and violent crimes.* Thousand Oaks, CA: Sage.

Hickey, E. (2005). *Sex crimes and paraphilia.* Upper Saddle River, NJ: Prentice-Hall.

Hodgins, S., & Janson, C-G. (2002). *Criminality and violence among the mentally disordered: The Stockholm metropolitan project.* New York: Cambridge University Press.

Holmes, R. M. (1983). *The sex offender and the criminal justice system.* Springfield, IL: Thomas.

Holmes, R. M. (1991). *Sex crimes.* Newbury Park, CA: Sage.

Holmes, R. M., & DeBurger, J. (1988). *Serial murder.* Newbury Park, CA: Sage.

Holmes, R. M., & Holmes, S. T. (Eds.). (1998). *Contemporary perspectives on serial murder.* Thousand Oaks, CA: Sage.

Holmes, R. M., & Holmes, S. T. (1999). *Serial murder* (2nd ed.). Thousand Oaks, CA: Sage.

Holmes, R. T., & Holmes, S. T. (2000). *Murder in America* (2nd ed.). Thousand Oaks, CA: Sage.

Holmes, R. M., & Holmes, S. T. (2002a). *Sex crimes: Patterns and behavior* (2nd ed.). Thousand Oaks, CA: Sage.

Holmes, R. M., & Holmes, S. T. (2002b). *Current perspectives on sex crimes.* Upper Saddle River, NJ: Sage.

Holmes, R. M., & Holmes, S. T. (2003). *Profiling violent crimes: An investigative tool* (3rd ed.). Thousand Oaks, CA: Sage.

Howlett, J. B., Hanfland, K. A., & Ressler, R. K. (1986, December). The violent criminal apprehension program VICAP: A progress report. *FBI Law Enforcement Bulletin, 55,* 14–22.

Janus, E. S. (2000). Sexual predator commitment laws: Lessons for law and the behavioral sciences. *Behavioral Sciences and the Law, 18,* 9–21.

Jung, J. (2000). *Psychology of alcohol and other drugs: A research perspective.* Thousand Oaks, CA: Sage.

Kafka, M. P. (2003). Sexual offending and sexual appetite: The clinical and theoretical relevance of hypersexual desire. *International Journal of Offender Therapy and Comparative Criminology, 47,* 439–451.

*Kansas v. Hendricks.* (1997). 117 S. Ct. 2072.

Kennerley, H. (2000). *Overcoming childhood trauma: A self-help guide using cognitive behavioral techniques.* New York: New York University Press.

Kimmel, M. S., & Plante, R. F. (Eds.). (2004). *Sexualities, identities, behavior, and society.* New York: Oxford University Press.

Kline, C. (1995). *The Jeffrey Dahmer murders: Unpublished research in forensic psychology, psychiatry and the law.* San Diego, CA: Author.

Klinteberg, B. A. F., Humble, K., & Schalling, D. (1992). Personality and psychopathy of males with a history of early criminal behavior. *European Journal of Personality, 6,* 245–266.

Knafla, L. A. (Ed.). (2002). *Crime, gender and sexuality in criminal prosecutions.* New York: Greenwood Press.

Krips, H. (1999). *Fetish: An erotic of culture.* Ithaca, NY: Cornell University Press.

Kosson, D., Smith, S., & Newman, J. (1990). Evaluating the construct validity of psychopathy on black and white male inmates: Three preliminary studies. *Journal of Abnormal Psychology, 99,* 250–259.

Lancaster, R. N., & Di Leonardo, M. (Eds.). (1997). *The gender/sexuality reader: Culture, history, and political economy.* New York: Routledge.

Landsberg, G., Rock, M., Berg, L., & Smiley, A. (2002). *Serving mentally ill offenders: Challenges and opportunities for mental health professionals.* New York: Springer.

Langevin, R., & Lang, R. A. (1985). *Erotic preference, gender identity, and aggression in men: New research studies.* Hillsdale, NJ: Erlbaum.

Lanier, M., & Henry, S. (2004). *Essential criminology* (2nd ed.). Boulder, CO: Westview Press.

Laplanche, J., & Pontailis, J. B. (1973). *The language of psycho-analysis.* New York: Norton.

Laws, R. D., Hudson, S. M., & Ward, T. (2000). *Remaking relapse prevention with sex offenders: A sourcebook.* Thousand Oaks, CA: Sage.

Leigh-Kile, D. (2001). *Sex symbols.* London: Vision Paperbacks.

Levy, K. N., & Platt, S. J. (1999). Attachment theory and psychoanalysis: Further differentiation within insecure attachments. *Psychoanalytic Inquiry, 19,* 541–575.

Lewis, M., & Feiring, C. (1991). Attachment as personal characteristic or a measure of environment. In J. L. Gewirtz & W. M. Kurtines (Eds.), *Intersections with attachment* (pp. 3–21). Hillsdale, NJ: Erlbaum.

Liebert, J. A. (1985). Contributions of psychiatric consultation in the investigation of serial murder. *Intentional Journal of Offender Therapy and Comparative Criminology, 29,* 187–200.

Lowman, R. L. (2001). Constructing literature from case studies: Promise and limitations of the method. *Consulting Psychology Journal, 53,* 119–123.

Lykken, D. T. (1995). *The antisocial personalities.* Hillsdale, NJ: Erlbaum.

MacCulloch, M. J., Snowden, P. R., Wood, P. J. W., & Mills, H. E. (1983). Sadistic fantasy, sadistic behavior, and offending. *British Journal of Psychiatry, 143,* 20–29.

Main, M. (1995). Recent studies in attachment. In S. Goldberg, R. Muir, & J. Kerr (Eds.), *Attachment theory: Social, developmental, and clinical perspectives* (pp. 47–71). Hillsdale, NJ: The Analytic Press.

Main, M., Kaplan, N., & Cassidy, J. (1985). Security in infancy, childhood, and adulthood: A move to the level of representation. In I. Bretherton & E. Waters (Eds.), *Growing points of attachment theory and research: Monographs of the Society for Research in Child Development, 50,* 66–104.

Malamuth, N. M., & McLlwraith, R. D. (1988). Fantasies and exposure to sexually explicit magazines. *Communication Research, 15,* 753–771.

Maletsky, B. (1990). *Treating the sexual offender.* Newbury Park, CA: Sage.

Martens, W. H. J., & Palermo, G. B. (2005). Lonliness and associated violent antisocial behavior: analysis of the case reports of Jeffrey Dahmer and Dennis Nilsen. *International Journal of Offender Therapy and Comparative Criminology, 49,* 298–307.

Masters, B. (1993). *The shrine of Jeffrey Dahmer.* London, UK: Hodder and Stoughton.

Masters, R., & Robertson, C. (1990). *Inside criminology.* Englewood Cliffs, NJ: Prentice-Hall.

Matthews, J. (1996). *The eyeball killer.* New York: Zebra.

Maxmen, J. S., & Ward, N. G. (1995). *Essential psychopathology and its treatment* (2nd ed., rev. for DSM-IV). New York: Norton.

Maxwell, J. A. (1996). *Qualitative research design: An interactive approach.* Thousand Oaks, CA: Sage Publications.

McGrath, J. E., & Johnson, B. A. (2003). Methodology makes meaning: How both qualitative and quantitative paradigms shape evidence and its interpretation. In P. Camic, J. Rhodes, & L. Yardly (Eds.), *Qualitative research in psychology: Expanding perspective in methodology and design.* Washington, DC: American Psychological Association.

McGrath, R. J. (1991). Sex offender risk assessment and disposition planning: A review of empirical findings. *International Journal of Offender Therapy and Comparative Criminology, 35,* 329–350.

McGuire, R., Carlisle, J., & Young, B. (1965). Sexual deviations as conditioned behavior. *Behavior Research and Therapy, 2,* 185–190.

Mednick, S. A., Moffitt, T., & Stack, S. (Eds.). (1987). *The causes of crime: New biological approaches.* Cambridge, MA: Cambridge University Press.

Meloy, J. R. (1992). *The psychopathic mind: Origins, dynamics and treatment* (2nd ed.). Northvale, NJ: Aronson.

Meloy, J. R., & Gacono, C. B. (2000). Assessing psychopathy: Psychological testing and report writing. In C. B. Gacono (Ed.), *The clinical and forensic assessment of psychopathy: A practitioner's guide* (pp. 231–249). Mahwah, NJ: Erlbaum.

Miles, M. B., & Huberman, A. M. (1994). *Qualitative data analysis: A sourcebook of new methods.* Beverly Hills, CA: Sage Publications.

Millon, T., Simonsen, E., & Birket-Smith, M. (1998). Historical conceptions of psychopathy in the United States and Europe. In T. Millon, E. Simonsen, M. Birket-Smith, & R. D. Davis (Eds.), *Psychopathy: Antisocial, criminal, and violent behavior* (pp. 3–31). New York: Guilford.

Moffitt, T., Lynam, D., & Silva, P. (1994). Neuropsychological tests predicting male delinquency. *Criminology, 32,* 277–300.

Money, J. (1990). Forensic sexology: Paraphilic serial rape (biastophilia) and lust murder (erotophonophilia). *American Journal of Psychotherapy, 64,* 26–36.

Money, J., & Lamacz, M. (1989). *Vandalized lovemaps: Paraphilic outcome of seven cases in pediatric sexology.* Buffalo, NY: Prometheus Books.

Money, J., & Werlas, J. (1982). Paraphilic sexuality and child abuse: The parents. *Journal of Sex and Marital Therapy, 8,* 57–64.

Moorman, C. (2003). *Parent talk: How to talk to your children in language that builds self-esteem and encourages responsibility.* New York: Fireside Edition Books.

Newton, M. (2000). *The encyclopedia of serial killers.* New York: Checkmark.

O'Donohue, W. O., Letourneau, E. J., & Dowling, H. (1997). Development and preliminary validation of a paraphilic sexual fantasy questionnaire. *Sexual Abuse: A Journal of Research, 9,* 167–178.

O'Neill, M. L., Lidz, V., & Heilbrun, K. (2003). Adolescents with psychopathic characteristics in a substance abusing cohort: Treatment process and outcomes. *Law and Human Behavior, 27,* 299–314.

Palermo, G. B. (2004). *The faces of violence* (2nd ed.). Springfield, IL: Charles C Thomas.

Palermo, G. B., & Farkas, M. A. (2001). *The dilemma of the sexual offender.* Springfield, IL: Charles C Thomas.

Palermo, G. B., & Kocsis, R. N. (2005). *Offender profiling: An introduction to the sociopsychological analysis of violent crime.* Springfield, IL: Charles C Thomas.

Perdue, W., & Lester, D. (1974). Temperamentally suited to kill: The personality of murderers. *Corrective and Social Psychiatry and Journal of Behavioral Technology, Methods, and Theory, 20,* 13–15.

Podolsky, E. (1966). Sexual violence. *Medical Digest, 34,* 60–63.

Poythress, N. G., Edens, J. F., & Lilienfeld, S. O. (1998). Criterion-based validity of the Psychopathic Personality Inventory in a prison sample. *Psychological Assessment, 10,* 426–430.

Pratt, J. (2000). Sex crimes and the new punitiveness. *Behavioral Sciences and the Law, 18,* 135–151.

Prendergast, W. E. (2003). *Treating sex offenders: A guide to clinical practice with adults, clerics, children, and adolescents* (2nd ed.). Binghamton, NY: Haworth Press.

Prentky, R. A., Burgess, A. W., & Carter, D. L. (1986). Victim responses by rapist type: An empirical and clinical analysis. *Journal of Interpersonal Violence, 1,* 73–98.

Prentky, R. A., Burgess, A. W., Rokous, F. R., Lee, A., Harman, C., Ressler, R., & Douglas, J. (1989). The presumptive role of fantasy in serial homicide. *American Journal of Psychiatry, 146,* 887–891.

Protter, B., & Travin, S. (1987). Sexual fantasies in the treatment of paraphiliac disorders: A bimodal approach. *Psychiatric Quarterly, 58,* 279–297.

Purcell, C. (2000). An Investigation of Paraphilias, lust murder and the case of Jeffrey Dahmer: An investigative model. Fresno, CA: Doctoral Dissertation.

Putnam, F. W. (1997). *Dissociation in children and adolescents: A developmental perspective.* New York: Guilford Press.

Rada, R. T. (1978). Psychological factors in rapist behavior. In R. T. Rada (Ed.), *Clinical aspects of the rapist* (pp. 109–123). New York: Grune & Stratton.

Raine, A. (1993). *The psychopathology of crime: Criminal behavior as a clinical disorder.* San Diego, CA: Academic Press.

Raine, A. (1998). Antisocial behavior and psychophysiology: A biosocial perspective and a prefrontal dysfunction hypothesis. In D. M. Stoff, J. Breiling, & J. D. Maser (Eds.), *Handbook of antisocial behavior* (pp. 289–303). New York: Wiley.

Reckless, W. C. (1973). *The crime problem* (5th ed.). Englewood Cliffs, NJ: Prentice Hall. (Original work published 1950.)

Reckless, W. C. (1961). A new theory of delinquency and crime. *Federal Probation, 25,* 42–46.

Reckless, W. C., & Dinitz, S. (1967). Pioneering with self-concept as a vulnerability factor in delinquency. *Journal of Criminal Law, Criminology and Police Science, 58,* 515–523.

Reckless, W. C., Dinitz, S., & Murray, E. (1956). Self-concept as an insulator against delinquency. *American Sociological Review, 21,* 744–746.

Reinhardt, J. M. (1957). *Sex perversions and sex crimes: A psychocultural examination of the causes, nature, and criminal manifestations of sex perversions.* Springfield, IL: Charles C Thomas.

Ressler, R. K. (Ed.). (1985). Violent crimes. *FBI Law Enforcement Bulletin, 54,* 1–31.

Ressler, R. K., Burgess, A. W., & Douglas, J. E. (1988). *Sexual homicide: Patterns and motives.* Lexington, MA: Lexington Books.

Ressler, R. K., Burgess, A. W., Harman, C. R., Douglas, J. E., & McCormack, A. (1986). Murderers who rape and mutilate. *Journal of Interpersonal Violence, 1,* 273–287.

Rice, M. E. (1997). Violent offender research and implications for the criminal justice system. *American Psychologist, 52,* 414–423.

Rothbard, J. C., & Shaver, P. R. (1994). Continuity of attachment across the lifespan. In M. B. Sperling & W. H. Berman (Eds.), *Attachments in adults: Clinical and developmental perspectives* (pp. 31–71). New York: The Guilford Press.

Salekin, R., Rogers, R., & Sewell, K. (1996). A review and meta-analysis of the Psychopathy Checklist and Psychopathy Checklist—Revised: Predictive validity of dangerousness. *Clinical Psychology: Science and Practice, 3,* 203–215.

Salekin, R., Rogers, R., & Sewell, K. (1997). Construct validity of psychopathy in a female offender sample: A multitrait-multimethod evaluation. *Journal of Abnormal Psychology, 106,* 576–585.

Sanford, L. (1992). *Strong at the broken places: Overcoming the trauma of childhood abuse.* New York: Avon Books.

Sapp, M. (2004). *Cognitive-behavioral theories of counseling: traditional and nontraditional approaches.* Springfield, IL: Charles C Thomas.

Schlesinger, L. B. (2003). *Sexual murder: Catathymic and compulsive homicides.* Boca Raton, FL: CRC Press.

Schore, A. N. (2003). *Affect disregulation and disorders of the self.* New York: W. W. Norton & Company.

Schroeder, M., Schroeder, K., & Hare, R. D. (1983). Generalizability of a checklist for the assessment of psychopathy. *Journal of Consulting and Clinical Psychology, 51,* 511–516.

Schwartz, A. E. (1992). *The man who could not kill enough.* New York: Carol Publishing.

Scully, D., & Marolla, J. (1985). Riding the bull at Gilley's: Convicted rapists describe the rewards of rape. *Social Problems, 32,* 251–263.

Serrin, R. C. (1991). Psychopathy and violence in criminals. *Journal of Interpersonal Violence, 6,* 423–431.

Serin, R. C., Peters, R. D., & Barbaree, H. E. (1990). Predictors of psychopathy and release outcome in a criminal population. *Psychological Assessment, 2,* 419–422.

Shipley, S. L., & Arrigo, B. A. (2001). The confusion over psychopathy (II): Implications for forensic (correctional) practice. *International Journal of Offender Therapy and Comparative Criminology, 45,* 407–420.

Shipley, S. L., & Arrigo, B. A. (2004). *The female homicide offender: Serial murder and the case of Aileen Wuornos.* Upper Saddle River, NJ: Prentice Hall.

Siegel, L. (1998). *Executive functioning characteristics associated with psychopathy in incarcerated females.* Unpublished doctoral dissertation, California School of Professional Psychology, San Diego.

Simon, L. (2000). An examination of the assumptions of specialization, mental disorder, and dangerousness in sex offenders. *Behavioral Sciences and the Law, 18,* 275–308.

Simon, R. I. (1996). *Bad men do what good men dream: A forensic psychiatrist illuminates the darker side of human behavior.* Washington, DC: American Psychiatric Press.

Simpson, J. A., & Rholes, W. S. (1997). *Attachment theory and close relationships.* New York: Guilford Press.

Small, M. (2004). *Opposite directions: A story of sexual compulsion.* Lincoln, NE: iUniverse, Inc.

Spencer, A. P. (1999). *Working with sex offenders in prison and through release to the community: A handbook.* Scotland: Jessica Kingsley Publishers.

Sroufe, L. A. (1983). Infant-caregiver attachment and patterns of adaptation in preschool: The roots of maladaptation and competence. In M. Perlmutter (Ed.), *Minnesota Symposia in Child Psychology, 16,* 41–83.

Sroufe, L. A., & Fleeson, J. (1996). Attachment and the construction of relationships. In W. W. Harup & Z. Rubin (Eds.), *Relationships and development* (pp. 51–71). Hillsdale, NJ: Erlbaum.

Stake, R. E. (1995). *The art of case study research.* Thousand Oaks, CA: Sage.

Stake, R. E. (1998). Case studies. In N. K. Denzin & Y. S. Lincoln (Eds.), *Strategies of qualitative inquiry* (pp. 86–109). Thousand Oaks, CA: Sage.

Steadman, H. J., McGreevy, M., Morrissey, J., Callahan, L., Clark, T., Robbins, P., & Cirincione, C. (1993). *Before and after Hinckley: Evaluating insanity defense reform.* New York: Guilford Press.

Steuerwald, B. L., & Kosson, D. S. (2000). Emotional experiences of the psychopath. In C. B. Gacono (Ed.), *The clinical and forensic assessment of psychopathy: A practitioner's guide* (pp. 111–135). Mahwah, NJ: Erlbaum.

Stone, M. H. (1998). The personalities of murderers: The importance of psychopathy and sadism. In A. E. Skodol (Ed.), *Psychopathology and violent crime: Review of psychiatry series* (pp. 29–52). Washington, DC: American Psychiatric Press.

Sullivan, T., & Maiken, P. (1983). *Killer clown.* New York: Grosset & Dunlap.

Tanay, E. (1976). *The murderers.* Indianapolis, IN: Bobbs-Merrill.

Terr, L. (1992). *Too scared to cry: Psychic trauma in childhood.* New York: Basic Books.

Tithecott, R. (1999). *Of men and monsters: Jeffrey Dahmer and the construction of the serial killer.* Madison, WI: University of Wisconsin Press.

Vetter, H. (1990). Dissociation, psychopathy, and the serial murderer. In S. A. Egger (Ed.), *Serial murder: An elusive phenomenon* (pp. 73–92). New York: Praeger.

Vold, G. B., Bernard, T. J., & Snipes, J. B. (2002). *Theoretical criminology* (5th ed.). New York: Oxford University Press.

Walker, S. (2006). *Sense and nonsense about crime and drugs: A policy guide* (6th ed.). Belmont, CA: West/Wadsworth.

Ward, T., Laws, R. D., & Hudson, S. M. (Eds.). (2002). *Sexual deviance: Issues and controversies.* Thousand Oaks, CA: Sage.

Weeks, J., Holland, J., & Waites, M. (Eds.). (2003). *Sexualities and society: A reader.* Cambridge: Polity Press.

White, L. S. (2001). *Mass murder and attempted mass murder: An examination of the perpetrator with an empirical analysis of typologies.* Unpublished doctoral dissertation, California School of Professional Psychology, Fresno.

Widom, C. (1997). Child abuse, neglect, and witnessing violence. In D. M. Stoff, J. Breiling, & J. D. Maser (Eds.), *Handbook of antisocial behavior* (pp. 159–170). New York: Wiley.

Winn, S., & Merrill, D. (1980). *Ted Bundy: The killer next door.* New York: Bantam.

Yarvis, R. M. (1995). Diagnostic patterns among three violent offender types. *Bulletin of the American Academy of Psychiatry and the Law, 23,* 411–419.

Yin, R. K. (1989). *Case study research: Design and methods.* Newbury Park, CA: Sage Publications.

Young, S. (2003). *Courtesans and Tantric consorts: Sexualities in Buddhist narratives, iconography, and ritual.* Belmont, CA: Wadsworth.

Zevitz, R., & Farkas, M. A. (2000). Sex offender community notification: Managing high-risk criminals or exacting further vengeance? *Behavioral Sciences and the Law, 18,* 375–391.

# INDEX

Lightning Source UK Ltd.
Milton Keynes UK
14 January 2010

148612UK00001B/54/P